Constructing and Reconstructing Childhood

Constructing and Reconstructing Childhood:
Contemporary Issues in the Sociological Study of Childhood

Edited by

Allison James and Alan Prout

Routledge
Taylor & Francis Group

LONDON AND NEW YORK

First published in 1997
by Routledge
2 Park Square, Milton Park, Abingdon, Oxon, OX14 4RN

Transferred to Digital Printing 2010

A catalogue record for this book is available from the British Library

Library of Congress Cataloging-in-Publication Data are available on request

ISBN 0 7507 0703 8 cased
ISBN 0 7507 0596 5 paper

Cover design by Caroline Archer

Typeset in 11/13pt Garamond by
Graphicraft Typesetters Ltd., Hong Kong.

2011001350

Publisher's Note
The publisher has gone to great lengths to ensure the quality of this reprint but points out that some imperfections in the original may be apparent.

Contents

Contents

Acknowledgments

Headline from *The Daily Mirror*, 9 December 1986, used by kind permission of Mirror Group Newspapers, Ltd.

Headline from *The Daily Mirror*, 11 October 1986, used by kind permission of Mirror Group Newspapers, Ltd.

Headline from *The Daily Record*, 8 January 1988, used by kind permission of Mirror Group Newspapers, Ltd.

Grateful acknowledgment is made to Tavistock for permission to reproduce the cover of the book, *Dangerous Families: Assessment and Treatment of Child Abuse*, by Dale, P. *et al.* (1986).

Preface to Second Edition

When the First Edition of *Constructing and Reconstructing Childhood* (hereafter CRC) appeared in 1990 the sociology of childhood was only just beginning to emerge as a distinct sub-discipline. Individuals and research groups existed in several different countries but they were scattered and communication between them, although developing, was partial — depending as it did on somewhat separate and certainly incomplete networks between academics and diverse, associated practitioners. Theoretical and empirical discussion was consequently somewhat limited. Six or seven years later the field has cohered remarkably: research centres and programmes have appeared and existing ones become more visible; conferences and seminars have mushroomed; a new journal has been established; courses on the sociology of childhood are now available and a number of important texts on childhood have been published. At the same time there is a growing recognition of childhood as a legitimate and problematic concern for research in sociology and cognate disciplines. For example, family sociology which we argued (following Alanen, 1988) had, rather surprisingly, rendered children almost invisible, has made some important moves in remedying its neglect (Brannen and O'Brien, 1996). In other disciplines, for example human geography and social anthropology, childhood is emerging as a significant area of study (for example, Valentine, forthcoming; James, 1993; Reynolds, 1996; Toren, 1993; Steedman, 1995). The traditional consignment of childhood to the margins of the social sciences or its primary location within the fields of developmental psychology and education is, then, beginning to change: it is now much more common to find acknowledgment that childhood should be regarded as a part of society and culture rather than a precursor to it; and that children should be seen as already social actors not beings in the process of becoming such. In short, although much remains to be done and these encouraging developments need to be taken much further, a significant change has occurred.

We would like to think that CRC made a contribution to this process. Certainly it posed a challenge to what we then characterized as the dominant and dominating conceptual pair of socialization and development.

In essence we argued that between them they represented childhood and children as natural, passive, incompetent and incomplete and in doing so foreclosed a series of important questions for theory and empirical research, framing the field with ideas which in other areas of social science were regarded as obsolete, outmoded or under productive. In setting out the 'emergent paradigm' we suggested an alternative view which gathered together and focused more recent and innovative thinking: from interactionist accounts we drew on the notion of children as agents in, as well as products of, social processes and from the influence of social constructionism we emphasized the social, cultural and historical variability of childhood and its irreducibility to a given biological reality.

Theoretically the field has moved on considerably, in some senses cohering but in others showing signs of new but productive divisions. From one point of view the emergent paradigm simply proved to be a rallying point for co-thinkers who were engaged in contemporaneous work which had come to the same or similar conclusions (see for example Jenks, 1982). But as more opportunities for exchange were created, and as the discussion in these various forums went on, it became clear that by emphasizing some of its tenets (or combining them in novel ways) distinctly different positions were beginning to emerge. Elsewhere, in a separate volume (James, Jenks and Prout, 1997), these are discerned as four main theoretical positions: the socially constructed child; the tribal child; the minority group child; the social structural child. These reflect not only different methods and approaches to the childhood studies — some emphasizing childhood as a conceptual space, while others engage with children as social actors — but they also represent differing positions with respect to the broader sociological questions of universalism/particularism and structure/agency.

This is not the place to expound and unpack these positions at the length required. Rather it seems more appropriate and timely to revisit the main components of the emergent paradigm identified in 1990, briefly assessing its tenets in the light of developments since its first publication. The notion of childhood as a social construction, the first point of the paradigm, has had a major impact and in some ways might be thought of as what Lee (1996) has termed the 'industry standard'. Certainly writers or researchers who do not acknowledge the constitution of childhood within socially and historically situated discourse or who fail to give weight to its variability and relativity are currently more or less guaranteed a much more critical reception than was previously the case. Major contributions from Stainton-Rogers and Stainton-Rogers (1992), Burman (1994) and Jenks (1996) have extended the argument and strengthened the case against biologically reductionist approaches to childhood by clearly illuminating some of the ways in which it is constituted through discourse. In a reworking of his original chapter Hendricks reflects in this volume on a different set of historical discourses, thereby further underlining the contingent character of childhood. To quote Jenks (1996: 32), the child is 'a status of person which is comprised through a series of, often heterogeneous, images, representations, codes and constructs'. Indeed, it is now often argued that it is more correct to talk of 'childhoods' rather than childhood.

However, it is in the very strength of the social constructionist account in opposing the notion of childhood as a given fact, particularly a biological one, that some indications of its limits are beginning to emerge. The first of these concerns the social and political implications of the relativism implied by the social constructionist literature in the face of the political, social and economic maltreatment ventured against children on an international scale. So whilst in the First Edition of CRC a number of contributors, for example Woodhead and Boyden, exposed the practical problems of a universalistic conception of childhood, voices are now raised to question how far it is wise to travel along the road of relativism (Stephens, 1995). These questions are also, of course, at the centre of debates about children's rights (see, for example, Freeman, 1996 and Archard, 1993). In Postscripts to their original chapters both Woodhead and Boyden acknowledge this problem but nonetheless remain insistent that the cultural specificity of particular childhoods has to be recognized. For Woodhead this entails developmental psychology reframing, not simply rejecting, notions of 'children's needs' and situating an understanding of these within the particularities of the cultural context. This is all the more crucial given the now widespread acceptance of children's rights where the 'best interests of the child' are taken as the base-line for social and political action. But who defines those interests remains problematic, a point which Boyden takes up explicitly in the postscript to her chapter. Though welcoming the ratification of the UN Convention on the Rights of the Child by many countries, Boyden remains cautious as to how, in practice, these rights are being interpreted and asks in whose interests are the 'best interests' of the child being addressed.

The second locus of debate concerns the biology of childhood bodies and the extent to which children are subject to its dictates, a discussion addressed in the First Edition of this volume by Solberg's questioning of age as a useful concept for understanding children's competence. As Prout (1997, forthcoming) explores, such discussions can now be placed in the wider question of the role of non-discursive practices in the construction of different versions of childhood. He suggests that, whilst there has been a lack of interplay between the two rapidly expanding topics of sociological enquiry of the body and childhood, both fields might benefit from a theoretical reconsideration of the unproductive counterposition of the 'material' and the 'social'. In this perspective new questions about the socially and biologically 'unfinished' character of the body (Shilling, 1993) might find a potentially rich field in the study of children. Though unchanged from the original Solberg's chapter still provides a provocative challenge to traditional biological determinism by demonstrating that the physical abilities and social competencies of same-aged children vary according to the familial expectations placed upon them. Similarly Kitzinger's thought provoking account of child sexual abuse remains a pertinent reminder, in the light of increasing anxiety and concern about the loss of childhood innocence (see James and Jenks, 1996), that children are not simply at the mercy of their bodies. As her chapter emphasizes it is the ways in which those bodies are thought about and acted upon which makes children vulnerable to particular discourses of power.

The understanding of childhood as a variable in social analysis, the second tenet of the paradigm, has also seen some major steps forward. In the First Edition of CRC Jens Qvortrup made a strong case for using children as the unit of account and demonstrated the difference this could make to social statistics. The European Centre's project 'Childhood as a Social Phenomenon' extended this work enormously. Not only did it produce empirical data (in the form of a huge international survey using existing data sources and looking at childhood in different societies) but it also tackled theoretical and methodological questions. In the former Qvortrup formulated an important part of the ground on which the contemporary sociology of childhood stands: namely the suggestion that although its membership may be constantly changing, childhood forms a permanent part of the social structure. In this view 'the childhood' of a society, and what is happening to it, becomes a key sociological question. In its main publication, Childhood Matters (Qvortrup *et al.*, 1994), contributors developed other important aspects of this central thesis; for example, parallels and differences between women and children (Alanen); the feminization of modern childhood (Jensen); the potential of viewing childhood as a social class (Oldman); social trends in the institutionalization and individualization of childhood (Nasman); the economics of childhood (Wintersberger) and methodologies for making children count in social statistics (Saporiti). In the Postscript to his chapter in this volume Qvortrup shows the important advances which have been made internationally in the collection of child-centred statistics while at the same time remaining cautious about their use. As he convincingly demonstrates the interpretation of statistics can be used to prop up particular ideologies of childhood.

This emphasis on 'the childhood' of a society, which might be analyzed by quantitative as well as qualitative methods, nonetheless meets a number sticking points which are now the source of continuing debate within the new social studies of childhood. Most fundamental perhaps is Christensen's (1997, forthcoming) questioning of whether childhood is an analytical category or rather an object of empirical enquiry to which the analytical resources of the social sciences should be brought — a suggestion which raises pointed comparisons with the analytical status of terms such as 'women' and 'the aged'. Second, is the danger that in collectivizing children into 'childhood' significant differences (of gender, class, ethnicity, disability etc.) between children are underplayed. Frones for example argues:

> There is not one childhood, but many, formed at the intersection of different cultural, social and economic systems, natural and man-made physical environments. Different positions in society produce different experiences (Frones, 1993).

Third is the extent to which looking at childhood as a feature of social structure stands in danger of recapitulating some of the problematic features of more traditional ways of studying children. These approaches, as we argued in our background discussion to the emergent paradigm tend to accentuate the socially developing child as an outcome of socialization processes rather than as an actor in society.

Our third and fourth tenets, have proved somewhat less subject to debate. All those engaged in the making of a new sociology of childhood have, almost by definition, a commitment to children's social relationships and cultures as 'worthy of study in their own right' (Prout and James, 1990: 8–9) and that children should be looked upon as social actors. True, we have heard it objected that children cannot be seen outside of their relationships with adults — but it was never our claim that they could and we in fact implicitly repudiated such a position by our suggestion that pioneering studies of children's culture (such as those carried out by the Opies) had remained on the margins of social science precisely because they tried to grasp childhood as a 'world apart' (see Chapter 10). That we did not state the position more strongly signified not our belief that children could be studied apart from adults but rather that within the 'emergent paradigm' such a prospect should not be entertained. In admitting that some of the very early work on childhood, including some of our own (James, 1979a and

1979b) had been written from such a perspective (in its efforts to grasp the child's point of view) we argued strongly that, though understandable, it was not a tenable position to hold. It is this view which since 1990 we have consistently argued for and would suggest (see James, Jenks and Prout, 1997 forthcoming) that through an insistence on the agency of children the concept of children's culture can provide a critical dimension to the literature on cultural reproduction.

Looking at children not only as outcomes of social processes but as actors within them has gained widespread acceptance; for example, it is at the core of the ESRC's 'Children 5–16 Research Programme' — a sign perhaps of its starting to be integrated into mainstream UK social science thinking — and many contributors to Childhood Matters constantly return to this point. However, why the idea that children might be considered as social actors has received a relatively easy reception is a matter of speculation: it chimed with the already central debate in sociology about structure and agency; a substantial interactionist literature making the same assumption already existed; it followed a logic parallel to that found in feminist accounts of women; and so on. Nevertheless, this should not lead to complacency for its acceptance is far from complete and, as James, Jenks and Prout argue (1997 forthcoming), the conception of children as socially developing, with its emphasis on children as inadequately socialized future adults, still retains a powerful hold on the social, political, cultural and economic agenda — as Hunt and Frankenberg's chapter on the multiple re-representations of American childhood in Disneyland, reminds us. The key task, then, is to develop further substantive studies which situate children's agency in specific settings. Mayall *et al.* (1996) do exactly this in their work on children's health in school. As they write:

> Children here are regarded as social actors, who aim to order their own lives in interaction with adults. But they are a minority group who lack power to influence the quality of their lives (Mayall *et al.*, 1996, p. 207).

In characterizing children as a minority group these authors begin to tease out the practices which constrain children — thus linking sociological study to a political agenda which includes but is not exhausted by the concept of 'rights'.

Our suggestion that ethnography may be the most important methodology for studying children was in part linked to these questions of agency and action. Children are largely excluded from formal power but already in 1990 the literature contained enough to suggest that in the flow of everyday interaction the picture may appear differently.

Ethnographic approaches we believed could bring researchers close enough to this action to elaborate on this through close attention to children's everyday lives in different settings. A body of work, represented by some of the studies cited above, have begun to do this and others including ourselves (James and Prout, 1995; 1996) have begun to theorize these possibilities. In retrospect, however, our claims for the primacy of ethnography seem somewhat one-sided as others have begun to grapple with ways of including children in survey and other methodologies. The work of the European Centre, the Australian Living Standards Study and the British Household Panel Study are notable examples. The use of participatory methods for work with children is also well under way in the field of development (see Postscripts to Woodhead and Boyden this volume) and are also begining to be be used for work with children in other settings (see James, 1993). Advances it seems are being made on several fronts, including that of research ethics (see Morrow and Richards, 1996), and a productive interchange is occurring between them.

Finally, the emergent paradigm made much of the double hermeneutic of childhood research — the sense in which social science constitutes a phenomenon and does not simply reflect it. Much of the above discussion can now find a counterpart in policy discussions. The Save the Children Fund, for example, in its document to the UN World Summit on Social Development highlighted six problems in current planning for children: a failure to collect child specific information; lack of recognition of children's productive contribution; no participation of children in decision-making; the use of an inappropriate 'standard model of childhood'; the pursuit of adult interests in ways which render children passive; and lack of attention to gender and generational relationships. Similarly, links between the approach of CRC and research on children in development (see Johnson *et al.*, 1995) and debates about children's rights (see Freeman, 1996) are beginning to be made and, as Glauser documents in the Postscript to his chapter, these have brought about some significant policy changes in relation to children. What remains however, is a gap between on the one hand research and innovative policy thinking and the other frameworks for action which practitioners in given localities and contexts can use and develop. In addition as Glauser cautions, while welcoming such moves we must nonetheless explore the significance and ramifications for children of this open embrace of 'childhood' onto policy and political agendas.

As we commented at the outset, then, the last six years have seen the expansion, multiplication and connectedness of many disparate networks of discussion and debate about innovative approaches to childhood. All of this is to be encouraged and perhaps in the next years we can expect an even greater engagement between the worlds of research and practice. We look forward to the discussions and fierce debates we might predict from such an encounter.

References

ALDERSON, P. (1993) *Children's Consent to Surgery*, Milton Keynes, Open University Press.

ALANEN, L. (1988) 'Rethinking childhood', *Acta Sociologica*, **31**, 1, pp. 53–67.

ARCHARD, R. (1993) *Children: Rights and Childhood*, London, Routledge.

BRANNEN, J. and O'BRIEN, M. (Eds) (1996) *Children in Families: Research and Policy*, London, Falmer Press.

BURMAN, E. (1994) *Deconstructing Developmental Psychology*, London, Routledge.

CHRISTENSEN, P. (1997 forthcoming) *The Cultural Performance of Childhood Sickness*, Hull University, Phd Thesis.

FREEMAN, M.F. (1996) 'The moral status of children', Paper to the International Conference on Children's Rights, University of Ghent.

FRONES, I. (1993) 'Changing childhood', *Childhood*, **1**, 1.

JAMES, A. (1979a) 'Confections, concoctions and conceptions', *Journal of the Anthropology Society of Oxford*, **10**, 2, pp. 83–95.

JAMES, A. (1979b) 'The game of the name: Nicknames in the child's world', *New Society*, **48**, 871, pp. 632–34.

JAMES, A. (1993) *Childhood Identities: Self and Social Relationships in the Experience of the Child*, Edinburgh, Edinburgh University Press.

JAMES, A. and JENKS, C. (1996) 'Public perceptions of childhood criminality', *British Journal of Sociology*, **47**, 2, pp. 315–31.

JAMES, A. and PROUT, A. (1995) 'Hierarchy, boundary and agency: Toward a theoretical perspective on childhood' in AMBERT, A. (Ed) *Sociological Studies of Childhood*, **7**, pp. 77–101.

JAMES, A. and PROUT, A. (1996) 'Strategies and structures: Towards a new perspective on children's experiences of family life', in BRANNEN, J. and O'BRIEN, M. (Eds) *Children and Families: Research and Policy*, London, Falmer Press.

JAMES, A., JENKS, C. and PROUT, A. (forthcoming) *Theorising Childhood*, Cambridge, Polity Press.

JENKS, C. (Ed) (1982) *The Sociology of Childhood — Essential Readings*, London, Batsford.

JENKS, C. (1996) *Childhood*, London, Routledge.

JOHNSON, V., HILL, J. and IVAN-SMITH, E. (1995) *Listening to Smaller Voices: Children in an Environment of Change*, London, Actionaid.

MAYALL, B., BENDELOW, G., STOREY, P. and VELTMAN, M. (1996) *Children's Health in Primary Schools*, London, Falmer Press.

MORROW, V. and RICHARDS, M. (1996) 'The ethics of social research with children: An overview', *Children and Society*.

LEE, N. (1996) Personal Communication.

PROUT, A. (Ed) (forthcoming) *Childhood Bodies*, London, Macmillan.

PROUT, A. and JAMES, A. (1990) 'A new paradigm for the sociology of childhood? Provenance, promise and problems', in JAMES, A. and PROUT, A. (Eds) *Constructing and Reconstructing Childhood*, Basingstoke, Falmer Press.

QVORTRUP, J., BARDY, M., SGRITTA, G. and WINTERSBERGER, H. (1994) (Eds) *Childhood Matters*, Aldershot, Avebury.

REYNOLDS, P. (1996) *Traditional Healers and Childhood in Zimbabwe*, Athens, Ohio, Ohio University Press.

SAVE THE CHILDREN FUND (1995) *Towards a Children's Agenda*, London, Save the Children Fund.

SHILLING, C. (1993) *The Body and Social Theory*, London, Sage.

STAINTON-ROGERS, R. and STAINTON-ROGERS, W. (1992) *Stories of Childhood: Shifting Agendas of Child Concern*, London, Harvester Wheatsheaf.

STEEDMAN, C. (1995) *Strange Dislocations: Childhood and the Idea of Human Interiority, 1780–1930*, London, Virago.

STEPHENS, S. (1995) (Ed) *Children and the Politics of Culture*, Princeton, Princeton University Press.

TOREN, C. (1993) 'Making history: The significance of childhood cognition for a comparative anthropology of mind', *Man*, **28**, 3.

VALENTINE, G. (forthcoming) 'Children should be seen and not heard: The production and transgression of adults' public space', *Urban Geography*, **17**, 2.

Introduction

Constructing and Reconstructing Childhood

The twentieth century is said to be 'century of the child' and perhaps at no other time have children been so highly profiled. The ideology of the child-centred society gives 'the child' and 'the interests of the child' a prominent place in the policy and practices of legal, welfare, medical and educational institutions. Whole academic discourses, especially in psychology and medicine, are devoted to understanding the particular qualities of children and in magazines and on television popularized versions of these frequently appear. But despite this rhetoric any complacency about children and their place in society is misplaced, for the very concept of childhood has become problematic during the last decade. This volume of essays reflects these contemporary concerns by exploring the ways in which childhood is socially constructed. This means, as we shall show, exploring the ways in which the immaturity of children is conceived and articulated in particular societies into culturally specific sets of ideas and philosophies, attitudes and practices which combine to define the 'nature of childhood'.

At the heart of current debates lies the question: what is a child? This is not just a matter of semantics but a question increasingly central to academic and professional practice. For example, in 1979 the International Year of the Child was launched. Not for the first time the television screens and hoardings of affluent western societies depicted sick and starving children. What was new, however, was the gradual emergence of the concept 'the world's children' in the official discourses of international agencies such as UNICEF and WHO. This confronted the West with images of childhood contrasting strongly with those familiar to them. The consequences of famine, war and poverty for children threw the very idea of childhood into stark relief. The 'world's children' united 'our' children and 'their' children only to reveal the vast differences between them.

Nearly ten years later western societies experienced a growing consciousness over child abuse, particularly child sexual abuse, which again challenged traditional beliefs about childhood. Media coverage and debate made public the more private lives of those children who have no access to what John Holt some years ago described as the mythic 'walled garden' of 'Happy, Safe, Protected, Innocent Childhood' which all children ideally inhabited (1975: 22–23). A recent charity advertisement plays upon this theme: it depicts a thin and ragged child staring blankly at the camera. Her country of origin is Britain, not the Third World. For professionals involved with children this mismatch between the 'real' and the 'ideal' is not news; what is new, however, is the extent to which the 'ideal' is having to be currently reassessed within the public domain.

This growing unease is reflected in changes in academic interests also. Concern has been developing about the way in which the social sciences have traditionally conceptualized and dealt with children and childhood. Nascent during the 1970s, the debates of the 80s are by now wide-ranging but attention centres on the inadequacy of the dominant frameworks for the study of childhood. The last decade has seen a number of different attempts to address these problems within the social sciences and history: Richards (1974) and Richards and Light (1986) offered a critique of psychological accounts of child development; Aries (1962) initiated a new historical debate about 'the invention of child-hood'; MacKay (1973) and Denzin (1977) developed an alternative approach to traditional concepts of socialization. These initiatives were innovative within their own disciplines but only gradually has the need for their synthesis become apparent.

Similarly, researchers have been restricted within national boundar-ies. Opportunities to discuss and exchange ideas have only been cre-ated during the last two or three years through such interdisciplinary events as the 'Ethnography of Childhood Workshops'. The first of these, held at King's College, Cambridge in 1986 and organized by Judith Ennew, has led to further meetings in Canada and Zimbabwe. Equally important has been the European initiative for the study of childhood as a social institution (see Qvortrup, this volume).

One result of these developments is that it has become quite clear that a new paradigm for the study of childhood is emerging, though for many it remains implicit. The task of making this emergent paradigm explicit is far from complete and remains the major priority for those involved in the study of childhood. Indeed this priority was the inspira-tion for collecting together these essays. Drawing on the writings of an international group of both academics and professionals involved with children, it is intended that this volume should further the debate and discussion necessary for the theoretical and empirical development of the new paradigm. In this sense, the book is an opportunity for some of the main innovators in the field to have their work presented to a wider audience in a way that locates it firmly within a comprehensive rethink of childhood sociology.[1]

Central Tenets of the Emergent Paradigm

The emergent paradigm promises to consolidate and continue the change in direction initiated by the research of the 1970s. It is possible, even at this stage, to abstract some of the predominant and characteristic features of the emergent paradigm. These are represented in the individual contributions to this volume which, taken together, provide an overview of the new directions.

First, and of prime importance, childhood is, within this paradigm, to be understood as a social construction. That is, the institution of childhood provides an interpretive frame for understanding the early years of human life. In these terms it is biological immaturity rather than childhood which is a universal and natural feature of human groups, for ways of understanding this period of human life — the institution of childhood — vary cross-culturally although they do form a specific structural and cultural component of all known societies. Hendrick discussess the shifting historical constructions of childhood in nineteenth and twentieth century England. His paper focuses on two related themes: first, the change from an ideal childhood fragmented in the main by geography and by class experience to one that was much more uniform and coherent; second, the political and cultural struggle to extend the changing concept of childhood among the population throughout the century. These issues are given a contemporary focus by Qvortrup who argues that the absence of children from official statistics and social accounting methods is a function of their conceptual marginality in everyday life. This marginality he sees as the result of a material devaluation but emotional elevation of 'the child'. This absence of children from official statistics can be contrasted with the prolific visual representation of children in western popular culture. Through a detailed analysis of Disneyland, Hunt and Frankenberg analyze the attempt to universalize an idealized version of childhood which is embedded and enfolded in conventional family values.

The second theme is that childhood, as a variable of social analysis, can never be entirely separated from other variables such as class, gender, or ethnicity. Kitzinger, for example, suggests that sexual exploitation is an inbuilt risk when the current ideological and structural position of children in western societies, a position which locates them in an idealized world of innocence and joy, is intersected by gender relations premised on male dominance. The point is amplified by Boyden in her assertion that during the twentieth century, a specifically European conception of childhood was exported to the Third World. Its values were essentially those of the white, urban middle class. But in the Third World this has had the effect of rendering deviant or criminal much of working class life and many of children's everyday activities. This globalization of a particular concept of childhood finds a counterpart in the assumption of some kind of universal experience for all children. In this volume Hunt and Frankenberg show how a hygienic and idealized version of North American childhood is articulated in the complex representations of Disneyland, representations which through mass media and international marketing now traverse the globe. Whilst, therefore, comparative historical and cross-cultural analysis reveals a variety of childhoods rather than a single, simple phenomenon, this is being undercut by current trends towards a 'world' view of childhood. Woodhead's chapter echoes these themes, cogently arguing that the universalizing rhetoric of 'children's needs' hides specific social and cultural choices. Nevertheless, as he cannily points out, since 'need' is a social construct, one particular version could gain wide, even worldwide, acceptance; in that sense childhood could became a universal concept.

The third important feature of the emergent paradigm is that childhood and children's social relationships and cultures are worthy of study in their own right, and not just in respect to their social construction by adults. This means that children must be seen as actively involved in the construction of their own social lives, the lives of those around them and of the societies in which they live. They can no longer be regarded as simply the passive subjects of structural determinations. Solberg, for example, focuses on the working life of children in Norway. Using data from several empirical studies she analyzes a variety of the work in which children are involved, and shows how these activities affect the 'social age of children' and contribute to the organization of everyday life in modern urban families.

Ethnography has been taken up as a methodology which has a particular role to play in the development of a new sociology of childhood since it allows children a more direct voice in the production of sociological data than is usually possible through experimental or survey styles of research. Similarly, fieldwork-based research encourages researchers to focus on the ongoing roles which children play and the meanings they themselves attach to their lives. James and Prout illustrate their argument about the importance of the social construction of time in the analysis of childhood by ethnographic material which focuses on the present, ongoing social lives of children rather than their past or future.

Finally, it can be said that to proclaim a new paradigm of childhood sociology is also to engage in and respond to the process of reconstructing childhood in society. Woodhead unpacks the concept of children's needs as inscribed in the practice and ideology of childcare professions. He shows how psychological concepts, often taken as objective and scientific criteria for judging the adequacy of parenting, rest on a set of implicit assumptions. In this sense, childhood is a phenomenon in relation to which the double hermeneutic (Giddens, 1979) of the social sciences is acutely present. Although this theme runs through many of the papers in this volume, Glauser directly addresses the ethical and political problems which this presents to the researcher. Using his own research with street children in Paraguay he explores the ways in which the language and models of research adopted create the 'reality' of childhood discovered and questions whose interests this serves.

The background to the emergence of this new approach to childhood is complex and often contradictory and, at this stage, a claim to novelty through a complete disjuncture with past work would be both premature and unhelpful. In our view, although the current movement towards a new sociology of childhood displays the clearly identifiable shifts in focus, emphasis and direction outlined above, it is prudent to keep an open mind on whether these represent a break or a continuity with the past. Although it is possible to identify these features as belonging to a new paradigm for the study of childhood it is clear that the paradigm exists more as a potential or possibility than as an already completed set of theoretical postulates. Prout and James tackle both these issues in an analysis of the origins and obstacles of the emergent paradigm. The immediate purpose of this book, then, is not to 'announce' a new paradigm but to bring together some of the elements that *may* form its basis. Our intentions are to state what these elements are, to acknowledge their provenance and to present readers with the work of some of those who are currently exploring new directions. Our hope is that this, in itself, will be productive of further progress.

Allison James and Alan Prout
December, 1989

Note

1   In such a collection as this, it is possible to select only a limited number of contributions. There are many working in this field who are not represented in this
volume but to whom we are all indebted. In particular we would like to mention
Judith Ennew, Pamela Reynolds and Jill Swart.

References

ARIES, P. (1962) *Centuries of Childhood*, London, Jonathan Cape.

DENZIN, N. (1977) *Childhood Socialization*, San Francisco, Jossey-Bass.

DREITZEL, H.P. (Ed) (1973) *Childhood and Socialization*, London, Collier-Macmillan.

GIDDENS, A. (1979) *The Central Problems of Social Theory*, London, Macmillan.

HOLT, J. (1975) *Escape from Childhood*, Harmondsworth, Penguin.

MACKAY, R. (1973) 'Conceptions of Children and Models of Socialization', in DREITZEL,
H.P. (1973) *Childhood and Socialization*, London, Collier-Macmillan.

RICHARDS, M.P.M. (Ed) (1974) *The Integration of a Child into a Social World*, Cambridge, Cambridge University Press.

RICHARDS, M. and LIGHT, P. (Ed) (1986) *Children of Social Worlds*, Cambridge, Polity
Press.

Chapter 1

A New Paradigm for the Sociology of Childhood? Provenance, Promise and Problems

Alan Prout and Allison James

Introduction: The Nature of Childhood

The title of this volume, *Constructing and Reconstructing Childhood*, captures the spirit within which it is conceived. First, we discussed in the introduction what we there called the 'emergent paradigm'. In this chapter we present it in precisely this light: an emerging and not yet completed approach to the study of childhood. Second, the title encapsulates what we feel to be the nature of the social institution of childhood: an actively negotiated set of social relationships within which the early years of human life are constituted. The immaturity of children is a biological fact of life but the ways in which this immaturity is understood and made meaningful is a fact of culture (see La Fontaine, 1979). It is these 'facts of culture' which may vary and which can be said to make of childhood a social institution. It is in this sense, therefore, that one can talk of the social construction of childhood and also, as it appears in this volume, of its re- and deconstrution. In this double sense, then, childhood is both constructed and reconstructed both for children and by children.

Attempting to describe and analyze the quality of that experience, researchers have, over the years, begun to develop new approaches to the study of childhood. One of the forerunners of this 'emergent paradigm', Charlotte Hardman, in 1973 compared her work on the anthropology of children to the study of women, arguing that 'both women and children might perhaps be called "muted groups" i.e., unperceived or elusive groups (in terms of anyone studying a society)' (1973: 85). In this discussion we suggest that the term 'muted' is indeed appropriate. The history of the study of childhood in the social sciences has been marked not by an absence of interest in children — as we shall show this has been far from the case — but by their silence. What the emergent paradigm attempts is to give a voice, to children through, as Hardman suggested, regarding 'children as people to be studied in their own right, and not just as receptacles of adult teaching' (*ibid* 87).

In what follows we trace the origins of this approach, analyze its benefits and outline some issues confronted in its further development. We show the ways in which the socio-political context made possible alternative approaches to childhood study as the experience of childhood changed for children. We locate these changes in relation to the new theoretical directions taken by the social sciences, described by Crick as 'a shift from function to meaning' which made possible the study of social categories rather than groups (1976: 2). Finally we point to the potential which the 'emergent paradigm' has for future developments in childhood sociology.

At this juncture it is useful, therefore, to reiterate what we see as the key features of the paradigm:

1. Childhood is understood as a social construction. As such it provides an interpretive frame for contextualizing the early years of human life. Childhood, as distinct from biological immaturity, is neither a natural nor universal feature of human groups but appears as a specific structural and cultural component of many societies.

2. Childhood is a variable of social analysis. It can never be entirely divorced from other variables such as class, gender, or ethnicity. Comparative and cross-cultural analysis reveals a variety of childhoods rather than a single and universal phenomenon.

3. Children's social relationships and cultures are worthy of study in their own right, independent of the perspective and concerns of adults.

4. Children are and must be seen as active in the construction and determination of their own social lives, the lives of those around them and of the societies in which they live. Children are not just the passive subjects of social structures and processes.

5. Ethnography is a particularly useful methodology for the study of childhood. It allows children a more direct voice and participation in the production of sociological data than is usually possible through experimental or survey styles of research.

6. Childhood is a phenomenon in relation to which the double hermeneutic of the social sciences is acutely present (see Giddens, 1976). That is to say, to proclaim a new paradigm of childhood sociology is also to engage in and respond to the process of reconstructing childhood in society.

It is clear that these six points represent merely a rough outline of the potential which the 'emergent paradigm' may hold for the study of childhood. Much more work needs to be done to integrate, theoretically develop and empirically elaborate these parameters. It is not certain whether these constitute the radical break with the past, as is sometimes claimed by those who are perhaps a little too enthusiastic for the study of childhood to be given recognition and status within mainstream sociology. Whilst it *is* certainly true that sociologists have devoted little attention to childhood as a topic of interest in itself and that many of the key concepts used to think about childhood are problematic, it is misleading to suggest that childhood is absent from the discourse of social scientists. On the contrary, 'the century of the child' can be characterized as such precisely because of the massive corpus of knowledge built up by psychologists and other social scientists through the systematic study of children. If the concept of childhood as a distinct stage in the human life cycle crystallized in nineteenth century western thought, then the twentieth century has seen that theoretical space elaborated and filled out with detailed empirical findings. Technologies of knowledge such as the psychological experiment, psychometric testing, sociometric mapping, ethnographic description and longitudinal surveys have all been applied to childhood and structured our thinking about children. They have also, and centrally to the concerns of this book, led to the growing imposition of a particularly western conceptualization of childhood for all children which effectively conceals the fact that the institution of childhood is a social construction (see Boyden, this volume). It is our task here, then, to situate what is new in the context of what has passed in order to judge its efficacy for contemporary concepts of childhood.

The complexity of the background to the emergence of the 'new' paradigm necessitates that we adopt an essentially thematic rather than historical account of the developments which allowed for, and at times precluded, changes in thinking about childhood. It is clear that psychological explanations of child development, announced early on in the twentieth century, have until recently dominated childhood study. They both supported and were supported by child-rearing/training practices, bridging the gap between theory and practice, parent and child, teacher and pupil, politician and populace. It is therefore predominantly developmental psychology which has provided a framework of explanation of the child's nature and indeed justified the concept of the naturalness of childhood itself. During this period, however, alternative voices have been raised, in the ideologies of populist movements and from changing paradigms within the social sciences. But for a long time these have gone unremarked and unheard or, indeed, have been silenced. The question now arises as to their salience in the 1990s, when, really for the first time, a reconstituted sociology of childhood has become more than the promise of a possibility. To begin to unravel the strands of these debates we begin at the beginning with the dominant explanatory frameworks.

Dominant and Dominating Accounts

A key concept in the dominant framework surrounding the study of children and childhood has been development and three themes predominate in relation to it: 'rationality', 'naturalness' and 'universality'. These have structured a mode of thought which stretches far beyond the disciplinary boundaries of psychology, influencing not only sociological approaches to child study but the socio-political context of childhood itself. The concept of 'development' inextricably links the biological facts of immaturity, such as dependence, to the social aspects of childhood. The universality of social practices surrounding childhood, which is the central focus of contemporary critiques, was consequently regarded as relatively unproblematic until the late 1970s. Resting on the assumed naturalness of childhood there was in fact little theoretical space within which to explore alternatives.

This dominant developmental approach to childhood, provided by psychology, is based on the idea of natural growth (see Jenks, 1982). It is a self-sustaining model whose features can be crudely delineated as follows: rationality is the universal mark of adulthood with childhood representing the period of apprenticeship for its development. Childhood is therefore important to study as a presocial period of difference, a biologically determined stage on the path to full human status i.e., adulthood. The naturalness of children both governs and is governed by their universality. It is essentially an evolutionary model: the child developing into an adult represents a progression from simplicity to complexity of thought, from irrational to rational behaviour. As an explanatory frame, it takes its inspiration from an earlier era, from the dawning of a scientific interest in society. During the nineteenth century western sociological theorists, the self-elected representatives of rationality, saw in other cultures primitive forms of the human condition. These they regarded as childish in their simplicity and irrational in their belief. Following on from Comte's theory of social evolution the 'savage' was seen as the precursor of civilized man, paralleling the way that the child prefigured adult life. Tylor, for example, argued that he could apply 'the often-repeated comparison of savages to children as fairly to their moral as to their intellectual condition' (1871: 31). The proximity of the savage to the natural world made Rousseau's child of nature an apt metaphor for social evolution during the nineteenth and early twentieth centuries.

The model of child development which has come to dominate western thought similarly connects biological with social development: children's activities — their language, play and interactions — are significant as symbolic markers of developmental progress. As activities they are seen to prefigure the child's future participation in the adult world. Little account is given of their significance to children's social life or to the variation which they reveal in the social context of childhood. The decreasing 'irrationality' of children's play as they mature is taken as a measure of an evolving 'rationality' of thought, charting the ways in which 'primitive' concepts become replaced by sophisticated ideas. The powerful and persistent influence of this explanatory framework can be illustrated through considering the impact of Jean Piaget's work on child development. In this respect it is significant that Piaget acknowledges the inspiration which Levy-Bruhl's work on 'primitive' thought had for the development of his own ideas. As Paul Light remarks, it is Piagetian approaches which have dominated work on cognition during the last quarter of the century, totally eclipsing 'earlier theoretical positions which attempted to ground an account of cognitive development in the child's social experiences' (1986: 170). In Piaget's account, child development has a particular structure, consisting of a series of predetermined stages, which lead towards the eventual achievement of logical competence. This is the mark of adult rationality. Within such a conceptual scheme children are marginalized beings awaiting temporal passage, through the acquistion of cognitive skill, into the social world of adults.

The singularity of 'the child' who constantly appears in both the title and the text of Piaget's writings is constructed around the twin assumptions of the naturalness and universality of childhood. Children do not have to appear: 'the child', as the bodily manifestation of cognitive development from infancy to adulthood can represent all children. As heirs to a western intellectual tradition centred on scientific rationality, 'the child' represented a laboratory specimen for the study of primitive forms of cognition and, indeed, children were brought into the laboratory to be studied. Representatives of pre-rational phases, children of various ages were used to discover the sequential process of the emergent rationality of 'the child'. Such an approach is consistent with the evolutionary perspective inherent in what Boas (1966) describes as nineteenth century cultural primitivism.

Piaget's work has been the inspiration for many other accounts of childhood and indeed for many social practices around children. For example it is his account of developmental stages in cognition which continues to inform contemporary western orthodoxies about child-rearing practices (see Urwin, 1985) and, as Walkerdine (1984) shows, it also lies at the heart of current educational thinking and practice. Indeed so much is this perspective incorporated into the everyday understanding of children in western societies that it is difficult to think outside it. For example, the common parental lament, 'its just a phase s/he's going through,' relies heavily on an implicit Piagetian model of child development, providing a biological explanation for a breakdown in social relationships. The challenge to this orthodoxy provided by contemporary approaches to childhood is the more remarkable given the pervasive dominance of developmental psychological models in everyday life.

The scientific construction of the 'irrationality', 'naturalness' and 'universality' of childhood through psychological discourses was translated directly into sociological accounts of childhood in the form of theories of socialization during the 1950s. At a time when positivism gripped the social sciences it offered a 'scientific' explanation for the process whereby children learnt to participate in society. Within structural functionalist accounts of society the 'individual' was slotted into a finite number of social roles. Socialization, therefore, was the mechanism whereby these social roles came to be replicated in successive generations. The theory puported to explain the ways in which children gradually acquire knowledge of these roles. However, it frequently failed to do so; 'how' socialization occurs was often ignored or glossed over by what Rafky describes as a 'vague, somewhat muddled . . . excess of "psychologising"' (1973: 44). Indeed, there is a great deal of theoretical slippage over this question of process: words like 'assimilate', 'induction' and 'accretion' inhibit discussion of the precise ways in which children become knowing subjects.

In her rethink of socialization theory, Tonkin (1982) demonstrates that the traditional model contains a fundamental confusion which accounts for such sleights of hand and indeed, it is recognition of this which paved the way for contemporary approaches. The importation of a psychological model directly into sociological theory collapsed together two definitions of what constitutes the subject; the individual as an instance of the species and the person as an instance of society.

As Tonkin notes, it is the individual who is the focus for classic psychology which is why, as she wryly comments, 'variations in the behaviour of a small number of university students may be held to instantiate variations at large in the world' (1982: 245). By contrast, within sociology it is the social aspects of personhood which are the paramount focus. It is these which are negotiated and manipulated in social relationships; the psychological aspects of individuals are residual in sociological explanation. Traditional functionalist accounts of socialization conflate these distinctions and ultimately fail to satisfactorily explain the process by which 'the individual acquires personhood'. (*ibid*: 245) As Jenks puts it: 'the social transformation from child to adult does not follow directly from physical growth' as is logically the case in traditional accounts of socialization (1982: 12).

The implicit binarism of the psychological model was uncritically absorbed into classical socialization theory. In such an account children are regarded as 'immature, irrational, incompetent, asocial [and] acultural' with adults being 'mature, rational, competent, social and autonomous' (Mackay, 1973: 28). They are, in effect, two different instances of the species. Socialization is the process which magically transforms the one into the other, the key which turns the asocial child into a social adult. The child's nature is therefore assumed to be different; for the model to work indeed this must be the case. The child is portrayed, like the laboratory rat, as being at the mercy of external stimuli: passive and conforming. Lost in a social maze it is the adult who offers directions. The child, like the rat, responds accordingly and is finally rewarded by becoming 'social', by becoming adult. In being constructed as unable to initiate interactions the child's nature is thus visualized as fundamentally different from an adult's. Elkin's account of the 1960s shows how this model was supposed to work: 'The socialising agents teach, serve as models, and invite participation. Through their ability to offer gratification and deprivations they induce cooperation and learning and prevent disrupting deviance' (1960: 101). Like a totalitarian regime of control, this model of socialization maintained the theoretical stability of functionalist accounts of society and indeed contributed to the production of the stasis of the functionalist world view. In so doing it generated a new series of problems related to the supposed failure of socialization in the everyday practices of some children.

Part of the reason for this mismatch between theory and practice is that the perspectives for the study of children derived from socialization theory were primarily based upon adult concern for the reproduction of social order. Children were of little account other than as passive representatives of the future generation which, as it turned out, was theoretically a heavy responsibility. Summarizing traditional approaches to socialization theory, Shildkrout comments that:

> ... child culture is seen as a rehearsal for adult life and socialisation consists of the processes through which, by one method or another, children are made to conform, in cases of 'successful' socialisation or become deviants in cases of 'failed socialisation' (1978: 109–10).

This neglect of the process of socialization, with undue emphasis placed upon its outcome, spawned a whole series of debates and moral panics about childhood. These focused upon the role of the family and the school as socializing agents with little weight given to consideration of the impact or meaning of these institutions in the lives of children. As important features in the social landscape of adults they were assumed, by adults, to be critical to the developmental progress of their children. Little attention was paid to the possibility of contradictions or indeed conflict in the socialization process. Tied to an implicit psychological model of child development, the sociological account of growing up was based on an inherent individualistic naturalism. All children who seemed to falter in the socialization process were potentially included in the new set of categories of 'child': school failures, deviants and neglected children. Failure to be harmoniously socialized into society's functioning meant, in effect, a failure to be human.

Dissenting Voices: A Challenge to Orthodoxy

The persistence of psychological explanations of the sociality of children both fed on and was fed by their ubiquity. In much the same way as the category 'women' was, in pre-feminist thinking, seen 'as some kind of universal' the category 'children' was within traditional explanations tied to what Hastrup has called 'the semantics of biology' (1978: 49). The biological facts of life, birth and infancy, were constantly used to explain the social facts of childhood with little account taken of any cultural component. It was the gradual growth in awareness that the meanings attached to the category 'child' and 'childhood' might differ across time or in space which began to destabilize traditional models of child development and socialization. As Danziger (1970) notes, the traditional model of socialization developed in the west, contained an implicit cultural bias, making it of little use for comparative purposes. The emergent paradigm, in contrast, begins with the assumption that a child is socialized by belonging to a 'particular culture at a certain stage in its history' (Danziger, 1970: 18).

There is no doubt that the growth of interpretive perspectives in the social sciences, especially symbolic interactionism and social phenomenology, gave an impetus to new directions in the study of childhood. In particular, they fostered an interest in children as social actors and childhood as a particular kind of social reality. For example the preoccupation with the social activities of everyday life — a concern that became central to interactionist sociology — allowed for the possibility of questioning that which previously had been seen as unproblematic. Within the interpretive tradition aspects of everyday life which are taken for granted are examined by 'bracketing them off'. The aim is to render them culturally strange by a process of detailed and critical reflection, thus bringing them into the sphere of sociological analysis. A second and crucial perspective is that social reality is not fixed, constant or unitary. Rather, social life is seen as being constantly created through the activities of social actors. It is an accomplishment of human beings and carried out on the basis of beliefs, perspectives and typifications which give rise to meaningful and intentional action. The explanation of social life requires grasping the meaning of it for participants in the context of its specific occurrence. These two features of interpretive sociology have combined to create a particular interest in the perspectives of low status groups in social organizations and settings. One such low-status group is, of course, children.

In the 1950s and 60s, then, interpretive sociologies were a potent source for the critique of the then dominant paradigm of structural-functionalism, from which conceptions of child socialization derived. This general critique reversed the structural-functionalist relationship between structure and agency, with interpretivists stressing the role of creative individual activity in the constitution of human society. An attack on prevailing notions of socialization was an integral part, summed up perhaps in Wrong's (1961) memorable accusation that Parsons held 'an over-socialised conception of man'. Phenomenological (Rafky, 1973) and interactionist (MacKay, 1973) alternatives, which gave children a more active role, were outlined. It was only a short step from this to the suggestion that the concept of childhood within socialization theory was itself faulty. MacKay summarized his position:

> If the two claims are correct, that children are competent interpreters of the social world and that they possess a separate culture(s), then the study of adult-child interaction (formerly socialisation) becomes the study of cultural assimilation, or, more theoretically important, the study of meaningful social interaction (1973: 31).

A second and later impetus to the new directions taken in the study of childhood came from structuralism, in its many forms, and from an upsurge of interest in semiology. Following the demolition of traditional models of socialization and critiques of child development, until this time the major routes which the study of childhood followed, these intellectual trends focused further attention on the ways in which processes of social classification not only structure the institutional arrangements of social life but our very mode of apprehending them. The possibilities of alternative world views, dissent, and hegemonic challenge which these intellectual debates opened up, paved the way for the suggestion that certain social groups might possess different views of the social world from the majority. Semiology became seen as increasingly important in the understanding of expressive meaning in everyday life and it produced a rich vein of symbolic analyses. Many of these focused on the use of nonverbal forms of symbolic expression by low status groups (see Hebdige, 1979) as well as on the power of language in shaping social reality (see Ricoeur, 1978).

Changes in the general intellectual climate during the 1970s initiated new directions in the study of childhood within many disciplines but it was perhaps from history that the opening moves were made. Although by no means the first historian to propose a radical critique of concepts of childhood, the work of the French historian Phillip Aries had a major impact on the social sciences. His dramatic and boldly stated contention that 'in medieval society the idea of childhood did not exist' was eagerly taken up by sociologists (1962: 125). It quickly became incorporated as an example of the variability of human societies, all the more useful because it looked not to the 'exotic' or 'primitive' but to a familiar western European past.

Aries's challenge to orthodoxy lay in his suggestion that the concept of childhood emerged in Europe between the fifteenth and eighteenth centuries, thus blasting a large hole in traditional assumptions about the universality of childhood. Making extensive use of medieval icons he argued that, beyond the dependent stage of infancy, children were not depicted. They were there as miniature adults only. However, from the fifteenth century onwards children began to appear as children, reflecting their gradual removal from the everyday life of adult society. According to Aries this was first fostered through the growth of new attitudes of 'coddling' towards children, which stressed their special nature and needs. Second was the emergence of formal education and long periods of schooling as a prerequisite for children before they assumed adult responsibilities. Initially only economically and practically possible for the upper classes, who alone had the time and money for 'childhood', these trends diffused downwards through society. Childhood became institutionalized for all.

Aries's work stimulated a flurry of historical work in relation to children and the family. Some of it offered support to Aries's idea of 'the discovery of childhood' whilst other work rejected the challenge. Lloyd De Mause (1976) for example retained the notion of childhood as a human universal, preferring to characterize early child rearing practices as so brutal and exploitative that they bear little resemblance to those of modern western societies. Childhood, he argued, is the same; it is parents who have changed. Aries's thesis was also increasingly the subject of critical scrutiny by other historians in relation to his historical method, evidence, and interpretation. The debate continues but one of the more interesting critiques can be found in Pollock (1983). Using 415 primary sources between 1500–1900, she comments that,

> Many historians have subscribed to the mistaken belief that, if a past society did not possess the contemporary Western concept of childhood, then the society had no such concept. This is a totally indefensible point of view — why should past societies have regarded children in the same way as Western society today? Moreover, even if children were regarded differently in the past, this does not mean that they were not regarded as children (1983: 263).

This is far from the sensationalism of Aries' original work, and ends with the more modest claim that whilst western societies both past and present make a distinction between children and adults, and accord children characteristics and treatment different from adults, the particular form of modern childhood is nevertheless historically specific.

Although there is no acknowledged link, this less grandiose formulation of the contention that childhood is socially constructed is supported by the earlier work of social anthropologists involved in culture and personality studies. These studies, designed to illustrate the infinite plasticity of culture and cultural relativity, focused on variations in child-rearing practices as the locus of difference. Benedict (1935), provides a well known example. Comparing childhood among the Zuni, Dobu and Kwakiutl she finds marked differences in terms of the responsibility children are allowed to assume, their degree of subordination to adults and the way the characteristics of gender are distributed. Earlier, Margaret Mead (1928), the chief representative of the 'culture-personality' school had sought, through her Samoan work, to counter the psychologist Stanley Hall's suggestion that adolescence is a period of natural rebellion through showing its absence in Samoa. However, despite this emphasis on the variability of childhood, such writers re-tained a conventional view of socialization as a moulding process carried out by adults. Those working within the culture-personality framework paid particular attention to child rearing practices, for these, they pos-ited, are the central means by which cultural traits are transmitted. Little attention was paid to childhood as a phenomenon in itself or to children as active participants in their own rearing process.

Anthropological interest in age as a principle of social differentia-tion and stratification is less well known. But it could be argued that the body of theory and ethnographic material (discussed in James and Prout, this volume) brought together under this rubric has had a more lasting impact on the current new thinking about childhood than the more apparently relevant work of the culture-personality writers. The now classic work of Eisenstadt (1956) on generational transition in modern societies is a reminder of the potential which this has. Writing from the perspective of Parsonian structural functionalism, but borrowing heavily from anthropology, Eisenstadt suggests that strong age grades are functional to the social stability of contemporary societies. In par-ticular he identifies youth subcultures as the means by which future adult familial and occupational roles can be both 'held at bay' and rehearsed in safety. This notion that strong age group affiliations among young people form a transitional stage which partially sequesters them from adult society reflects anthropological work on age systems cross-culturally.

From these beginnings the body of work on subculture was spawned. Functionalist theorists, such as Musgrove (1964), took Eisen-stadt's suggestion further through arguing that young people were a consumer defined class outside the structured differentiations of capit-alist society. This view was later rejected in the analyses emerging from the Centre for Contemporary Cultural Studies (see Hall and Jefferson, 1976). Combining Marxism and semiology, writers within this tradition, on the contrary, saw youth subcultures as expressing the contradictions and conflicts of the class structure. The most celebrated example is Cohen's (1972) analysis of skinheads. With their boots, braces, collarless shirts and cropped hair, Cohen describes the skinheads as attempting to magically recover the traditional English working-class community life that was fast disappearing in sixties urban reconstruction.

The emergence and later analysis of working-class youth subcul-tures as social groups with specific ideologies sparked off sociological interest in 'age' as a principle of social classification in *western* societ-ies. Other 'age' categories such as 'children' and 'the elderly' assumed new status as 'social problems' in the socio-political context of 'aging' populations and increasingly 'child-centred' societies. Paralleling the work on subcultural world views it was therefore suggested that younger children too might inhabit semi-autonomous social worlds whose meanings the adult world had yet to come to terms with. In 1973, for example, Hardman phrased her research in terms of seeking 'to discover whether there is in childhood a self-regulating, autonomous world which does not necessarily reflect early development of adult culture' (1973: 87). Semiological approaches tapped a rich vein in the language and concepts used by children: when it was no longer necessary to describe children's behaviour or language as pre-social or pre-rational, it became possible to contextualize it as expressive of their social world (see James, 1979a; 1979b).

Whilst the direct impact of these new theoretical perspectives on the empirical studies has generally been disappointing, one area, the sociology of schooling, stands out from this general rule. For example, the pioneering work of Hargreaves (1967) and Lacey (1970) on the meaning and process of social differentiation in the subcultures of secondary school pupils gave a powerful impetus to interest in children's views of their everyday life. Such work was given a theoretical voice in the (then) 'new perspectives' in the sociology of education (Young, 1971). In essence Young advocated the use of interpretive perspectives to shift the sociology of education away from its traditional concerns with the structural features of educational systems towards a questioning of the schooling process itself. This meant critically examining concepts such as 'achievement' 'ability' and 'knowledge' in terms of their meanings for those involved in the schooling process. The focus for study became the interactions between actors (mainly teachers and pupils) in concrete educational settings, which were at first classrooms but soon extended into other contexts in the lives of pupils. In this framework children, as school pupils, were transformed from objects of educational systems to active participants, paralleling the transformations of children's subjectivity in the remodelled perspectives on socialization. Although this perspective was itself far from uncontentious, one positive outcome was the creation of a whole new genre of empirical studies which described and analyzed pupil cultures and experiences, (see for example Woods, 1980).

Within psychology, which, as we have already shown, had always been the main arena for childhood research in the social sciences, doubting voices also began to be raised during the late 1960s. Here again interpretive perspectives combined with an awareness of cultural and historical relativism to produce a radical critique. In Britain the publication in 1974 of a collection edited by Martin Richards, and a similar North American one edited by Kessell and Siegel (1983), are widely regarded as landmarks of the new approach. The underpinnings of this were later described by Richards as:

> . . . the criticism of a psychology based on universal laws that were supposed to hold good across all societies and at all historical times. It was argued that such terms as 'the mother' and 'the child' not only conveyed a meaningless generality but also misrepresented the relationship between individual and social worlds and portrayed social arrangements as if they were fixed by laws of nature (1986: 3).

Although the focus remained on the individual, the recognition that childhood is socially constructed led to a heightened awareness of the social context within which psychological processes take place.

The research programme which these new perspectives engendered has been extremely fruitful. Two lines of enquiry, which were both stimulated by and constitutive of the new perspectives, illustrate the impact of interpretive methodology. The first centres on the experimental core of classical Piagetianism. The 'objectivity' of 'the experiment' was thrown into doubt by McGarrigle's and Donaldson's work (described in Donaldson, 1978) which, through the substitution of a 'naughty teddy' for the adult experimenter, showed children achieving apparently 'precocious' test results. It is suggested that these results could be accounted for by the fact that the experiment had, through the activities of the naughty teddy bear, become far more 'meaningful' to the child. The reassessment of Piaget which such work led to is not yet complete or resolved but Light (1986) has recently suggested that both the social context of adult-child relationships and the symbolic meanings which children bring to experiments, in terms of social rules and the objects used, may influence the 'results'.

The elucidation of rules and meanings in everyday life was a central aim of the second impact of interpretivism on psychology. Harre's (1979) notion of 'ethogenic method' might be seen as exemplifying its main tenets: a focus on the meaning system within which social actions take place; a concern with the way in which subjectivity and inter-subjectivity are constituted within language; and the objective of using common-sense understandings within research processes. The method is in principle not limited by the age of the social actors being studied but in practice much of the research carried out within this perspective has concerned children and youth. These have resulted in studies which have much in common with the educational and subcultural studies discussed earlier (see Marsh, *et al.*, 1978).

These then are some of the intellectual trends which have created a theoretically plausible space called the 'social construction of child-hood'. It would, however, be naive to imply that the establishment of such a space was made possible only by the community of social scientists. It is clear, for example, that the influence of interpretive philosophy within the social sciences was bolstered by the political possibilities which it seemed to offer. If social (and psychological) rea-lities are constructions of human understanding and intentional activity then they can be unmade as well as made. The more optimistic versions of this voluntarism suffused the radical political movements of the 1960s and 70s and underpinned much of its 'counter-cultural' thinking. Anti-colonial, civil rights, anti-psychiatry and the women's movements all suggested that social relationships were not fixed by social and psy-chological laws but could be reconstituted (through various forms of social and political struggle) on a different basis. Although the optimism about social change may have diminished over the last decade, at its most powerful, it began to question even the most taken-for-granted social relationships. Children and childhood, although not central to this questioning, played a small part in, for example, an upsurge of interest in children's rights (recently discussed in, Franklin, 1986).

In considering the question of the relationship between the social sciences and society we have already pointed to the way in which Piagetian developmental psychology has shaped the practices of prim-ary school teaching. In general, whilst sociology and psychology may seek only to understand the world as it is, their products, findings, terminology and ways of accounting for the world are nevertheless absorbed back into it and become constitutive of the societies into which they enquire. In this sense there can be no concepts of childhood which are socially and politically innocent. Where sixties radicalism saw itself as liberating children from oppression, we now see practi-tioners of the social sciences more cautiously acknowledging the role of their disciplines in the production of childhood in its present form.

Obstacles to and Prospects of Constructing a New Paradigm

The emergence of the new paradigm for the study of childhood has been traced along a somewhat tortuous path; as yet the paradigm is still relatively fluid and unformed, and there remain many obstacles which must be overcome before the sociology of childhood can be said to have a firm theoretical footing. In this last section we will indicate some of these.

First, it has to be recognized that the still dominant concepts of 'development' and 'socialization' are extraordinarily resistant to criticism. They persist despite all that has been said against them. Richards (1986: 3), for example, laments that despite widespread discussion of the need for cognitive and developmental psychology to locate itself within a social and cultural context, only a minority of recently published empirical research even faintly considers this possibility. Similarly, in sociology, the concept of socialization continues to dominate theory and research about children. The lack of change here stands out particularly sharply in, for example, the sociology of the family. Whilst thinking about women and the family has been revolutionized by feminist critiques, thinking about childhood remains relatively static, like the still point at the centre of a storm. There are, for example, huge differences in the treatment of most topics between Morgan's excellent *Social Theory and the Family* (1975) and his publication of (the equally excellent) *Family, Politics and Social Theory* a decade later (1985). Childhood, however, remains more or less unchanged, and is, if anything, more marginal in the second than in the first work.

It has to be acknowledged immediately that this state of affairs results in part from the productivity of the dominant position. It has, despite all the criticisms which we have made above, been extraordinarily productive in the creation of knowledge about childhood and any new developments will build on this foundation. Indeed, insofar as the emergent paradigm is being developed in relation to old ideas, these can be seen as part of its provenance. However, it is now clear that these ideas are no longer adequate. Their continued dominance is, in part, the responsibility of those who (like ourselves) have talked long on the sociology of childhood but published little. This book is a partial remedy for that but it also has to be acknowledged that there are some deep-rooted sources of resistance to the reconceptualizing of childhood within sociology. Ambert (1986) uncovers some of these in her survey of childhood in North American sociology. She suggests that children's relative absence is rooted in the same factors which excluded attention to women (and gender): that is, a male-dominated sociology that does not give worth to child care and still less to the activities of children themselves. This, allied to conservativism and a male-oriented career structure means that: '. . . the gate-keepers of the discipline . . . continue to place a high value on certain types of knowledge, data, theories and research methods. . . . One does not become a household name in sociology by studying children' (Ambert, 1986: 16).

Resistance to new ways of thinking about childhood extends beyond the confines of sociology. There is a correspondence between the concepts of the social sciences and the ways in which childhood is socially constructed. Notions like socialization are inscribed in the practices of teachers and social workers, for example, and this ensures that their critique extends into and meets a wider resistance. This is not simply a matter of habit, convenience, false consciousness or vested interests but of what Foucault refers to as 'regimes of truth' (1977). He suggests that these operate rather like self-fulfilling prophecies: ways of thinking about childhood fuse with institutionalized practices to produce self-conscious subjects (teachers, parents and children) who think (and feel) about themselves through the terms of those ways of thinking. 'The truth' about themselves and their situation is thus self-validating. Breaking into this with another 'truth' (produced by another way of thinking about childhood) may prove difficult. For example, the resilience of socialization as a dominant concept rests partly on the way in which notions of childhood are embedded within a tightly structured matrix of significations binding childhood with, and positioning it in relation to, the family. As Leena Alanen remarks,

> The triangularity of childhood, the family and socialization proves to be as moulded into one piece that cannot be broken into parts for separate consideration . . . blocking the possibilities of even imagining novel relationships between the three components (1988: 54).

Unlocking these relationships is one of the main theoretical tasks for the development of an alternative framework.

How can this be best approached? In one sense the emergent paradigm outlined here is the start of this process. The critique of previously hegemonic concepts has loosened some of the connections and allowed some of the 'creative imagining' of which Alanen speaks. For some time now it has been possible to think of a theoretical space in which, for example, children can be looked at as active social beings, constructing and creating social relationships, rather than as the 'cultural dopes' of socialization theory. Similarly, it is possible to posit age relationships as a serious dimension of analysis alongside those of class, gender and ethnicity, and work on this has already begun.

We believe, however, that it would be a mistake to think that the theorizing of childhood should, or can, take place outside of the theoretical debates of mainstream sociology. On the contrary, it needs to draw on the debates of the social sciences at large — and to contribute to them — if it is not to become an isolated and esoteric specialism. That outcome would be almost as damaging as no sociology of childhood at all, since it would relieve other branches of sociology from the necessity of thinking through the implications for their own treatment of childhood. The aim, rather, must be for a sociology of childhood which is coherent enough both to stand on its own but at the same time make a serious impact on other branches of the discipline. To achieve this its concerns must correspond and connect with wider sociological debates.

Paradoxically one of the most important strands of theoretical thinking to be taken into account has had most influence among psychologists interested in childhood. It concerns the attempt to situate child development in a social context, leading to what Harre (1986) has termed 'the step to social constructionism'. The project of integrating social and psychological perspectives has turned out to be a complex one. Straightforward attempts to give an increased weight to 'social context' is found to recapitulate the fundamental individual-society binarism which we have already criticized. As Ingelby (1986) has persuasively argued, 'development-in-a-social context' merely conjoins psychological processes and social context without specifying their links. That is to say, theories of development-in-a-social context assume an individual subject which exists separately from and pre-figures society. Ingelby's point here is borrowed from the post-structuralist perspectives of Henriques *et al.* (1984), who are themselves indebted to the ideas of Foucault. It is suggested here that the notion of a subject which exists outside of social relationships is a heritage of Cartesian dualism which has yet to be overcome in the social sciences. Whilst structuralism resolved this dualism (or binarism, as we have called it) by 'abolishing' the subject, making individuals merely the bearers of social relationships, post-structuralist thinking retains subjects by making them the effects of 'discourse'. This concept of discourse goes beyond De Saussure's (1983) parole/langue distinction by positing 'discourse' as sets of concepts and the language through which they are thought as inseparable from and and fused with social practices and institutions. Ideas, concepts, knowledge, modes of speaking, etc. codify social practices and in turn constitute them.

Within these discourses subject positions (such as 'the child') are created. Seen from this point of view, then, different discourses of childhood constitute childhood (and children) in different ways — not only as sets of academic knowledge but also in social practices and institutions. Ingelby illustrates the promise of discourse theory in understanding childhood as a social construction by reference to Walkerdine's (1984) work on nursery school. She shows how classroom activities such as 'playing hospitals', insert children into discursively constituted subject positions ('doctor', 'nurse', 'patient') which are already suffused with relations of power and gender. Nevertheless, children are able to

shift between discourses and in a striking illustration Walkerdine describes how a girl transforms the 'Wendy House' from a hospital into
a family, transforming the subject positions so that she as 'mother' is
able to order the doctor to 'eat up his dinner'.

Whilst not in the mainstream of their discipline, some psychologists, then, have taken up Foucault's work as a means of overcoming
individual-society binarism by grasping how subjects are produced within
and through discursive practices. Clearly an interest in *individual* consciousness remains an important concern of psychology even in this
radically transformed state and the work of psychologists such as Urwin
(1985) on the construction of power and desire in infantile psychic
development shows how fruitful it can be. But the issues involved in
the discussion of subjectivity and social relations also has an importance for sociologists and that this is so illustrates the extent to which
existing academic distinctions (such as that between sociology and
psychology) are dissolved by social constructionism. Indeed, because
discourse is conceptualized as traversing social institutions, practices,
everyday life and subjectivity, it has the effect of rendering untenable
many traditional sociological distinctions — for example those between
'macro' and 'micro' sociology (Silverman, 1985). Nevertheless, sociologists and social anthropologists might retain their distinctive concern(s)
by emphasizing the effects of discourse in the constitution of practices
and institutions rather than of subjectivity and psychic processes.
Armstrong (1983), for example, has shown how within pediatric medicine, shifts in discourse from pathology to the surveillance of normal
growth, reconstituted the body of the child in medical practice. In doing
so he shows how one extremely important twentieth century version of
childhood was constructed. In this volume several authors implicitly
draw, for part of their analysis, on the notion of childhood as a discursive formation (or formations) within which different types of children and childhood have been constituted: in Hendrick's review of the
historical review of the construction and reconstruction of childhood;
Glauser's deconstruction of the concept of 'street-child' in a Paraguayan
context; and Qvortrup's analysis of the constitution of childhood in
social statistics.

The application of discourse theory to childhood is, however, not
without its problems. First, is the question of biological and social factors in the construction of childhood; the extent to which childhood
as a text can be understood independently of childhood as a stage of
biological growth and maturity. If, as Armstrong suggests, the body of
the child was reconstituted by shifting discursive practices of medicine,
then are we to take the body as *only* a social construction (Bury, 1986)?

If so then consideration of, for instance, the different physical size of children and their relative muscular weakness compared to adults (of either sex) are not relevant to sociological explanations of, for example, inequalities of power between children and adults. This, however, seems an absurd example of what Timpanaro (1975) has called 'cultural determinism', that is exempting human beings from the rest of the animal kingdom by denying *any* effects of our biological and physical being (see Woodhead, this volume). But if we are to see childhood as *both* biological and social, as we argued at the outset of this chapter, what weight should be given to each factor? In some societies, for example, children are expected to do far more physically demanding work than they do in Europe and North America. Do we account for this as part of the cultural variability of childhood or do we accept that at some point biological facts constrain the argument and compel us to invoke ethical and political categories such as abuse and exploitation?

The second issue arises from the application of a strict logic to the notion that childhood is socially constructed, that is constituted in discourse. If this is so then there can be no such object as the 'real child' (or any variant on this theme such as 'the authentic experience of childhood'). Instead we must content ourselves with the analysis of how different discursive practices produce different childhoods, each and all of which are 'real' within their own regime of truth. This is difficult for many of those active within the sociology of childhood to accept. There is strong tendency to see the mission of sociology as debunking, demystifying and releasing childhood from the ideological distortions of dominant social theories and practices. Ethnographic methods, in particular, are advocated as means of getting nearer to the 'truth' about what childhood is like (see Gubrium and Silverman, 1989). Modern ethnographic methodology, however, concurs with discourse theory, at least to the extent that it rejects a naturalistic view of ethnographic data. All ethnographic material has to be understood reflexively, that is as a product of a research process in which a particular interpretation is made by an observer in relation to the settings in which the observations are made. But is it not possible for ethnography to make a claim to a weaker sense of authenticity in which previously unexplored or unreported aspects of childhood are made available and previously mute children empowered to speak? Much of the work on pupil's experience of schooling, for example, seems to fall into this category. Whilst not (usually) claiming to be privileged accounts of schoolchildren's lives (and in this sense claiming authenticity), such work has, within the limits of any situated interpretation, given voice to the previously silent.

These questions of social construction, subjectivity and authenticity are intimately bound up in the major theoretical debate of contemporary sociology: that is, the problem of the relationship between agency (or 'action') and structure in social life. The debate has a particular salience for the sociology of childhood, since it was from interpretive sociology that much of the impetus to re-examine the role of children as active, meaning-producing beings came. Interpretive sociology stresses the creative production ('agency') of social life rather than the determination of social behaviour by systems of social organization. For a period of time in the 1960s and 1970s there appeared to be two competing types of sociology: one stressed that the system of social relationships in society (the mode of production, power and domination, belief systems and ideology etc.); the other stressed the creative activity, purposes and negotiative interaction between individual actors. Attempts to unify these alternative versions of sociology have been a major aim of theorists such as Giddens in his theory of 'structuration.' Giddens argues that sociologists must grasp both agency and structure, that they are in fact different sides of the same coin: 'Every act which contributes to the reproduction of a structure is also an act of production, and as such may initiate change by altering the structure at the same time as it reproduces it' (1979: 69).

Although Giddens's attempt to resolve this debate has been criticized (Clegg, 1989), some such view of how structure and agency complement each other seems be an essential component in any new sociology of childhood. It is important to recover children as social actors (and their activity as a source of social change); as interpretivists have insisted, this in itself is not adequate. We need also, however, to grasp childhood as a social institution that exists beyond the activity of any particular child or adult. There must be theoretical space for both the construction of childhood as an institution and the activity of children within and upon the constraints and possibilities that the institutional level creates. This does seem to be possible; in this volume, for example, Kitzinger's analysis of child sexual abuse retains both structure and agency. By exploring the relationship between these two levels we can, then, begin to elucidate the links between given (and largely adult defined social institutions) and the cultures which children construct for and between themselves. This is important for at least two reasons. First, unless we do so, accounts of children's cultures will always run the risk of consigning themselves to the margins of both social and sociological concern. To a significant degree this is the fate of pioneers such as the Opies (1977, 1984), who despite the richness of the ethnographic archive which they assembled, present a picture of

childhood as a world apart. It is linked to the dominant adult culture
only as a sort of anachronistic attic containing the abandoned lumber
of previous times (see James and Prout, this volume). Second, if we
attempt to account for children as both constrained by structure and
agents acting in and upon structure, we can make a plausible claim that
such accounts, if rigorous, are 'authentic'. Not in the sense that they
reveal some hitherto timeless 'essence' of childhood but rather that they
accurately portray aspects of childhood as it is constituted at a particular moment in time and point in space.

Temporality, in fact, is a feature of childhood to which little attention has been paid. Whilst it is, of course, inherent to the notion of
psychological development it appears there only as a natural constant,
the background flow to the teleological unfolding of the child. In sociology, the concept of socialization acts as a kind of suppressor of
childhood's present tense, orientating analysis either towards the past
(what went wrong with socialization) or the future (what the goals of
socialization should be). This neglect of the present is unusual since
sociologists tend to conduct synchronic analyses, preferring to leave
the succession of events in time to historians. One solution would be
to fuse the historical and sociological enterprises. Fruitful though this
may be, the resulting synthesis would probably also treat time as if it
is simply the natural stuff within which events occur. What is needed
is a more thoroughgoing analysis of time as a social construction during
childhood. In the conclusion to this volume (see James and Prout) we
begin such an analysis.

Politics and Ethics in Researching Childhood

Finally, we turn to the importance of empirical studies of childhood, for
despite the emphasis of this chapter, we believe it would be a mistake
to see the way forward only in terms of theoretical development. Well
conducted empirical studies such as those done by Solberg, Kitzinger
and Glauser in this volume are essential counterparts to theoretical
work. Quite apart from this symbiosis between theory and empirical
enquiry, however, we believe that the sociology of childhood in particular needs many more studies which open up hitherto neglected
topics — children and work, politics, health, food, and so on. These in
themselves could begin to pry the sociology of childhood away from
the stereotyped topics of the family and schooling.

Throughout this introductory chapter we have stressed that the
social sciences are not neutral commentaries on childhood but active

factors in its construction and reconstruction. The processes by which this occurs are complex (Giddens, 1984) and only partially within the province of conscious agency. Nevertheless, recognition of the socially constitutive role of the social sciences seems to require that attention be paid to the social implications of sociological work. It is far from clear, however, how these issues are best handled. The traditional notion of the detached scholar has collapsed, but what will replace it? This is not a question unique to the sociology of childhood but is an issue of current debate throughout the social sciences (Silverman, 1985). Finch (1985), for example, in her discussion of the relationship between qualitative research and social policy, suggests that sociologists should see themselves as offering 'illumination' within broad policy debates rather than specific 'social engineering' solutions to social problems. She points out that the relationship of the social sciences to social policy (and, one might add, other processes by which society is con- stituted) is not a direct one. Decisions are made (or avoided) through complex political processes within which sociologists may (or may not) have an influential but rarely, if ever, a determining role. She argues for a 'democratic' approach in which sociologists provide insights for participants at *all* levels in institutions and societies. In particular she advocates that sociologists should be involved with and concerned about the 'grass roots' of organizations, that is, those who have the least formal power and influence, rather than simply directing their work towards 'top' policy makers (see Glauser and Boyden, this volume).

Although generally attractive, the application of this perspective to childhood presents some special problems. Despite our recognition that children are active social beings, it remains true that their lives are almost always determined and/or constrained in large measure by adults and there are few instances of children becoming organized at a 'grass roots' level to represent themselves independently. On the contrary, almost all political, educational, legal and administrative processes have profound effects on children but they have little or no influence over them. Child care proceedings, for example, are supposed to be taken 'in the best interests of the child' but the children concerned are fre- quently never consulted. Similarly, recent changes in social security regulations in England and Wales have made it much more difficult for young people to live independently of their families after the age of 16, encouraging them to remain in households which they may find uncongenial, unpleasant or downright dangerous. Whilst independent political action by children is not unknown (for example, the Burston school strike of 1914 or the role of children in the Soweto uprising of 1976) its history is frequently hidden or suppressed. This not only makes it difficult to incorporate into academic accounts but frustrates any continuity in children's political organization. Nevertheless, attempts by children to 'speak for themselves' persist. In Britain at the moment, for example, children taken into care by the state are beginning to form their own organizations and projects such as the Children's Legal Centre and telephone counselling services for children who feel they need help, are steps taken by sympathetic adults which also point in this direction.

Sociologists need to find a relationship to both children's own activity and to the social processes which shape and constrain children's lives but in which they themselves are not necessarily involved. This relationship must allow a degree of analytical detachment — so avoiding the trap of merely articulating the interests of particular groups — whilst at the same time not denying responsibility for the effects which it may have. This is not an easy position either to establish or to occupy and presents some difficult dilemmas. For example, the current concern with child sexual abuse centres on the need to protect children from sexual exploitation. But, as Kitzinger argues in this volume, many of the practices through which this protection is established themselves disable and depower children by confirming the traditional view of children as passive victims. How, then, can we contribute to combatting child abuse whilst at the same time questioning these assumptions? More generally, how can a sociology of childhood be practised in a way which is sensitive to the political and ethical problems it inevitably entails? We offer this collection of essays as a way of raising these problems, stimulating debate and making some contribution to their solution.

References

ALANEN, L. (1988) 'Rethinking childhood', *Acta Sociologica*, **31**, 1, pp. 53–67.
AMBERT, A.M. (1986) 'The place of children in North American sociology', in ADLER, P. and ADLER, P. (Ed) *Sociological Studies in Child Development*, Greenwich, Conneticut, JAI Press.
ARDENER, S. (Ed) (1978) *Defining Females: The Nature of Women in Society*, London, Croom Helm.
ARIES, P. (1962) *Centuries of Childhood*, London, Jonathan Cape.
ARMSTRONG, D. (1983) *The Political Anatomy of the Body: Medical Knowledge in Britain in the Twentieth Century*, Cambridge, Cambridge University Press.
BENEDICT, R. (1935) *Patterns of Culture*, London, Routledge and Kegan Paul.
BERNARDI, B. (1985) *Age Class Systems: Social Institutions and Polities Based on Age*, Cambridge, Cambridge University Press.
BOAS, G. (1966) *The Cult of Childhood*, London, Warburg Institute.

Bury, M. (1986) 'Social constructionism and medical sociology', *Sociology of Health and Illness*, **8**, 2, pp. 137–69.

Clegg, S.R. (1989) *Frameworks of Power*, London, Sage.

Cohen, P. (1972) *Subcultural Conflict and Working Class Community*, Birmingham, Centre for Contemporary Cultural Studies.

Cohen, S. (1971) *Images of Deviance*, Harmondsworth, Penguin.

Cohen, S. (1980) *Folk Devils and Moral Panics*, Oxford, Robertson.

Crick, M. (1976) *Explorations in Language and Meaning*, London, Malaby Press.

Danziger, K. (Ed) (1970) *Readings in Child Socialization*, London, Pergamon Press Ltd.

De Mause, L. (Ed) (1976) *The History of Childhood*, London, Souvenir Press.

De Saussure, F. (1983) *Course in General Linguistics*, London, Duckworth.

Denzin, N.K. (1977) *Childhood Socialization*, San Francisco, Jossey-Bass.

Donaldson, M. (1978) *Children's Minds*, London, Fontana.

Donzelot, J. (1979) *The Policing of Families*, London, Hutchinson.

Dreitzel, H.P. (Ed) (1973) *Childhood and Socialization*, London, Collier-Macmillan.

Eisenstadt, S.N. (1956) *From Generation to Generation*, London, Collier-Macmillan.

Elkin, F. (1960) *The Child and Society*, New York, Random House.

Finch, J. (1985) *Research and Policy: Uses of Qualitative Methods in Social and Educational Research*, Lewes, Falmer Press.

Foucault, M. (1977) *Discipline and Punish*, London, Allen Lane.

Franklin, B. (Ed) (1986) *The Rights of Children*, Oxford, Basil Blackwell.

Garfinkel, H. (1967) *Studies in Ethnomethodology*, Englewood Cliffs, NJ, Prentice Hall.

Giddens, A. (1976) *The New Rules of Sociological Method*, London, Hutchinson.

Giddens, A. (1979) *The Central Problems of Social Theory*, London, Macmillan.

Giddens, A. (1984) *The Constitution of Society*, Cambridge, Polity Press.

Gubrium, J.F. and Silverman, D. (1989) *The Politics of Field Research: Sociology Beyond Enlightenment*, London, Sage.

Hall, S. and Jefferson, T. (Eds) (1976) *Resistance Through Rituals: Youth Subculture in Postwar Britain*, London, Hutchinson.

Hardman, C. (1973) 'Can there be an anthropology of children?', *Journal of the Anthropological Society of Oxford*, **4**, 1, pp. 85–99.

Hargreaves, D.H. (1967) *Social Relations in a Secondary School*, London, Routledge and Kegan Paul.

Harre, R. (1979) *Social Being: A Theory of Social Psychology*, Oxford, Basil Blackwell.

Harre, R. (1986) 'The step to social constructionism', in Richards, M. and Light, P. (Eds) (1986) *Children of Social Worlds*, Cambridge, Polity Press, pp. 287–96.

Hastrup, K. (1978) 'The semantics of biology: Virginity', in Ardener, S. (Ed) *Defining Females: The Nature of Women in Society*, London, Croom Helm, pp. 49–65.

Hebdige, D. (1979) *Subculture: The Meaning of Style*, London, Methuen.

Henriques, J. et al. (Eds) (1984) *Changing the Subject: Psychology, Social Regulation and Subjectivity*, London, Methuen.

Ingelby, D. (1986) 'Development in a social context', in Richards, M. and Light, P. (Eds) (1986) *Children of Social Worlds*, Cambridge, Polity Press, pp. 297–317.

James, A. (1979a) 'The game of the name: Nicknames in the child's world', *New Society*, **48**, 871, pp. 632–34.

James, A. (1979b) 'Confections, concoctions and conceptions' in Waites, B. et al. (Eds) (1982) *Popular Culture: Past and Present*, London, Croom Helm, pp. 294–307.

Jenks, C. (1982) *The Sociology of Childhood: Essential Readings*, London, Batsford.

KESSEL, F.S. and SIEGEL, A.W. (Eds) (1983) *The Child and Other Cultural Inventions*, New York, Praeger.

LA FONTAINE, J.S. (1979) *Sex and Age as Principles of Social Differentiation*, London, Academic Press.

LACEY, C. (1970) *High Town Grammar: The School as a Social System*, Manchester, Manchester University Press.

LEVY-BRUHL, L. (1923) *Primitive Mentality*, London, Allen and Unwin.

LIGHT, P. (1986) 'Context, conservation and conversation', in RICHARDS, M. and LIGHT, P. (Eds) (1986) *Children of Social Worlds*, Cambridge, Polity Press, pp. 170–90.

MACKAY, R. (1973) 'Conceptions of children and models of socialization', in DREITZEL, H.P. (Ed) (1973) *Childhood and Socialization*, London, Collier-Macmillan, pp. 27–43.

MARSH, P. *et al.* (1978) *The Rules of Disorder*, London, Routledge and Kegan Paul.

MEAD, M. (1963) *Growing Up in New Guinea*, Harmondsworth, Penguin.

MEAD, M. (1928, 1969) *Coming of Age in Samoa*, Harmondsworth, Penguin.

MEAD, M. and WOLFSTEIN, M. (Eds) (1955) *Childhood in Contemporary Culture*, Chicago, Chicago University Press.

MEDRICH, E.A. *et al.* ((1982) *The Serious Business of Growing Up: A Study of Children's Lives Outside School*, Berkeley, University of California Press.

MORGAN, D.H.J. (1975) *Social Theory and the Family*, London, Routledge and Kegan Paul.

MORGAN, D.M.J. (1985) *The Family, Politics and Social Theory*, London, Routledge and Kegan Paul.

MORGAN, J. *et al.* (1979) *Nicknames, Their Origins and Social Consequences*, London, Routledge and Kegan Paul.

MUSGROVE, F. (1964) *Youth and the Social Order*, London, Routledge and Kegan Paul.

MUSGROVE, P.W. (1988) *Socialising Contexts*, London, Allen and Unwin.

OPIE, I. and OPIE, P. (1977) *The Lore and Language of Schoolchildren*, London, Paladin.

OPIE, I. and OPIE, P. (1984) *Children's Games in Street and Playground*, Oxford, Oxford University Press.

POLHEMUS, T. (Ed) (1978) *Social Aspects of the Human Body*, Harmondsworth, Penguin.

POLLOCK, L.A. (1983) *Forgotten Children: Parent–Child Relations from 1500 to 1900*, Cambridge, Cambridge University Press.

RAFKY, D.M. (1973) 'Phenomenology and socialization: Some comments on the assumptions underlying socialization', in DREITZEL, H.P. (Ed) *Childhood and Socialization*, London, Collier-Macmillan, pp. 44–64.

RICHARDS, M.P.M. (Ed) (1974) *The Integration of a Child into a Social World*, Cambridge, Cambridge University Press.

RICHARDS, M. and LIGHT, P. (Eds) (1986) *Children of Social Worlds*, Cambridge, Polity Press.

RICOEUR, P. (1978) *The Rule of Metaphor: Multidisciplinary Studies of the Creation of Meaning in Language*, London, Routledge and Kegan Paul.

SHILDKROUT, E. (1978) 'Roles of children in urban Kano', in LA FONTAINE, J.S. *Sex and Age as Principles of Social Differentiation*, London, Academic Press.

SILVERMAN, D. (1985) *Qualitative Methodology and Sociology*, Aldershot, Gower.

STEEDMAN, C. *et al.* (Eds) (1985) *Language, Gender and Childhood*, London, Routledge and Kegan Paul.

TIMPANARO, S. (1975) *On Materialism*, London, New Left Books.

TONKIN, E. (1982) 'Rethinking socialization', *Journal of the Anthropological Society of Oxford*, **13**, 3, pp. 243–56.

Tylor, E.B. (1871) *Primitive Culture*, Vol. 1, London, John Murray.

Urwin, C. (1985) 'Constructing motherhood: The persuasion of normal development', in Steedman, C. *et al.* (Eds) (1985) *Language, Gender, and Childhood*, London, Routledge and Kegan Paul, pp. 164–202.

Waites, B. *et al.* (Eds) (1982) *Popular Culture: Past and Present*, London, Croom Helm.

Walkerdine, V. (1984) 'Developmental psychology and the child-centred pedagogy: The insertion of Piaget into early education', in Henriques, J. *et al.* (Eds) (1984) *Changing the Subject: Psychology, Social Regulation and Subjectivity*, London, Methuen.

Woods, P. (1980) *Pupil Strategies: Explorations in the Sociology of the School*, London, Croom Helm.

Wrong, D. (1961) 'The oversocialized conception of man in modern sociology', *American Sociological Review*, **26**, pp. 184–93.

Young, M.F.D. (Ed) (1971) *Knowledge and Control: New Directions for the Sociology of Education*, London, Routledge and Kegan Paul.

Chapter 2

Constructions and Reconstructions of British Childhood: An Interpretative Survey, 1800 to the Present

Harry Hendrick

The purpose of this chapter is to survey some of the most important social constructions of British childhood since the end of the eighteenth century in order to illustrate the historical variability of the concept. Such a brief account is unable to do little more than point towards the principal identities, and the attributable 'prime movers of social change' (Anderson, 1980: 61). My hope is that a familiarity with these perceptions, as held by dominant interests within our society, will help to explain both the tenacity and the self-confidence of western interpretations of 'childhood'. The focus here is on four related themes. First, the gradual shift from an idea of childhood fragmented by geography — urban/rural — and by class life-experiences, to one that was intended to be much more uniform and coherent; second, the rise and development of what historians refer to as the 'domestic ideal' among the nineteenth-century middle classes, which helped to present 'the family' as the dominant institutional influence on age relations; third, the evolution of an increasingly compulsory relationship between the State, the family and child welfare; and, fourth, the political and cultural struggle to extend the developing constructions (and reconstructions) of childhood through all social classes, to *universalize* it.

Introduction

Let us begin by making clear what is meant by 'social construction'. The term has nothing to do with 'the cultures which children construct for and between themselves' (Prout and James, this volume). During our period, 'childhood' — both the institution and the construction of — was composed by adults; usually those of the professional middle class. This is not meant to sound conspiratorial. No attempt is being made to suggest that children's condition is entirely devoid of a biological dimension, nor to deny the effects of physical being, though the nature of the consanguinity between the social, the psychological and the biological is extraordinarily problematic. All the same, historians agree that 'ideas like parenthood and childhood are socially constructed and thus can be put together in diverse set of way's (Anderson, 1980: 60). We know also that whatever its historical mutability, there is always a relationship between conceptual thought, social action and the process of category construction and, therefore, definitions of childhood must to some extent be dependent upon the society from which they emerge.

Thus the supporting premise of what follows is that the numerous perceptions of childhood, which have been produced over the last two hundred years or so, can only be fully comprehended within the context of how different generations and social classes have responded to the social, economic, religious and political challenges of their respective eras. Throughout the nineteenth century, for example, the influences of Romanticism and Evangelicalism, the social and economic impact of the industrial revolution, and the combined effects of urban growth, class politics, the 'rediscovery' of poverty, imperialism and the 'revolution' in the social sciences, all made necessary new understandings and new practices. As these changes were involved with the building of an industrial state and, later on, a liberal industrial democracy, no part of the societal fabric was left unattended, or unreconstructed, not least those areas most relevant to this essay: family relationships, concepts of health, welfare and education, and the value of children as investments for the future. Similarly, twentieth-century influences, such as popular democracy, world wars, psycho-analysis and the 'Welfare State', have profoundly altered the ways in which 'childhood' has been 'put together'.

In 1800 the meaning of childhood was ambiguous and not universally in demand. By 1914 the uncertainty had been virtually resolved and the identity largely determined, to the satisfaction of the middle class and the respectable working class. A recognizably 'modern' notion of childhood was in place: it was legally, legislatively, socially, medically, psychologically, educationally and politically institutionalized. During these years the making of childhood into a very specific kind of age-graded condition went through several different stages or 'constructions' (and 'reconstructions'). Each new construction, which was manifested in a kind of public identity, may be observed in approximate chronological order as pertaining to Rousseauian Naturalism, Romanticism, Evangelicalism, the shift from wage-earning labour to 'childhood', the reclamation of the juvenile delinquent, schooling, 'Child

Study', 'Children of the Nation', psycho-medicine, and 'Children of the Welfare State'.

Prelude: Eighteenth-century Influences — The natural Child

There is a general agreement among historians of the modern period that from the late seventeenth century a new attitude towards children (and notions of childhood) began to manifest itself, so much so that the eighteenth century has been claimed as a 'new world' for them (Plumb, 1975). In the 1680s, the Cambridge neo-Platonist philosophers asserted the innate goodness of the child and in 1693 Locke published *Some Thoughts Concerning Education*, which included an attack on the idea of infant depravity, and portrayed children as *tabula rasa* (although with respect to ideas rather than to temperament and ability). Not that Locke was revolutionary in relation to child rearing methods, though he tended to oppose corporal punishment. Much more significant was his recognition that children were not all the same — they differed and, therefore, they were individuals (Sommerville, 1982: 120–27; Cunningham, 1995: 63–4; Hardyment, 1995: 1–15).

In effect, the eighteenth century heard a debate on the child's nature. At one extreme stood the infamous statement of John Wesley, the Methodist leader, which urged parents to 'break the will of your child', to 'bring his will into subjection to yours that it may be afterward subject to the will of God'. At the other extreme stood Rousseau, author of the seminal *Emile* (1762), and all those who, under his influence, invested their children with a new understanding and affection (Sommerville, 1982: 127–35; Hardyment, 1995: 24–9). In *Emile* Rousseau captured the imagination of Europe with his validation of Nature, which espoused the natural goodness of children and the corrupting effects of certain kinds of education. He was not alone in his attachment to Nature for the age was one of profound social changes, many of which expressed themselves in more sensitive responses to the natural world in general and, in particular, to animals, women and slaves (Plumb, 1975: 70; Thomas, 1983: 172–91, 301; Porter, 1982: 284–8).

Part of the originality of the educational theory propounded in *Emile* lay in the claim that from both the physiological and the psychological perspectives, the educator was to treat the child as 'a little human animal destined for the spiritual and moral life' who developed 'according to certain laws whose progression must be respected above all' (Boutet De Monvel, 1963: vii). No less significant in inspiring a new outlook was the book's philosophical emphasis on the child as *child*: 'We know nothing of childhood' — 'Nature wants children to be children before they are men'. Thus could children be valued as children, and not merely as adults in the making (although this view of childhood still saw it as a stage on the route to adulthood (Sommerville, 1982: 127–31; Cunningham, 1995: 65–9; Pattison, 1978: 58). This was the essential feature of Rousseau's radicalism and of his contribution to the new construction of childhood. Moreover, it was reiterated by numerous reformers throughout the nineteenth century, even though the majority of them lost the subtlety of Rousseau's innovative understanding of the child-nature relationship, reducing it to a crude view of children as distinguished merely by 'natural' incapacity and vulnerability' (Coveney, 1967: 40–4; Sommerville, 1982: 127–31).

The Romantic Child

The 'natural' child soon met up with the influences of Romantic and Evangelical revivals at the end of the eighteenth century, as well as the effect of the political economy of a growing child-labour force in factories and mines. Where the Romantics were concerned, in the works of Blake, Coleridge and Wordsworth, the child — enveloped in a concept of 'original innocence' derived from Rousseau — stood centrally in the search to investigate 'the self' and to express the Romantic protest against the 'Experience of Society'. In time, these objectives became sentimentalized and static in the hands of Victorian literature, but they began full of nuance and did much to provide children with an identity, not just of 'naturalness', but of significance for the evolution of humanity itself.

There were, however, initially two different views authenticated by Romanticism. One, associated with Blake, saw childhood not as a preparation for what was to come, but as the *source* of 'innocence', a quality that had to be kept alive in adulthood in order to provide nourishment for the whole life. Blake's vision, however, was confused by that of Wordsworth who changed the emphasis by bestowing upon children an infancy endowed with blessings from God, so much so that childhood came to be seen as the age where virtue was domiciled, and everything thereafter was downhill rather than upward towards maturity. The influential Wordsworthian perception of childhood was of a special (genderless) time of life, filled with childlike qualities, which was lost at the moment of its completion — it becomes 'a lost realm' since 'Growing up becomes synonymous with the loss of Paradise'

(Cunningham, 1995: 73–5; Pattison, 1978: 58; Carpenter, 1985: 9; Sommerville, 1982: 168–9).

Notwithstanding that one particular Romantic view came to dominate the continuing construction of childhood, we need to see that we are witnessing the putting together of a particular childhood, narrowly confined to an elite, as a literary, social and educational theme. Furthermore, we are witnessing a contest for a particular set of beliefs, to represent a particular form of society, which was to stand between eighteenth-century rationalism and nineteenth-century industrialism. In this struggle, the child was to be central to the 'reinstatement of Feeling' (Coveney, 1967: 29–33, 37, 40).

The Evangelical Child

In some respects the 'Romantic Child' was short-lived. Poets are no match for political economy. Both the reaction to the French Revolution — the suppression of liberties — and the impact of the industrial revolution — the demand for free labour and the destruction of the old 'moral economy' — pushed adult–child relations in the opposite direction to that promised by Romantic aspirations. Besides the reactionary political climate of the early nineteenth century, and the aggressiveness of the new capitalism, optimistic notions of childhood also found themselves pitted against the weight of the Evangelical Revival, with its belief in Original Sin and the need for redemption. In evangelical hands, human nature, having been tarnished in the fall from grace, was no longer 'pleasing to the author of our Being'. Thus in 1799 the *Evangelical Magazine* advised parents to teach their children that they 'are sinful polluted creatures'.

Hannah More, the evangelical founder of the Sunday School movement and 'scribe of the counter-revolution', not only denounced the 'the rights of man' and of women, but warned that in future society would be subject to 'grave descants on the rights of youth, the rights of children, the rights of babies' (Walvin, 1982: 45). 'Is it not', she wrote 'a fundamental error to consider children as innocent beings, whose little weaknesses may, perhaps, want some correction, rather than as beings who bring into the world a corrupt nature and evil dispositions, which it should be the great end of education to rectify?' (Quoted in Robertson, 1976: 421; but see also Rosman, 1984: 97–118). By the 1820s More had overtaken Maria Edgworth, a disciple of Rousseau, and author of the influential *Practical Education* (1801), in popularity, which suggests a retreat from the 'rational tenderness' approach to child-rearing and with it the view of the child as being not only of Nature, but also of Reason (Hardyment, 1995: 19–30).

In opposing both Rousseau and the Romantics, Hannah More never underestimated the importance of educating and rearing children. In part her conviction was rooted in a tradition born during the Reformation, which sought to register childhood as an age that warranted the investment of time, thought, concern and money. However, the nineteenth-century discussion on the meaning of childhood in an industrializing and urbanizing nation was very much the work of evangelicals who produced their own agenda for child welfare reform, largely through the promulgation of a Domestic Ideal with its emphasis on home, family, duty, love and respect (Heasman, 1962; Davidoff and Hall, 1987: 321–56). During the many debates, the optimism of the Rousseauian and Romantic views gave way to the pessimism and alarmism of evangelical thought. The loss occurred despite the continued, though fragmented, influence of the Romantic ideal where childhood was portrayed as being fundamentally different from adulthood; different, that is, in the sense of having its own nature, and not simply being an immature condition. The evangelicals grasped this difference, but they used it for their own purposes.

From Wage-earning to 'Childhood'

Prior to the closing decades of the eighteenth century, there were few voices, if any, raised against child labour. For most children labouring was held to be a condition which would teach them numerous economic, social and moral principles. By the end of the century, however, this view was being challenged as first climbing-boys and parish apprentices in cotton mills and then factory children in general came to be regarded as victims, as 'slaves', as innocents forced into 'unnatural' employment and denied their 'childhood'. During the course of the debates, between, say, 1780 and 1840s, a new construction of childhood was put together by participants, so that at the end of the period the wage-earning child was no longer considered to be the norm. Instead childhood was now seen as constituting a separate and distinct set of characteristics requiring protection and fostering through school education.

There are several explanations for this fundamental change of attitude towards the capabilities and responsibilities of children. Broadly speaking, many contemporaries were appalled, not only by the scale and intensity of the exploitation of young wage earners, but also by what was seen as their brutalization. These critics were equally appalled by the scale and intensity of the industrialization process itself, and they regarded the plight of the factory child — since factories were the most vivid representation of this process — as symbolic of profound and often little-understood changes in British society, changes that appeared to threaten what was held to be a *natural* order. In campaigning to restrain child labour, reformers — of varying persuasions — were in effect arguing about much else besides, including the direction of industrialization and, within this context, the meaning of progress. The 'childhood' they wished to promote was one that would be suitable for a civilized and Christian nation.

These objections, along with many others, to child labour had their roots in those eighteenth-century psychological, educational and philosophical developments already mentioned. For example, in opposition to, and paralleling the development of, *laissez-faire* capitalism, many critics projected the notion of a 'natural' and 'innocent' childhood, one opposed to the unremitting debasement of children through long hours, unhealthy conditions, corporal punishment and sexual harassment (of girls) (Cunningham, 1995: 138–45; Thompson, 1963: 331–59). Similarly, the evangelical attitude to children, though in conflict with the Romantic, also opposed their unregulated economic activity. This attitude emanated from the combined, and often contradictory, influences of evangelical opinion concerning human nature, the gathering pace of the bourgeois 'domestic ideal' and fears about the social and political behaviour of the mass of labouring men and women — a class in the 'making' — in the first few decades of the century. It saw the brutalization of children as contributing to the dehumanization of this class and, therefore, was to be avoided (many Romantics also shared this view to a certain extent). A not unconnected theme here was the anxiety of the middle and upper classes who looked on Chartism (the first mass working-class political movement) as indicative of unstable conditions which, in common with the recurring economic distress of the period, turned issues relating to public order into matters of national security (Rosman, 1984: 47–53; Davidoff and Hall, 1987: 93–4, 343; Hall, 1979; Pearson, 1983: 156–62).

The Health and Morals of Apprentices Act, 1802, which was intended to control conditions primarily for parish apprentices, proved ineffective with the expansion of industry and the introduction of steam power. But thereafter the reform campaign grew in vociferousness, assisted as it was by government investigative committees, agitational publications and rallies. If the Rousseauian, Romantic and Evangelical understandings of childhood underpinned much of the reformers' campaign, there were more specific arguments against child labour that also pointed to the child's special character. Reformers were quick to identify the physical and moral dangers. The former referred to damage to children's bodies through long hours, debilitating temperatures, polluted atmospheres, and beatings. The moral dangers were perceived chiefly as a lack of education and religious instruction and general precociousness. These 'utilitarian' arguments amounted to a warning that child labour threatened the reproduction of society (Cunningham, 1991: 65).

In addition, there were three critical factors in the reconstruction process (and the emphasis is on the prefix here since the arguments achieved so much of their power through being diffused with Rousseauian, Romantic and Evangelical sentiments). The first was the emergence of the view that child labour was not 'free' labour. A basic principle of *laissez-faire* political economy was that labour was free and, therefore, could make its own contract with employers. However, during the debate on the above mentioned Factory Act of 1802, it became clear that children were not equal participants in the making of a contract and, once this was accepted, therefore, it followed that child labour was different in kind from adult labour (Cunningham, 1991: 69–71; Driver, 1946: 47, 243).

Second, the image of the child as being 'unfree' soon came to be associated with another and in some respects more vigorous image, that of slavery. Many reformers from the late eighteenth century onward looked for inspiration to the anti-slavery movement of the period, and were quick to draw analogies between the lives of West Indian slaves and those of factory children. The analogy had first been used in respect of climbing boys, but it became much more potent in connection with factory children since both textiles and slavery were central to the British economy (Cunningham, 1991: 72; Drescher, 1981: 11–13; Driver, 1946: 53, 104–5). The effect of the comparison of child wage-earners to slaves furthered the view that their condition rendered them unfree.

The third factor was the debate concerning 'The Order of Nature'. The fear was that a natural order of parents, and more likely of fathers, supporting their children, was being inverted through the demand for child (and female) labour in factories at the expense of adult males. This was important since it affected not only the role of children, but also that of women as wives in relation to men as husbands and, more generally, the 'natural order' of patriarchal domesticity. Moreover, it had ramifications for the growing tension throughout industrialization between this 'natural' order (of course, itself a social construction) and the order of capitalist political economy. This led on, in the minds of those, like the Evangelical Tory, Lord Ashley, to a consideration of the 'order' of the nation at a time of great social and economic upheaval, where the neglect of children could easily lead not only to the damnation of souls, but also result in social revolution (Cunningham, 1991: 83–96; Thompson, 1963: 331–49; Pearson, 1983: 156–62).

In the debates of the 1830s, the 'fundamental categories' of analyis had become 'childhood-adulthood' (Driver, 1946: 244). Thus the substance of the child 'nature' in question was that it differed in kind from that of the adult. The age at which adulthood began had been undecided, but in 1833 a Royal Commission, drawing upon physiological evidence concerning puberty and having identified the associated change in social status, declared that at the age of 13 'the period of childhood . . . ceases' (Quoted in Driver; Cunningham, 1995: 140). The Commission led on to the Factory Act, 1833, the first piece of effective legislation, which prohibited selective employment of children under 9, and limited the working day to eight hours for those aged between 9 and 13. This was the principal success of the reformers' campaign: to establish the distinctive quality of child labour and, thereby, of children. It soon followed that such a quality implied a nature that should be common to all children, after allowing for the 'natural' differences of social position. By 1837, a reformer compaigning on behalf of climbing boys, who were still unprotected by legislation could claim: '*They* are, of all human beings, the most lovely, the most engaging, the most of all others claiming protection, comfort, and love. They are CHILDREN' (Quoted in Cunningham, 1991: 64). In this sense, the campaign to reclaim the wage-earning child for civilization was one of the first steps along the road of what can be described as the social construction of a *universal* childhood. Although at the time this made little difference in practice, the ideal situation had been formulated and posed, and for the rest of the century, reformers, educationalists and social scientists strove to make real the ideal through two further reconstructions: the reformed juvenile delinquent and compulsorily schooled child.

The Delinquent Child — The Child As *Child*

Perhaps there was no more obvious attempt at the conscious universalization of 'childhood' than that which occurred with the mid-nineteenth-century reconstruction of juvenile delinquency (Pearson, 1983, Ch. 7). The arguments surrounding the evolution of the concept of juvenile delinquency focused upon the perceived conflict between 'Innocence and Experience' (we shall see here the perversion of these

Romantic virtues). The clue to the new attitude being proclaimed by reformers can be found in this quotation from M.D. Hill, the Recorder of Birmingham:

> The latter [the delinquent] is a little stunted man already — he knows much and a great deal too much of what is called life — he can take care of his own immediate interests. He is self-reliant, he has so long directed or misdirected his own actions and has no little trust in those about him, that he submits to no control and asks for no protection. He has consequently much to unlearn — he has to be turned again into a child (quoted in May, 1973: 7).

No wonder, then, that Micaiah Hill, in a prize-winning essay, asked 'Can these be children?' Hill voiced a common theme throughout the literature when he wrote that understandings of middle or upper-class childhood were 'utterly inapplicable to that of a child brought up to vagrant habits' (Quoted in Pearson, 1982: 167). Of course, this implied that he and other reformers were using a concept of childhood that was at odds with what they saw as the childhood of the poor and the neglected. Clearly, by this time (1850s) the intention was to make these children conform to a middle-class notion of a properly constituted childhood, characterized by a state of dependency.

The campaign for reform produced the Youthful Offenders Act, 1854, which, together with further Acts in 1857, 1861 and 1866, was significant for a number of reasons. Most importantly, for our purposes it provided the initial recognition in legislative terms of juvenile delinquency as a separate category (prior to the Act only children under 7 were presumed to be incapable of criminal intent), thereby extending 'childhood' beyond the traditional first seven years to under 16 (for non-indictable offences). Accordingly, the legislation defined the extended 'childhood' as 'different'; reinforced the view that they were not 'free' agents; drew attention to the child–parent relationship with the latter being expected to exercise control and discipline; and emphasized the danger of those in need of 'care and protection' becoming delinquents (Walvin, 1982: 152–3; May, 1973: 7–29).

Here was a critical turning-point in the legislative history of age relations, second only in significance to the Education Acts of the 1870s and 1880s. For under construction was a carefully defined 'nature', albeit the subject of much debate, which also contained a return to a mythical condition of childhood. Hence the phrase 'he has to be turned *again* into a child' (my emphasis). At the heart of this particular reconstruction process lay the 'care and protection' clauses of the legislation.

These clauses took the Romantic approach to childhood and fused it with Evangelical convictions to produce an image of the 'innocent' child, who needed to be given the protection, guidance, love and discipline of what Mary Carpenter called '*the family*', by which she meant an idealized notion being generated through the Domestic Ideal. However, where poor parents failed to rear such a child, it was determined that 'parental' discipline for delinquents should be provided by reformatory schools (Carpenter, 1853: 298–99; May, 1973: 7–29; Pearson, 1983: 165; Pinchbeck and Hewitt, 1973: 471–7).

At the core of the reconstruction as a whole, and the reason why it is so important in the history of childhood, was the successfully advanced belief of Carpenter that 'a child is to be *treated as a child*' (Quoted in Manton, 1976: 109). 'What physiologists tell us', she wrote, justifies representing 'the child in a perfectly different condition from the man' (Carpenter, 1853: 293). The problem was believed to be that young delinquents and, by implication, all those neglected working-class children exhibited features which were the reverse of 'what we desire to see in childhood'. Such children were 'independent, self-reliant, advanced in knowledge of evil, but not of good, devoid of reverence for God or man, utterly destitute of any sound guiding principle of action . . .' In a revealing passage, Carpenter continued: 'That faith or trust so characteristic of childhood, which springs from a sense of utter *helplessness* [my emphasis], from a confidence in the superior power and wisdom of those around', scarcely existed in the child in need of proper parental care. Thus children had to be restored to 'the true position of childhood'. The child 'must be brought to a sense of dependence by re-awakening in him new and healthy desires that he cannot himself gratify, and by finding that *there is a power far greater than his own to which he is endebted for the gratification of these desires.* [my emphasis]' (*Ibid:* 297–9).

In order to understand the significance of developments in the concept of juvenile delinquency for this particular construction of childhood, it has to be remembered that the movement to create a separate order of juvenile justice emerged from three sources: the debate on child labour, the economic and political upheavals of the 1830s and 1840s, and the increasing popularity of the school as a means of class control. Consequently, the writings of reformers were the products of deeply held and widely debated convictions about the nature of the social order at a time when the middle class was anxious about what it deemed to be the rebellious and aggressive attitudes and behaviour of those young people (and their parents) who frequented the streets of urban areas (May, 1973). On the broader level, the question facing politicians, philanthropists and reformers was how to build a healthy, co-operative society, one with a cohesive social and moral fabric, to replace the chaos and immorality that appeared to be widespread, even in an increasingly respectable mid-Victorian Britain (Selleck, 1985: 101–15; Pearson, 1983: 162–7; 171–9). The new conception of juvenile delinquency, with its implicatons for the universalization of an ideal childhood, was part of the answer (May, 1973: 29).

The Schooled Child

In their approach to the reformation of the juvenile delinquent, many commentators made the implicit assumption that, in the long run, only education would prevent the 'dangerous classes' from continually reproducing their malevolent characteristics. The work of reform of 'habits of order, punctuality, industry and self-respect', advised one enquirer, must 'begin with the young . . . They are the depositories of our hopes and expectations' (Quoted in Pearson, 1983: 182); while a Justice of the Peace warned: 'I have no other conception of any other means of forcing civilisation downwards in society, except by education' (Quoted in Johnson, 1970: 96–8, 104). Similarly, a government report noted that there was a need to produce educated men who 'can be reasoned with' (Quoted in Colls, 1976: 97). Mary Carpenter had these sentiments in mind when she portrayed reformation as the necessary step towards 'willing obedience' which, in the coming age of industrial democracy, was an essential condition of 'rule by consent' (Quoted in Pearson, 1983: 179–82).

The evolution of the concept of delinquency and the introduction of compulsory schooling, while not exactly chronologically hand-in-hand, were, as has just been shown, ideologically related. Thus there was nothing coincidental in mid-nineteenth century penologists and social investigators seeking to return children to their 'true position', as it also involved making them more amenable to the classroom. The fact that it was a minority of children who were delinquent in some way or another was irrelevant to the basic restructuring of what a proper childhood should be. The notion of this childhood was as much concerned with images and establishing norms as with real rates of delinquency. For the reformers, precocity (and the perceived independence of spirit that accompanied it) and effective schooling were irreconcilable. The reconstruction of the 'factory child' through the prism of dependency and ignorance, was a necessary precursor to mass education in that it helped to prepare public opinion for shifts in the child's identity: from wage-earner to school-pupil; for a reduction in income of working-class families, as a result of loss of children's earnings; and for the introduction of the State into the parent–child relationship.

But in what ways did the school seek to alter children's 'nature', thereby creating a virtually new construction of childhood? It threw aside the child's 'knowledge' derived from parents, community, peer group, and personal experience. Instead it demanded a state of ignorance. Secondly, it required upon pain of punishment, usually physical, a form of behaviour, accompanied by a set of related attitudes, which reinforced the child's dependence and vulnerability and, in terms of deference towards established authorities, its social class (Humphries, 1981, Chs 2–3; Hendrick, forthcoming). Thirdly, the ability of children to work for wages was no longer viewed from the perspective of their exploitation by adults, but rather from that of their own moral weakness: wage-earning children were not 'proper' children and, therefore, had to be made 'innocent' of such adult behaviour, and the school was the institutional means of achieving this end. Fourthly, in claiming the legal and moral right to inflict physical punishment upon children, the school reinforced the idea of the child as being in 'need' of a *particular* form of discipline for, although children had always been assaulted in their capacity as employees, wage labour had obscured what was coming to be regarded as an essential feature of their new condition (Hendrick, 1992: 42). Fifthly, it further institutionalized the separation of children from society, confirming upon them a separate identity: their proper place was in the classroom. Finally, the school emphasized the value of children as investments in future parenthood, economic competitiveness, and a stable democratic order.

There is no doubt, then, that in the last quarter of the nineteenth century the school played a pivotal role in the making of a new kind of childhood. It was not alone in this process, for as the century came to a close other agencies and philosophies were also reconceptualizing the child's condition (Hendrick, 1994, part II and Hendrick, forthcoming). But the classroom and the ideological apparatus of education were crucial because they demanded — indeed, could not do without — a truly *national* childhood, one that ignored (at least theoretically) rural/urban divisions, as well as those of social class (Hurt, 1979, *passim*). Schooling, as has just been shown above, did more than merely declare a particular definition of childhood. By virtue of its legal authority, and on a daily basis through teachers and school attendance offices, it was able to impose its vision upon pupils (many, perhaps the majority, of whom were unwilling to accept this 'reconstruction' of what they should be) and upon their parents (many of whom showed a similar relunctance) (Hurt, 1979, Chs 7 and 8). This construction was intended to directly involve *all* children and was meant to be as inescapable as it was visible, for in denoting them as 'pupils', the school was a constant and omnipotent reminder of who they were.

The 'Child-study' Child

One reason why the schooling process was so significant was that it helped to give rise to what became known as the Child Study movement (1880s–1914). The 1880s was an important decade in the history of children's welfare since, partly under the impact of schooling and partly as a result of a growing concern about poverty and its possible political consequences, it saw the beginning of 'a prolonged and unprecedented public discussion of the physical and mental condition of school children' (Sutherland, 1984: 6–13). One development, above all others, turned children into attractive research-subjects, namely, the opportunities afforded to investigators by mass schooling. Earlier in the century the focus of attention had been on distinct groups of children, such as factory workers and delinquents, but now it was the entire school population. In fact, the school was crucial in making children available to professionals: sociologists, psychologists, doctors and educationalists, all of whom sought to produce 'scientific' surveys of the pupils (Sutherland, 1984: 5). In this way, just as children were being dramatically constructed as 'school pupils' under the weight of 'education' (itself searching for scientific status as a subject), they also found themselves being examined under the influence of 'science', whose main institutional forum was the Child Study movement.

For some time there was a growing interest in how children developed, the immediate origins of which were separate articles published in *Mind* by Darwin and Hippolyte Taine in 1877, followed in 1881 by 'Babies and Science', written for the *Cornhill Magazine* by James Sully, Professor of Philosophy and Psychology at London University. These articles heralded a number of important studies in the closing decades of the century, the most notable being, from Germany, Wilhelm Preyer's *The Mind of the Child* (1888) and, from the USA, Stanley Hall's seminal essay on 'The Content of Children's Minds' (1883) (Wooldridge, 1995).

Besides the influence of Hall's writings, the impetus behind the movement came from three main sources. Mass schooling had revealed the extent of mental and physical handicap among the pupils and this attracted the attention of politicians and philanthropists, as well as of social and natural scientists; biologists and natural historians saw a close affinity between racial development and that of the child and looked to Child Study to further their knowledge; and, at a time when poverty was being 'rediscovered', there was a growing anxiety about racial degeneration. In general, teachers, doctors, psychologists, scientists, sociologists, educationalists and middle-class parents were anxious about the quality of the child population and this was combined with an interest in the details of human development (Wooldridge, 1995: 19).

Child Study spawned two organizatons in the 1890s: the first, the Child Study Association (1894), was formed largely under the inspiration of Hall, and argued for 'a scientific study of individual children by psychological, sociological and anthropometric methods' and for the examination of the 'normal as well as the abnormal' (Keir, 1952: 10). The Association's journal, the *Paidologist* claimed that it would help parents 'with observations of the periods and aspects of child life'; it would attract teachers by offering them 'guiding principles'; and that it would prove to be of interest to those involved in 'education, psychology, biology and medicine'. The emphasis of the Association was on the individual child, rather than the condition of the child population as a whole. It wished to gain 'insight into child nature' in order to offer 'a more precise unfolding of the human mind, and of the way in which this was modified by the environment'. The second group to be founded was the more medically oriented Childhood Society (1896), which owed its orgins to two committees: one established by the BMA in 1888, and the other by the 7th International Congress of Hygiene and Demography in 1891. The membership tended to come from medicine, education and statistics. The main interest of the Society lay in the mental and physical condition of children, especially racial considerations. In 1907 the two groups merged to become the Child Study Society, but by 1914 the movement as a whole was in decline as educational psychology rapidly fulfilled its role (Wooldridge, 1995, Ch. 2).

None the less, during its brief life the Society conducted a number of investigations and actively promoted its findings, thereby diffusing knowledge about the nature and conditions of childhood. In effect, Child Study helped to spread the techniques of natural history to the study of children, showing them to be 'natural creatures'; through its lectures, literature, and the practice of its influential members, it popularized the view that the child's conception differed from that of adults, that there were marked stages in normal mental development; and that there were similarities between the mental worlds of children and primitives (Wooldridge, 1995: 47).

The significance of the movement in the reconstruction of childhood (along 'scientific' lines) was that (in conjuction with developments in educational psychology), it was part of a more comprehensive movement towards enveloping childhood in a world of scientific experts of one sort or another. Childhood was no longer something that occurred 'naturally'. As we have seen, from the eighteen-century onwards there had been a growing interest in the nature, meaning and specificity of childhood, and of how it related to the big questions of human development. Under the impact of post-Darwinian science, the fear of racial deterioration, the ongoing revolution in the social sciences and the beginnings of preventive medicine, Child Study was seen to be increasingly relevant to understandings of, and solutions to, a number of dominant problems of the period and, therefore, it was considered to be socially and politically important. Thus the movement served to position the social, educational, psychological and racial importance of childhood, and of children, in terms of education, social welfare and mental and physical health.

'Children of the Nation'

Child-Study, as has been observed, owed its inspiration to 'a heady combination of utilitarian calculation and romantic sentiment' (Wooldridge, 1995: 19). However, the movement was itself part of a much broader development concerning children and childhood in the late nineteenth century. We have already noted the importance of schooling in terms of providing opportunities for 'scientific' research, and for providing the stimulus for the 'unprecedented' public discussion of the physical and mental condition of children. Given this to be so, it has been suggested that between the 1880s and c. 1914, children, and child welfare, achieved a new social and political identity as they came to be seen, in the words of Sir John Gorst, the Tory reformer, as being 'of the Nation' (Quoted in Hendrick, 1994: 41; also Hendrick: forthcoming). This can best be understood as a shift of emphasis from the mid-nineteenth century concern with rescue, reform and reclamation, mainly through philanthropic and Poor Law interventions, to the involvement of children in a consciously designed pursuit of the national interest, which included the post-Boer war movement for 'national efficiency', education, racial hygiene, responsible parenthood, social purity and preventive medicine. The latter was of particular significance as the emphasis in children's health changed from 'sickly survival to the realisation of potential' (Baistow, 1995, title).

In each of these areas the State was becoming more interventionist through legislation (and through forming new relationships with local government authorities and charitable agencies). It is well known that among the most significant legislative Acts were those covering the age of consent (1885), infant life protection (1872 and 1897), the prevention of cruelty to, and neglect of, children (1889), the school feeding of 'necessitous' children (1906), school medical inspection (and treatment) (1907), a juvenile justice system (1908), and infant welfare (1918). The implementation of these measures meant that through their everyday involvement in children's lives, welfare bureaucracies of national and local government, and of philanthropy, imposed what, to all intents and purposes were, certain class dominated, and 'expert' formulated, concepts of childhood on the general population. Both state and charitable welfare provision made a number of assumptions (many of which were derived from psycho-medicine) about what constituted a proper childhood and its 'natural' conditions.

However, it could be argued that an important feature of this reconstruction of childhood, and of child welfare legislation in particular, was a concern with children's rights, and that 'it was the state alone which could enforce these rights' (Cunningham, 1995: 161). This view necessitated a sharp separation of childhood from adulthood, and the recognition of children's peculiar needs and characteristics. 'Childhood and adulthood . . . became almost opposites of one another' (*Ibid*: 160). Of course, protecting children, and their rights, was 'in harmony with the larger purposes of the state in securing the reproduction of a society capable of competing in the harsh conditions of the twentieth century' (*Ibid*: 161). This was clearly expressed by Dr T.N. Kelynack, a leading medical journalist and public health activist, who wrote:

> the world of childhood has been an undiscovered or at least unexplored land. The child is a new discovery. Realizing at last the wealth, power, requirements of this long-neglected treasury, minds and hearts everywhere are awakening to a realization of opportunities and responsibilities, and in all sections of society eagerness is being manifested to understand and serve the child (Quoted in Hendrick, 1994: 42).

And why was this?

> The child of today holds the key to the kingdom of the morrow; the child that now is will be the citizen of coming years and must take up and bear the duties of statesmanship, defence from foes, the conduct of labour, the direction of progress, and the maintenance of a high level of thought and conduct . . . (Kelynack quoted in Wooldridge, 1995: 23).

Such assumptions and aspirations, whether focusing on children's 'rights' or their role as 'the citizen of tomorrow', demanded a subject conformity, that not only continued to *universalize* childhood, making it even more coherent and ordered, but also consolidated the idea of it as a period marked by vulnerability and, therefore, requiring protection. The incapacitated child, vulnerable, innocent, ignorant and dependent, was entirely suited to be a member of the twentieth-century family, the 'haven' within a liberal-capitalist system, sustained by a popular vote (Hendrick, 1992: 49). In an age of fierce imperial, political, military and economic national rivalries, in addition to domestic anxieties regarding poverty, class politics, social hygiene and racial efficiency, children were being reconstructed as material investments in national progress.

The Psychological Child (in the Psychological Family)

By 1918, childhood was well on its way to being conceptually 'modern': it had been broadly shaped by nineteenth-century notions derived from Romanticism, Evangelicism and middle-class 'domesticity', it was increasingly defined in relation to educational, medical, welfarist and psychological jurisdictions, and was clearly separate from adulthood. However, given the importance of 'time' in understandings of childhood (see James and Prout, 'Re-Presenting Childhood' in this volume), it is important to recognize that the inter-war period saw further significant refinements of the conceptualization of childhood, through, on the one hand, psychology, in particular the work of Cyril Burt on individual differences and that of Susan Isaacs on child development and, on the other hand, through the psychiatrically dominated Child Guidance movement (Wooldridge, 1995: 73–135; Thom, 1992; Rose, 1985: 176–96). The different strands of psychology, psychoanalysis and psychiatry are extremely complex and difficult to disentangle and, therefore, the emphasis here is not on describing them, but on claiming their importance for yet another reconstruction of childhood. If the earlier reconstruction through welfare (1880–1918) had emphasized the child's body (though with a mental health dimension), the psychological child would be one of the Mind in terms of emotions, fantasies, dreams, instincts and habits (Hendrick, 1994: 1–7).

The specific targets for Burt's applied psychology were three groups of abnormal children: the delinquent, the backward and the gifted (this focus alone, from an influential psychologist, put child nature in general under the spotlight). Within this framework Burt developed a moral psychology in which mental conditions were given pre-eminence over the economic. Thus he attached great importance to the family, and to the role of the mother in the rearing of emotionally balanced children. Strained family relations produced the nervous child, for it was in family relationships that 'the real difficulty resides'. A properly functioning family was essential for mental health since 'Nearly every tragedy of crime is in its origins a drama of domestic life' (Quotations in Wooldridge, 1995). This was particularly true of juvenile delinquents, whose condition, said Burt, arose from a misdirection of a high level of 'energy' which produced unconscious 'complexes' (Rose, 1985: 195). These complexes related to the child's mental life involving fantasies and conflicts, the resolution of which was to be solved through psychoanalysis striving to 'disengage all the implicated motives of the child, unconscious as well as conscious' (*ibid*). Such a view of the child's emotional world pointed towards a depth and breadth of meaning that had hitherto been barely appreciated.

Susan Isaacs was probably the most significant child psychologist of her generation and, therefore, was extremely influential in promoting a psychological construction of childhood since her ideas reached a wide and varied audience via a number of avenues: published studies of the intellectual and social development of children; her experimental school — Malting House — in Cambridge; the establishment by her of the Department of Child Development at the London Institute of Education; her work as a propagandist for nursery education; her problem page in *Nursery World* and in *Home and School*; her evidence to the Consultative Committee of the Board of Education; and her role in introducing educational psychologists to the work of such seminal figures as Freud, Piaget and Klein (Wooldridge, 1995: 111; Rose, 1985: 189–900; Urwin and Sharland, 1992: 185–7).

In her examination of children's intellectual growth, Isaacs showed that they have the same mechanisms of thought as adults do 'They know less than adults and have less developed minds than adults; but they do not understand the world in fundamentally different ways from adults' (Wooldridge, 1995: 121). Where the social development of young children was concerned, she portrayed them as 'naive egoists' and claimed that their aggressiveness was due to their egotistical desire for 'possessions, power and attention'. The reasons for this lay in the unconscious, a world for the infant that was dominated by basic wishes, fantasies and fears. Isaacs informed mothers as to the importance of these and advised that leaving the child free to choose its own form of expression was usually the best course (Rose, 1985: 189). Much of the early life of children was taken up with the control of their impulses and the understanding of their anxieties. Only in this way could the child's ego be free 'for the possibility of real development — in skill and understanding, and stable social relations' (Quoted in Wooldridge, 1995: 126). In essence, an 'understanding, liberal, tolerant attitude was to be encouraged to the vicissitudes of the mental and emotional growth of the child' (Rose, 1985: 189).

If two strands of psychological reconstruction of children are evident in the work of Burt and Isaacs, the third and most overtly institutional influence was in the development of Child Guidance Clinics of the 1920s and 1930s, through both their practice and their research (Rose, 1985; Thom, 1992). The significance of the clinics was that they took 'nervous', 'maladjusted' and delinquent children and 'treated' them, producing as they did a new perspective on the nature of childhood. Under the clinics' influence child psychiatry was consolidated as a distinct realm of medicine as childhood was given 'its own repertoire of disorders: . . . of personality (timidity, obstinacy . . .); behaviour disorders (truancy, temper tantrums . . .); habit disorders (nail biting, thumb sucking . . .); "glycopnec" disorders (migraine, insomnia . . .)' (Rose, 1985: 179). However, perhaps the special significance of the clinics was their role in distributing a new understanding of childhood among a number of different professionals: teachers, probation officers, social workers, school attendance officers, and doctors and psychiatrists. This made it possible to 'regard the clinic as the fulcrum of a comprehensive programme of mental welfare'. Furthermore, the clinics were propagandist, through radio talks, popular publications, lectures and its association with parent–teachers organizations, in promoting certain views of happy families and happy children which were dependent upon a new tolerance of, and sympathy for, the child (*ibid*: 203–4).

From Burt and Isaacs, from psychological and psychiatric textbooks, from the clinics and from educational psychology came the message, actively promoted throughout the professions of psycho-medicine, teaching, social work, and penology, that 'childhood' mattered. This significance bestowed upon childhood was made visible in three main contexts: the mind of the child; the child in the family; and child management. Childhood, it was explained, had an inner world, one that reached into the unconscious and was of great significance for adult maturity, the efficient functioning of family and, ultimately, for political stability: 'The neglected toddler in everyone's way is the material which becomes the disgruntled agitator, while the happy contented child is the pillar of the State' (Riley, 1983: 59–108; Rose, 1985: 188–91; quotation in Urwin and Sharland, 1992: 191; see also: 174–99).

The Child of the Welfare State

This child had two main identities: as a *family member*, and as a *public responsibility*. These identities, insofar as they were 'new' (and both were heavily dependent upon the psychologizing of the child throughout the inter-war period), were rooted in three main sources: wartime experiences, in particular the evacuation process; the theories of maternal deprivation and family cohesion associated with the leading figures in Child Guidance; and the Curtis report on child care in children's homes, which was followed by the Children Act, 1948.

The evacuation process in 1939 (described by one psychoanalyst as 'a cruel psychological experiment on a large scale') had involved the removal of nearly one million unaccompanied children together with half a million mothers with pre-school children from their urban homes in large industrial cities to reception areas in regions less likely to be bombed. The main social and psychological impact of this mass movement of children and mothers was to reveal the extent of urban poverty and slum housing, the tenacity of the ordinary working-class family in sticking together, the relatively poor physical and mental condition of thousands of children, and the existence of what was coming to be known as the 'problem family' (that is, the family who found it difficult or impossible to cope emotionally, economically, mentally, physically, and so on, without assistance from social workers and other state agencies). Evacuation, it was claimed, had shone a torchlight into the darkest corners of urban Britain, and what was revealed was both shocking and frightening in its implications for racial efficiency, emotional stability and post-war democracy (Macnicol, 1986; Calder, 1971; Inglis, 1989; Holman, 1995).

But the evacuation experience also had important consequences for theories of child care and for the psychological significance of family relationships. The Cambridge Evacuation Survey, conducted by a team of psycho-medics, revealed, as had Child Guidance Clinics, 'the crucial importance of family ties and of the feelings of parents and child towards one another'. But whereas the clinics had a small number of patients, evacuation provided the experts with many hundreds of thousands of subjects (Rose, 1990: 161). For those psychiatrists, such as John Bowlby, who had researched the effects of early separation of young children from their mothers, the evacuation experience confirmed their views. Separation produced an 'affectionless character' and it was character disorder that was the root cause of anti-social behaviour (Quoted in Rose, 1990: 162; see also Urwin and Sharland, 1992: 194, and Riley, 1983). This line of thinking about children's mental health became significant in the post-war climate as concern was expressed about the mental hygiene of the population. In such a climate of opinion, 'The troubles of childhood were of particular concern . . . [for] . . . a scheme of preventive mental health, not only for themselves, but because they were sure warning of greater problems to come, and they were treatable by early intervention.' (Rose, 1990: 163). Here, then, was a portrait of childhood, couched almost entirely in psycho-analytical terms, which looked upon children as being significant members of an organic population.

Furthermore, where the reconstruction of childhood is concerned, all these influences played a part in what might be called the 'discovery' of children 'in care'. Nor should the influence of the pronatalist drive to rejuvenate the family be overlooked (pronatalism grew out of an anxiety about the low birth rate) (Riley, 1982: 150–96). However, first we need to remind ourselves that the politics of the 1940s brought forth what was conspicuously thought of as a 'Welfare State' in which citizens had evidence of their *citizenship* through their right to free social and health services. This deliberate democratization of citizenship began to be formulated during the war-time debates on post-war reconstruction with one eye on sustaining a healthy and growing population and the other on the growth of communism throughout Europe and Nationalism throughout the Empire. In addition to the government's commitment to full employment, and the Education Act, 1944, there were four major welfare Acts regarded as underpinning the creation of the Welfare State: the Family Allowances Act (1945), the National Health Service Act (1946), the National Insurance Act (1946) and the National Assistance Act (1948).

The Children Act, 1948, has to be set within the context of this legislative record. Prior to the passing of the Act, the Curtis Committee on children in care (1946) found:

> a lack of personal interest in and affection for the children which we found shocking. The child in these Homes was not regarded as an individual with his rights and possessions, his own life to live and his own contribution to offer. He was merely one of a large crowd, eating, playing and sleeping with the rest . . . Still more important, he was without feeling that there was anyone to whom he could turn who was vitally interested in his welfare or who cared for him as a person (Quoted in Rose, 1990: 167; see also Hendrick, 1994: 214–17).

This sentiment was enshrined in the Act, whose main principles included the establishment of local-authority Children's Departments, a new emphasis on boarding-out in preference to residential homes, restoration of children in care to their natural parents, and greater emphasis on adoption where appropriate.

In many respects, the principal theme of the Act, distinguishing it from previous child welfare legislation, was that local authorities responsible for a child in care were 'to exercise their powers with respect to him so as to further his best interests and to afford him opportunity for the proper development of his character and abilities' (quoted in Hendrick, 1994: 218). The child 'was a citizen of a democracy, a citizen with rights, and these included the right to a family life' (quoted in Rose, 1990: 167). Thus the publicly cared-for child was to be treated as an individual, to have rights and possessions, to be treated as a person; and wherever possible to be put into either an adoptive 'family' or returned to his or her natural parents. Childhood had been reconstructed on two levels, both of which had their origins throughout the inter-war period: as an *individual* citizen in a welfare democracy, and as a member of a family (Hendrick, 1994: 22–8). Moreover, insofar as the child in care was a 'public' child, it was viewed from the perspective of a kind of 'domestic ideal' (itself driven by pronatalism), whose late eighteenth early nineteenth-century paternity was now emblazoned with psychoanalytic understanding.

'Contemporary' Childhood

Thereafter, identifying constructions or reconstructions of childhood in the 1960s, 1970s or 1980s becomes more difficult, at least for the historian. In many respects the 1960s stands as an enigmatic decade, so commonly referred to by a generation of the 'chattering classes' (of both the Left and the Right) while so far from being known in any accurate historical sense. Images of youth cultures and 'teenage' revolts are one thing, but notions of childhood, as far as this decade is concerned, are something altogether different.

The golden age of welfare was already beginning to tremor with self-doubt by the end of the 1960s, and its end was confirmed by the Labour Minister Anthony Crosland in 1975, long before the New Right gained the political and intellectual ascendency, when he publicly warned that 'The party is over' (quoted in Glennerster, 1995: 167). And yet, at the same time as right-wing think tanks saw some of their more extreme ideas being put into practice in relation to economic and to a lesser extent social policy, and the Children's Rights Movement of the 1960s seemed to have lost ground, a new attitude towards children developed through the 'rediscovery' of child physical abuse to which was added, in the 1980s, child sexual abuse. It hardly needs to be said that media and political campaigns around child abuse were never straightforward in their concern for children, whose sufferings have often been hijacked by special interest groups in order to spread their own and primarily adult influences, whether they be of the feminist, Marxist, medical or religious variety. However, to his credit, Nigel Parton, one of the most influential left-wing figures in the debate, admitted that in his earlier work he ignored 'the child in child abuse' as well as 'the impact of power relations on children's lives' (Parton, 1990: 10–18. See also the influence of Ennew, 1986). And Parton is only one of many social scientists who have begun to recognize the existence of children as people — indeed, from the time of its conception, this volume (James and Prout, 1990) was testimony to the growing appreciation of the need for adult society to look beyond the traditional interest of psychologists in child development, to a deeper and more subtle understanding of the child's social world and of the adult–child relationship (Chisholm, *et al*.) 1990; James, 1993; Quortrup, *et al.* 1994; Mayall, 1994; Jenks, 1996).

Equally significant in the continuing, but often contradictory, processes of reconstruction are organizations that have emerged since the Year of the Child (1979), whose objectives are not those of the traditionally passive and often repressive protection of children. Instead, they represent a new Children's Rights Movement as they seek to listen to children's grievances and to campaign on their behalf: e.g., the Children's Legal Centre, Childline, and EPOCH (End Physical Punishment of Children), and the Children's Rights Development Unit. Similar progressive developments include the famous Gillick judgement of 1985, where the House of Lords upheld the legality of doctors giving contraceptive advice to children without parental knowledge or consent, and the abolition in 1986 of corporal punishment in state schools. On the other hand, the much vaunted The Children Act, 1989, though providing provision for 'listening' to children's viewpoint has, it seems, done little to enhance their rights. In sexual abuse cases children's evidence is no longer so unconditionally accepted as true and, since the murder of Jamie Bulger in 1993 by two 10-year-old boys, most commentators agree that public and legal attitudes towards children have hardened. It is difficult to assess the extent to which all this constitutes a meaningful 'reconstruction' of childhood.

But another aspect of this question is the popularity in certain quarters of the belief that childhood has been eroded, lost or has suffered a 'strange death' (Jenks, 1996). While the wide gulf between the poor child and the majority of more affluent children troubles many contemporary observers, others are equally concerned that there has been an 'increase of violence and disturbance among the young' who, having been given 'the best of everything', nevertheless feel 'cheated, purposeless and confused' (Seabrook, 1982). There is a similar concern for the so-called end of innocence (or the 'fall' of childhood), important features of which are said to be the 'sexualization of childhood from the innocence — and ignorance — of the past to the more wordly wise child of today . . . in a commercial, fashion-conscious age, boys and girls are so preoccupied with how they look and dress that they can no longer enjoy mucking about and having fun — that they are missing out on the pleasures of childhood' (Humphries, *et al.*, 1988: 147). A recent twist to this theme has been the suggestion that with the Bulger murder, 'the innocence of childhood has finally come of age' (Jenks, 1996: 118).

However, the most controversial thesis (advanced by Neil Postman, an American media sociologist) claims that childhood is 'disappearing', mainly through the influence of television, but also by the use of child models in the advertising of children's clothes and adult products, the tendency of children's clothes to resemble adult fashions, the increasing violence of juvenile crime, and the gradual replacement of traditional street games by organized junior sports leagues (in America). The child, in having gained access to the world of adult information (mainly through television) has been 'expelled from the garden of childhood' (Postman, 1983: 192).

In such a climate of opinion, 'children become alien creatures, a threat to civilisation rather than its hope and potential salvation' (Cunningham, 1995: 179). Television is regarded as dangerous because 'it places before children images of the good life hardly consonant with the delayed gratification endorsed by Postman and before him by a long tradition within Christianity'. This vision of the good childhood, is not one of freedom and happiness; 'rather it is good behaviour, a deference to adults, and a commitment to learning skills essential for the adult world' (*ibid*: 180). Notwithstanding this critical appraisal, it has been suggested that modern society has seen a 'collapse of adult authority', which 'took effect at varying rates'. The 'collapse' is said to be witnessed by the growth in parental spending on children, and the search by parents for 'emotional gratification' from children. (*ibid*: 182–5; also Zelizer, 1985).

This view, together with that of 'disappearing' childhood, is countered by those who argue that children 'remain subject to authority relations' (Hood-Williams, 1990). The power and control of adults over children is described with reference to Weber's notion of 'patriarchal authority' (meaning 'the probability that a command with a specific content will be obeyed by a given groups of persons'), as 'age-patriarchy', which refers to an imbalance of power, control, and resources manifesting themselves through adult control — expressed as a demand for obedience — over children's space, bodies and time. This is not to say that there is an absence of affection between parents and children for, just as between husband and wife within the patriarchal marriage, so 'one of the tasks of some modern childhoods is to be companionable, to be fun, to be loved and loving as well as to meet the more traditional requirements to respect, honour and, above all, to obey' (*ibid.* 158).

We have here an answer to the claim that the parental search for 'emotional gratification' has entailed a shift in power towards children. On the contrary, it has positioned children in a similar fashion to the ideal 'bourgeois' wife and mother in her historical role as 'the angel in the home': pampered and loved, an essential ornament serving as testimony to domestic bliss, but subservient to male power (Davidoff and Hall, 1987). With reference to the heaping upon children of consumer goods, we know that adults have far greater control over 'the meaning and availability of consumer goods', which subordinates children's choices 'towards consumption patterns that do not seriously conflict with those of adults' (Oldman 1994: 47–7). Moreover, since toys usually reach children as 'gifts', and we know from anthropological studies that gifts 'are a very special form of exchange which require their own reciprocities', clearly 'gifts are not given "freely". Some return is expected' (Hood Williams, 1990: 162).

Conclusion

This survey has shown that since at least the eighteenth century there have been several authoritative social constructions (and reconstructions) of childhood. From the perspective of adults, these different understandings have shared the intention to identify the existence of 'childhood'; to define the desirable state of 'childhood'; to incorporate the concept into a larger philosophy concerning the meaning of life; and to control 'childhood', whatever its nature. From the beginning of our period, each construction sought to mould 'childhood' as a singular noun; the plural posed too many conceptual and political problems. In the eighteenth and for most of the nineteenth century, the plurality of 'childhoods' made it difficult to capture the desired condition and to secure agreement on what it should be. Consequently, disciples of Rousseau, Romantics, Evangelicals, child-labour reformers, anti-slavers, penologists, educationalists, moralists, psycho-medics and advocates of all aspects of child welfare struggled to regularize competing identities, through what was a developing conception of *proper* 'childhood', designed to secure universal approval. For most of this century what became a widely accepted construction of childhood by, say, 1914, has been elaborately and carefully refined in accordance with the principles of medicine, psychology and education on the one hand and, on the other, in relation to the political goals of universal welfare and a popular commitment to the family.

The extent to which each 'construction' was a 'reconstruction' is difficult to determine and, ultimately, it is not that important an issue. Contemporaries probably assumed conceptual originality, but there was always some degree of overlap among the expanding and changing perceptions, certainly in their ideological imperatives (and we should never forget the *political* nature of the social construction of childhood). The different constructions stretched out towards three related and paralleling objectives. The first was a uniformity and coherence necessary to unite the urban and the rural, capable of embacing different social-class experiences, and focusing on the supposedly 'natural' state of childhood. Secondly, the font of this uniformity and coherence was to be the family, sanctified by religion and personified from the early nineteenth century by a largely middle-class 'domestic ideal', with its emphasis on order, respect, love, duty and clearly defined age and gender distinctions. Here the child could live out a *proper* childhood in a *natural* environment. Thirdly, from the end of the nineteenth century a compulsory relationship involving the State, the family and public health and welfare services was legislated into practice. This built upon ideals of domesticity and, through psycho-medicine, reinforced the 'natural' childhood in terms of education, socialization and the culture of dependency. Of course, none of this just happened. It was a consciously executed political and cultural enterprise and, therefore, was often fiercely contested territory as the different beliefs concerning the 'nature' of childhood struggled for supremacy. And not least important among the contestants were children themselves.

References

ANDERSON, M. (1980) *Approaches to the History of the Western Family: 1500–1914*, London, Macmillan.

BAISTOW, K. (1995) 'From sickly survival to the realistion of potential: Child health as a social project', *Children Society*, **9**, pp. 20–35.

BOUTET DE MONVEL, A. (1963) 'Introduction', Rousseau, J.J. *Emile*, London, Dent.

CALDER, A. (1971) *The People's War*, London, Panther.

CARPENTER, H. (1985) *Secret Gardens: The Golden Age of Children's Literature*, London, Allen and Unwin.

CARPENTER, M. (1853) *Juvenile Delinquents: Their Condition and Treatment*, London, Cash.

CHISHOLM, L. *et al.* (1990) *Childhood, Youth and Social Change: A Comparative Perspective*, London, Falmer Press.

COLLS, R. (1976) '"oh happy English children": Coal, class and education in the North-East', *Past and Present*, **73**, pp. 74–99.

COVENEY, P. (1967) *The Image of Childhood*, 2nd ed., Harmondsworth, Peregrine Books.

CUNNINGHAM, H. (1991) *The Children of the Poor: Representations of Childhood Since the Seventeenth Century*, Oxford, Basil Blackwell.

CUNNINGHAM, H. (1995) *Children and Childhood in Western Society since 1500* London, Longman.

DAVIDOFF, L. and HALL, C. (1987) *Family Fortunes: Men and women of the English middle class 1788–1850*, London, Hutchinson.

DRESCHER, S. (1981) 'Cart Whip and Billy Roller: Or anti-slavery and reform symbolism in industrializing Britain', *Journal of Social History*, **15**, 1, pp. 3–24.

DRIVER, C. (1946) *Tory Radical: The Life of Richard Oastler*, New York, Oxford University Press.

ENNEW, J. (1986) *The Sexual Exploitation of Children*, Cambridge, Polity Press.

GLENNERSTER, H. (1995) *British Social Policy since 1945*, Oxford, Blackwell.

HALL, C. (1979) 'The early formation of Victorian domestic ideology', in BURMANM, S. *Fit Work for Women*, London, Croom Helm, pp. 15–32.

HARDYMENT, C. (1995) (Ed) *Perfect Parents: Baby-care Advice Past and Present*, Oxford University Press.

HEASMAN, K. (1962) *The Evangelicals in Action*, London, Geoffrey Bles.

HENDRICK, H. (1992) 'Changing attitudes to children, 1800–1914', *Genealogists' Magazine*, **24**, 2, pp. 41–9.

HENDRICK, H. (1994) *Child Welfare England: 1870–1989*, London, Routledge.

HENDRICK, H. (forthcoming) *Children, Childhood and English Society, 1880–1990*, Cambridge University Press.

HOLMAN, B. (1995) *The Evacuation*, The Lion Press.

HOOD-WILLIAMS, J. (1990) 'Patriarchy for children: On the stability of power relations in children's lives', in CHISHOLM, L. *et al.*, *Childhood, Youth and Social Change: A Comparative Perspective*, Basingstoke, Falmer Press, pp. 155–71.

HORN, P. (1974) *Children's Work and Welfare 1780s–1880s*, London, Macmillan.

HUMPHRIES, S. (1981) *Hooligans or Rebels? An Oral History of Working Class Childhood and Youth, 1889–1939*, Oxford, Blackwells.

HUMPHRIES, S., MACK, J. and PERKS, R. (1988) *A Century of Childhood*, London, Sidgwick and Jackson.

HURT, J.S. (1979) *Elementary Schooling and the Working Classes: 1860–1918*, London, RKP.

INGLIS, R. (1990) *The Children's War: Evacuation 1939–45*, London, Fontana.

JAMES, A. (1993) *Childhood Identities: Self and Social Relationships in the Experience of the Child*, Edinburgh University Press.

JENHS, C. (1996) *Childhood*, London, Routledge.

JOHNSON, R. (1970) 'Educational policy and social control in early Victorian England', *Past and Present*, **49**, pp. 96–119.

KEIR, G. (1952) 'A history of child guidance', *British Journal of Educational Psychology*, **22**, pp. 5–29.

MACNICOL, J. (1986) 'The effect of the evacuation of schoolchildren on official attitudes to state intervention', in SMITH, H.L. *War and Social Change: British Society in the Second World War*, Manchester University Press.

MANTON, J. (1976) *Mary Carpenter and the Children of the Street*, London, Heinemann.

MAY, M. (1973) 'Innocence and experience: The evolution of the concept of juvenile delinquency in the mid-nineteenth century', *Victorian Studies*, **17**, 1, pp. 7–29.

MAYALL, B. (1994) (Ed) *Children's Childhoods: Observed and Experienced*, London, Falmer Press.

OLDMAN, D. (1994) 'Adult–child relations as class relations', in QUORTRUP, J. *et al.*, *Childhood Matters: Social Theory, Practice and Politics*, Aldershot, Avebury, pp. 43–58.

PARTON, N. (1990) 'Taking child abuse seriously', in Violence Against Children Study Group, *Taking Child Abuse Seriously*, London, Unwin Hyman, pp. 7–24.

PATTISON, R. (1978) *The Child Figure in English Literature*, Athens, University of Georgia Press.

PEARSON, G. (1983) *Hooligan: A History of Respectable Fears*, London, Macmillan.

PINCHBECK, I. and HEWITT, M. (1973) *Children in English Society*, London, RKP.

PLUMB, J.H. (1975) 'The new world of children in eighteenth-century England', *Past and Present*, **67**, pp. 74–95.

PORTER, R. (1982) *English Society in the Eighteenth Century*, Harmondsworth, Penguin.

POSTMAN, N. (1983) *The Disappearance of Childhood*, London, W.H. Allen.

QVORTRUP, J. *et al.* (1994) *Childhood Matters: Social Theory, Practice and Politics*, Aldershot, Avebury.

RILEY, D. (1983) *War in the Nursery: Theories of the Child and Mother*, London, Virago.

ROBERTSON, P. (1976) 'Home as a nest: Middle class childhood in nineteenth-century Europe', in DE MAUSE, L. *The History of Childhood*, London, Souvenir Press.

ROSE, N. (1985) *The Psychological Complex: Psychology, Politics and Society in England, 1869–1939*, London, RKP.

ROSE, N. (1990) *Governing the Soul: The Shaping of the Private Self*, London, Routledge.

ROSMAN, D. (1984) *Evangelicals and Culture*, London, Croom helm.

SEABROOK, J. (1982) *Working-Class Childhood: An Oral History*, London, Gollancz.

SELLECK, R.J.W. (1985) 'Mary Carpenter: A confident and contradictory reformer', *History of Education*, March, pp. 101–15.

SOMMERVILLE, J. (1982) *The Rise and Fall of Childhood*, London, Sage.

SUTHERLAND, G. (1984) *Ability, Merit and Measurement: Mental Testing and English Education*, Oxford, Clarendon Press.

THOM, D. (1992) 'Wishes, anxieties, play, and gestures: Child guidance in inter-war England', in COOTER, R. *In the Name of the Child. Health and Welfare, 1880–1940*, London, Routledge, pp. 200–19.

THOMAS, K. (1983) *Man and the Natural World: Changing Attitudes in England, 1500–1800*, Harmondsworth, Penguin.

THOMPSON, E. (1963) *The Making of the English Working Class*, London, Gollancz.

URWIN, C. and SHARLAND, E. (1992) 'From bodies to minds in childcare literature: Advice to parents in inter-war Britain', in COOTER, R. *In the Name of the Child. Health and Welfare, 1880–1940*, London, Routledge, pp. 174–99.

WALVIN, J. (1982) *A Child's World: A Social History of English Childhood, 1800–1914*, Harmondsworth, Penguin.

WOOLDRIDGE, A. (1995) *Measuring the Mind*, Cambridge University Press.

ZELIZER, V. (1985) *Pricing the Priceless Child: The Changing Social Value of Children*, New York, Basic Books.

Chapter 3

Psychology and the Cultural Construction of Children's Needs

Martin Woodhead

Introduction

Children's psychological 'needs' are at the heart of contemporary public concern, part of the everyday vocabulary of countless numbers of social welfare workers and teachers, policy-makers and parents. Conceptualizing childhood in terms of 'needs' reflects the distinctive status accorded to young humanity in twentieth century western societies. It is widely regarded as a progressive and enlightened framework for working with children. It gives priority to protecting and promoting their psychological welfare, by contrast with former times and other societies, where adult priorities have centred more on children's economic utility, their duties and obligations, rather than their needs, (Newson and Newson, 1974; Hoffman, 1987).

It may seem somewhat presumptuous to challenge the ubiquity of this way of thinking about children. But by systematically analyzing the concept of 'need', I hope to show that this seemingly innocuous and benign four-letter word conceals in practice a complex of latent assumptions and judgments about children. Once revealed, these tell us as much about the cultural location and personal values of the user as about the nature of childhood. My conclusion, provocatively, is that our understanding and respect for childhood might be better served if 'children's needs' were outlawed from future professional discourse, policy recommendations, and popular psychology.

This chapter is a by-product of nearly two decades spent exploring the borderlands between child psychology, education and social welfare, especially relating to children under 5 years. I have encountered numerous statements about children's needs on the way, a small selection of which are reproduced below.

The first is taken from a policy document on nursery education which stated that:

There is now considerable evidence pointing to the importance of the years before five in a child's education — and to the most effective ways of providing for the *needs*, and potential, which children display at this age . . . most *needs* could be met by part-time nursery education (Department of Education and Science 1972, para. 16, my emphasis).

Social work professionals have framed their recommendations in similar terms:

It is the responsibility of the worker to be aware of the *needs* of the child — *needs* appropriate to his age (para. 2.6) . . . One of the most essential *needs* of the young child is that of continuity in his experience of being cared for (British Association of Social workers, undated, para. 4.12, my emphasis).

Evidently, both education and social work professionals are in little doubt about the existence of 'children's needs'; indeed, in many cases they are the foundation on which policies and practices are built. A clear example is in the debate about day care for the children of working parents. One prominent child-care expert has taken up a very firm position:

My ideal society has no day nurseries, residential nurseries or crèches in it. None at all. Babies and very small children each *need* a 'special' and continuous person or people and they *need* to have their daily lives based on somewhere they know as 'home' (Leach, 1979: 161, my emphasis).

One of the clearest examples of framing statements about children's welfare in terms of an understanding of their needs can be found in the writings of the former Director of the National Children's Bureau, Mia Kellmer-Pringle. She argued against full-time day care as follows:

Full-time mothering is unique in the sense that the mother has the time and hence the patience, to develop sensitivity to her baby. This enables her to recognize and adapt to his very special, individual *needs* . . . The *need* for love and security is met by the child experiencing from birth onwards a stable, continuous, loving and mutually enjoyable relationship with his mother or mother figure . . . The same applies to her ability to meet the second *need*, for new experiences. These are essential for the mind as food is for the body . . . It is very difficult to meet this *need* either in a day nursery or by child minders, essentially because they provide a group setting whereas this learning and stimulation is *needed* on a one-to-one basis (Kellmer-Pringle, 1976: 97–8, my emphasis).

These needs, along with two further 'basic needs' (for praise and recognition and for responsibility) have been elaborated in detail (Kellmer-Pringle, 1975: 1980).

All the examples so far have been from British sources. But the concept of 'children's needs' is much more extensively used than this. It even found a place in the United Nations Declaration of the Rights of the Child, Principle 6, which begins:

> The child, for the full and harmonious development of his personality, *needs* love and understanding. He shall, wherever possible, grow up in the care and under the responsibility of his parents, and in any case in an atmosphere of affection and moral and material security; a child of tender years shall not, save in exceptional circumstances, be separated from his mother . . . (United Nations, 1959, my emphasis).

Finally, the specification of children's needs is a perennial activity. This is illustrated by my final example, which returns to the topic of nursery education, but was prepared over fifteen years after the first:

> A variety of *needs* . . . were drawn to our attention. . . . Young children *need* to be with adults who are interested and interesting, and with other children to whom they may relate. They *need* to have natural objects and artefacts to handle and explore. They *need* opportunity to communicate through music and imaginative play . . . These *needs* can only be met if an appropriate environment is provided with adults who understand something of child development and are ready and able to listen, encourage and stimulate (House of Commons, 1988, para. 5.1, my emphasis).

Clearly, in each of these cases, it is possible to view the concept of 'need' merely as shorthand, an economical way of conveying the author's conclusions about the requirements of childhood. There are certainly virtues in condensed prose! But arguably such expressions may also be serving as a very credible veil for uncertainty and even disagreement about what is 'in the best interests of children'. Philosophers have frequently drawn attention to complexities in the concept of 'need' that are rarely recognized in everyday use, (e.g., Taylor, 1959). Its use in social welfare policy has been analyzed by Walton (1969), Smith (1971), and Bradshaw (1972). Applications in educational thinking have been considered by Hirst and Peters (1970), Dearden (1972), Wilson (1973), and Wringe (1981).

One way of beginning to understand the latent meaning in 'need' statements is by substituting other expressions for 'need'. Thus, while 'want' would convey the idea of a child's demands, 'should have' implies that an observer is judging what is desirable for the child. But 'need' is endowed with a more complex meaning structure. And it also makes a more powerful impact on the reader than either 'want' or 'should have'.

In part this is because the extracts quoted earlier appear to be describing qualities of childhood which are timeless and universal. Identification of needs appears to be a matter of empirical study by the psychologist, or close observation by professional or parent. This apparently 'factual' basis of needs is signalled in the extracts themselves. Caring adults are described as able 'to *recognize* and *adapt* to' the child's needs, or become '*aware* of the needs of the child', or respond to the needs 'which children *display* at this age'. In each case there is a strong implication that, provided the adult is sufficiently astute, needs can be identified mainly or solely through observing children themselves.

But the authority of 'need' statements does not only come from their apparently straightforward descriptive quality. They also convey considerable emotive force, inducing a sense of responsibility, and even feelings of guilt if they are not heeded. This power comes partly from the connotation of helplessness and passivity of any individual who is 'in need', and partly from the implication that dire consequences will follow if the need is not met through appropriate intervention. This combination of descriptive and imperative authority provides a persuasive basis for defining policy. But are 'need' statements quite so robust as they seem? To find out, we need to look more closely at their formal structure.

The Concept of Children's Needs

Statements of the form 'X needs Y' generally make an assumption about the goal of meeting the need as well as the consequence of failing to do so. They are, in effect, an abbreviation of 'X needs Y, for Z to follow'. Indeed the significance of the relationship between X and Y only gains its strength when Z is known. So it is important to note that Z is rarely made explicit. Usually it is unstated, or incompletely stated, presumed as a shared understanding between author and reader. There is one exception in the extracts cited above, (the United Nations Declaration of the Rights of Child) which helps clarify the formal structure of statements about children's needs, as follows: 'The child (X), for the full and harmonious development of his personality (Z), needs love and understanding (Y)'. This example can be understood as making a factual statement (or hypothesis) about the relationship between X, Y and Z, in which Y is seen as a pre-requisite for Z. In other words it could be restated more simply in the form: 'Children that are not given love will grow up emotionally unstable'.

So, the first step in evaluating a 'need' statement is to identify the outcome Z and test the descriptive claim that Y is a necessary condition to achieve it. But this only gets us part of the way towards appreciating the power in claims about children's needs.

The examples cited at the beginning of this chapter suggest much more than just an empirical relationship between X, Y and Z. They also imply a desirable relationship, that Z is a desirable goal for X, and Y is the way to achieve it. In other words, statements about children's needs convey an element of judgment about what is good for them and how this can be achieved. It is this aspect of such statements that imbues them with emotive force, implying an imperative for action.

To take a more straightforward example, if an amateur gardener receives the expert advice: 'Your plants need water', it is most likely intended to do more than just inform about the factual relationship between plants (X), water (Y), and the unstated outcome, growth (Z). Not unreasonably, it also implies that where plants are concerned, growth is desirable. The gardener would be expected to fill up the watering can without delay; after all the survival of the plants is at stake. In other words, the expert's statement presumes a totally uncontroversial value judgment about what is good for plants. The same applies to the statement 'children need love'. The desirability of emotional stability is so generally accepted that we hardly recognize there to be an unstated goal; the existence of an implicit value judgment is not at all self-evident.

To summarize the analysis so far, I have argued that concealed beneath the apparent simplicity and directness of 'need' statements is a highly condensed combination of both empirical and evaluative claims. They are often not fully specified, but depend on a consensus of knowledge and values between author and reader, horticultural adviser and gardener, social-worker and client, policy-maker and community, etc. A more explicit statement of the sentiment 'A child needs love' might read: 'It is desirable for a child to grow up emotionally secure. A child who is not given love will not grow up emotionally secure. Therefore a child should be given love.'

Besides economy of words, what is the significance of condensing this set of ideas into such a short and compelling phrase as 'children need love' with all the power and connotations discussed earlier? Why is this construction so much more frequently used than, for example, 'parents should give love to their children' or 'society should make sure children are loved'? These alternatives are not so bizarre as they seem at first sight. After all, judgments about what is desirable for children and how to achieve it are made by parents, by teachers, by policy makers, by society — not by the children themselves! Unless, that is, we are attributing to children themselves a sense of the prospect of emotional security that lies ahead, and an understanding of the kinds of experience that will promote it. I will consider this possibility in a moment. But from the analysis so far I think it should already be clear why statements of policy are so frequently framed in terms of 'children's needs'.

A statement which appears to describe qualities of children's nature as young humanity has a very different status to a judgment by parents, teachers, experts or politicians about what is good for them. Identification of 'need' with children themselves has the effect of reducing the task to an empirical one, of better understanding the natural course of development, rather than a matter of cultural or personal values, of deciding what is good for them. If needs can be identified with children's nature, with universal qualities of their biological and psychological make-up, then the evidence of scientific enquiry can provide the basis of social and educational policy and practice. But, if, on the other hand, needs have to be seen as cultural construction, superimposed on children 'in their best interests' as future adult members of society, personal values and cultural ideologies have a much bigger part to play and the politician's or practitioner's authority is substantially diminished. To put it bluntly, the one appears mainly a matter of establishing 'the facts', the other appears as also a matter for personal choice and political discussion.

I have set these up as extremes — between 'needs' as intrinsic to children, part of their make-up, and 'needs' as a cultural construction. But in the rest of the chapter I shall argue that the picture is more complex than that. I want to suggest that there are at least four distinct bases for establishing children's needs. In trying to unravel them in the rest of the chapter, I shall be guided by a deceptively simple question, namely: when we speak of children as having needs, where exactly are their needs?

Where Are Children's Needs?

Needs in Children's Nature

As noted above, much of the authority of statements about children's needs comes from assuming that the needs are a property of children themselves, something that they possess, endowed by nature, and detectable in their behaviour. Needs are most literally identified with children's nature when used in the noun form, 'X has a need for Y'.

Kellmer-Pringle's four basic needs (for love and security, for new experiences, for praise and recognition, and for responsibility) come into this category. They are identified with the biological/psychological make-up of young humanity — their instincts, drives, motives, wants. This is clear from the analogy (in the quotation cited at the outset) between the need for new experiences and the need for food; which seems to imply that there are regulatory processes within the organism for monitoring the level of need and initiating behaviour, in accordance with basic homeostatic principles (Mace, 1953).

On this model, 'need' is complementary to 'want', provided we can assume that the organism's actions are congruent with its needs. Where children are concerned we can as a rule say that the need for food *is* an intrinsic drive signalled in infancy by rooting for the breast, as well as a distinctive pattern of crying, which is differentiated by care-givers from other types of cry (Thoman, 1975).

But what of the need for love, new experiences, praise and recognition, and responsibility? Can these be literally identified with the psychological make-up of the individual such that in some sense (to follow the formal proposition given earlier) X has a drive to seek out Y in order to achieve the state of Z? To focus on the 'need for love and security', the most influential theorist, John Bowlby was careful to avoid referring to 'needs' or 'drives'. But he did view children's attachment behaviour as closely analogous to patterns of imprinting observed in non-human species (Bowlby, 1969: 224, 272–3). It is certainly true that young infants are predisposed to pay attention to the human face and seek proximity, comfort and nutrition from care-givers (Schaffer, 1984). They also protest vigorously if they are separated from attachment figures, at least after about 7 or 8 months of age (Schaffer and Emerson, 1964) and this is not greatly modified by the cultural setting in which they have been brought up (Kagan *et al.*, 1978).

On this evidence, it seems reasonable to conclude that a general predisposition to seek out enduring human relationships is a feature of the infant. But it is much less clear to what degree this is linked to specific features of early nurturing environments, as in '. . . a stable, continuous, loving and mutually enjoyable relationship with his mother or mother figure' (Kellmer-Pringle) or '. . . a "special" and continuous person or people and . . . daily lives based on somewhere they know as home' (Leach). Specification of these particularities of 'need' and ways in which they can be met seem to have a rather different kind of knowledge base. They are for the most part based on an inference from beliefs and evidence about the undesirable consequences of deprivations.

Needs and Psychological Health

Whereas in the first model the need Y is identified as lying within the child, the emphasis of the second model is on the outcome Z, as a universal quality of psychological well-being in children. Giving children sufficient of Y is seen as a prerequisite for Z, but without presuming that they have any intrinsic drive to achieve it. This is a pathological approach to defining children's needs, analogous to a doctor diagnosing that a child needs a heart operation. The diagnosis is based on a judgment about the desirability of a particular outcome, i.e., physical health, and a prescription of how to achieve it. There is no sense in which the doctor's diagnosis is referring to the drive structure of the child. This is essentially a teleological basis for defining need, which in this case is most commonly associated with pathological models of children's welfare. Particular experiences in early childhood are being judged according to their consistency with later mental health, and projected on to children as their 'needs'.

This model has been widely applied in child welfare work, again very largely through the influence of John Bowlby. Indeed, several of the extracts quoted at the beginning of this chapter are derivative from his famous statement about maternal deprivation:

> What is believed to be essential for mental health is that an infant and young child should experience a warm, intimate, and continuous relationship with his mother (or permanent mother substitute — one person who steadily 'mothers' him) in which both find satisfaction and enjoyment (Bowlby, 1953: 13).

'Need' here does not presume qualities that are intrinsic to children; it is an inference from the relationship between certain qualities of mothering and a valued consequence for children. In many respects this is a powerful basis for prescribing for childhood, which acknowledges the relative helplessness and dependency of the infant and the important role of care-givers who (whether by native instinct, social learning or parent education courses) have the disposition to give love and affection.

Much research has centred on the validity of the claim that particular qualities in early relationships have repercussions for mental health. Studies have focused on the numbers of adults that fulfil a caring role, the patterns of care, and the reversibility of early deprivations. For example, Tizard *et al.* (1974, 1978) conducted a long-term follow-up study of children who had spent much of their infancy (up to four and a half years) in institutions and were then placed either with adoptive parents, with their natural parents, or remained in an institution. Despite the very different life experiences of these children, and the evidence that in some respects the effects of early deprivation were reversible, consistent long-term effects of institutionalization were found right through to the age of 16 (Hodges and Tizard 1989a, 1989b). Some of the most consistent results were based on teachers' reports of behaviour problems. Reporting on the data when children were 8 years old, Tizard concluded:

> . . . it seemed to us possible that all the children's problems at school stemmed not from a conduct disorder of the usual kind, but from two basic characteristics, both concerned with their social behaviour — an almost insatiable desire for adult attention, and a difficulty in forming good relationships with their peer group, although often they got along much better with younger and older children (Tizard and Hodges, 1978: 114).

It is an easy step to infer from such evidence that children 'need' the loving care of which these institutional children are deprived. After all, such statements have a sound foundation in systematic research. The problem is that global inferences neglect the cultural context of particular child care arrangements in which the children's development was embedded, and the cultural definitions of mental health and psychological adjustment that the research presumed. These can be variable even within one social setting, as cross-generational research has shown. For example, Wadsworth (1986) has argued that differences in cultural attitudes toward the consequences of divorce during different epochs may modify the impact of that trauma on children. Wadsworth cites evidence from a 1946 cohort for which an association was found between the experience of parental separation or divorce during children's first five years and the incidence of criminal convictions among boys by the age of 21. He postulates a series of transmission pathways that might account for this relationship, including the social stigma associated with divorce at that time, which may have altered the relationship of children to significant adults with whom they came into contact. Most important, he recognizes that the effect of this transmission pathway might be specific to the era in which these children grew up, during which professionals were encouraged to hold strong expectations that children would be severely adversely affected by the experience.

Psychologists are only beginning to tease out the complex social processes that can modify, amplify, or alleviate the impact of early childhood experiences (e.g., Woodhead 1988, Rutter 1989). But the inadequacy of making simplistic inferences about children's needs from such complex and often context-specific processes is already abundantly clear.

Needs and Social Adjustment

Despite the utility as well as persuasive power of applying a pathological paradigm to child welfare judgments, normative relationships are all too readily interpreted as if they were universally valid prescriptions for childhood. The clearest example concerns the number of adults who take care of children. On the evidence available to him at the time Bowlby (1953) argued that children have a predisposition to become attached to one major figure (the theory of 'monotropism'). This is reflected in the claims quoted earlier. Monotropism has certainly been the normal pattern in western society although it does underestimate the role of fathers and other members of the family as primary care-givers (Osborn *et al.*, 1984). Monotropism is also adaptive in a society which emphasizes maternal care in a nuclear family. But for other cultures other patterns are equally adaptive, and so in their terms, equally consistent with mental health. For example, on the basis of cross-cultural evidence, one reviewer concluded that infants generally seem able to form strong and secure relationships with up to five, possibly ten, 'caretakers' (Smith, 1979: 504; Smith, 1980). And Weisner and Gallimore (1977) have described the special place of sibling care in traditional African societies. Clearly multiple caretaking may orient children to patterns of relationships in adult life other than monotropism (Zukow, 1989). But there is little justification for translating the observation that normative patterns of early rearing are culturally adaptive into a judgment that these patterns are necessary prerequisites of mental health.

The point has been made most clearly by analogy with two species of monkey, (Schaffer, 1977). Bonnets are gregarious creatures, and share care of infants widely within the group. By contrast, pigtails live in closely-knit family units and are exclusive in their patterns of care. Each pattern is in its own terms adaptive, though an individual brought up in one pattern might find it difficult to adapt to the other:

> A bonnet-reared child is unlikely to become an effective pigtail parent; any particular cultural tradition rests on continuity between child rearing, personality development, and social setting. Yet that is very different from equating any one such tradition with mental health and all other traditions with ill health (Schaffer, 1977: 110).

Of course, there is no direct parallel within the cultural complexities of human society. But the general perspective certainly applies (e.g., Super and Harkness, 1983).

Within this perspective, models of children's welfare based on a concept of need could still have some validity, but they would be relative, not absolute. Thus within a particular cultural framework, X_1 might be said to need Y_1 for Z_1 to follow. But within another cultural framework a different need might be equally vociferously argued for; hence X_2 might be said to need Y_2 for Z_2 to follow; X_3 need Y_3 for Z_3, and so on. This is similar to a pathological model, but it recognizes that determination of need depends as much on appreciation of the particular constellation of relationships in the social environment (past, present and future) as it does on knowledge of universal qualities of human nature. So when it comes to making statements of policy or offering professional advice, personal and cultural values are much more strongly implied. A statement about children's needs would depend on value-judgments, stated or implied, about which patterns of early relationship are considered desirable, what the child should grow up to become, and indeed what makes for the 'good society'.

By way of illustration, consider Kellmer-Pringle's fourth basic children's need — for responsibility. This is a highly valued attribute amongst western nations where individualism, independent thinking, flexibility and assertiveness are the routes to personal achievement. Thus in a cross-national study of parents' attitudes to children Hoffman (1987) found that parents in the USA laid stress on the importance of a child 'becoming a good person', being 'independent and self-reliant'. By contrast in countries, (such as Turkey, the Philippines and Indonesia) where children's economic contribution is highly valued, parents placed much greater stress on 'deference to elders' and 'obedience'. Presumably parents in the two societies would view their children's 'needs' quite differently.

In short, while in certain very general respects, 'need' statements may have universal validity, detailed prescriptions about children's needs are normative, and depend on a judgment about processes of cultural adaptation and social adjustment. This conclusion could have import-ant implications for any inter-cultural generalizations. For instance, it could be argued that the emphasis in the United Nations Declaration (quoted at the outset) on the need for maternal care, which was informed by western family arrangements and research, risks being ethnocentric.

Needs and Cultural Prescriptions

There is one other common usage of the concept of children's needs which is even further removed from an understanding of children's nature, their mental health, or their social adjustment. It is most clearly illustrated by the policy statements on early education quoted at the outset. Take the conclusions of the House of Commons Select Commit-tee in 1988. In what sense do children 'need to be with adults who are interesting, . . . need to have natural objects . . . to handle, need . . . to communicate through music and imaginative play'? Such educational needs are largely a cultural construction. They are illustrated in even more extreme form by such claims as 'children need to learn physics, pottery and parent craft'. These needs are certainly not a part of the psychological make up of individual children, nor even a prerequisite for their psychological well-being, either in absolute or relative terms. There is a weak sense in which children in western society deprived of educational opportunities may be culturally maladapted, but there is plenty of room for argument about the appropriate criteria for judging that.

To understand the ubiquity of such 'need' statements we have to consider the relationship between experts who make such authoritative pronouncements (in this case educators) and clients who receive them (usually parents on behalf of their children). Framing professional judg-ments in terms of 'children's needs' serves to direct attention away from the particular adult value-position from which they are made. Projected onto children themselves, they acquire spurious objectivity. In this way, cultural prescriptions for childhood are presented as if they were intrin-sic qualities of children's own psychological make-up.

Human Nature or Cultural Construction?

When policy recommendations and professional advice are expressed in terms of children's needs, they give an impression of universal objectivity. It is tempting to accept them at face value as authoritative statements of fact. But beneath the veneer of certainty I have argued there lies a complicated array of personal and cultural values alongside empirical claims about childhood.

Framing prescriptions in terms of children's needs may serve important functions for those who make them, notably the greater authority that comes from projecting their decision-making criteria onto the child. But as a consequence they fail to differentiate several quite distinct bases for making prescriptions about what is in the best interests of children. Four categories of usage have been distinguished: 'need' as a description of children's psychological nature; 'need' as an inference from what is known about the pathological consequences of particular childhood experiences; 'need' as a judgment about which childhood experiences are most culturally adaptive; and 'need' as a prescription about which childhood experiences are most highly valued in society. These are not just matters of emphasis. The different usages have quite different statuses, which become merged and confused when rendered into apparently unproblematic generalizations about children's 'needs'.

In a homogeneous society, where the findings of psychological research derive from and feed back into a shared normative framework of cultural values and practices, these distinctions might not seem too important. But when the reference point is a culturally diverse society like Britain, and especially when it is a group of societies as diverse as the United Nations, simple generalizations about children's needs are much more problematic. In these circumstances, it becomes imperative to disentangle the scientific from the evaluative, the natural from the cultural.

How much better it might be to abandon this problematic way of construing childhood altogether? This would help break down the mystifications that are locked in much professional language, forcing those who make judgments about what is and is not in children's interests to make explicit and justify their decision-criteria, and unveil their assumptions for external scrutiny.

In drawing these conclusions, I want to emphasize that I am not suggesting that judgments about the adequacy of children's care, education and welfare are to be avoided — on the contrary. Despite the diversity of cultural arrangements for child rearing, it is clearly imperative to establish consensus on the boundaries of minimal adequacy; although even this task may be problematic, as comparative studies of child abuse have discovered (Korbin, 1981). Neither am I arguing that the perspectives on childhood that inform these judgments are a purely cultural construction. Children inherit a distinctively human nature as well as being brought up in a particular culture. Their dependency on others to protect their interests during the long period of human immaturity known as childhood means that judgments must continually be made by those responsible for them; although the length of their dependency and the cultural articulation of what is in their best interests will vary from society to society and from time to time.

The challenge is not to shy away from developing a perspective on childhood, but to recognize the plurality of pathways to maturity within that perspective. This is all the more important at a time when the influence of child psychology is extending well beyond the societies (notably North America and Europe) from which dominant theories and research data have been derived. For example a 'Handbook of Asian Child Development and Child Rearing Practices' has been prepared by mainly Thai child development experts explicitly to assimilate western child development theory into Third World contexts. The following brief extract vividly illustrates the profound but largely unacknowledged issues that are raised by the enterprise:

> Asian parents have a long history of well developed cultures behind them. They are mostly agriculturalists who are submissive to the earth's physical nature. Thus many of their traditional beliefs and practices prevent them from seeking and using the new *scientific* knowledge in child-rearing.
>
> The Handbook of Child Rearing may require parents to change many of their beliefs, attitudes, values, habits and behaviours. Therefore, many necessary changes will be met with some resistance. For example, giving the child more of the independence the child *needs* and making less use of power and authority during adolescence will shake the very roots of those Asian families where authoritarian attitudes and practice are emphasized. (Suvannathat *et al.*, 1985: 4–5, my emphasis).

Cross-cultural research has always held a respectable, albeit marginal role in psychological work, (e.g., Warren, 1980). But it is only in the last ten years or so that consideration of cultural and social context has begun to occupy centre-stage as an integral element in mainstream theory and research, (e.g., in the USA: Bronfenbrenner, 1979; Kessen, 1979; Kessel and Siegel, 1983; in the UK: Richards, 1974; Richards and Light, 1986). Whether the emerging 'cultural constructivist' perspective on child development will make sufficient impact to modify the assumptions in the extract above remains to be seen. If it does not, as seems likely, and western culture and values continue to be promoted in the guise of science, then a gradual process of homogenization of child-rearing patterns seems inevitable. In the long term, such trends could have important implications for the concept of 'children's needs'. The arguments in this chapter in favour of a more explicit, culturally sensitive, perspective on childhood will lose much of their force. Children's needs will become universal.

Note

An earlier version of this chapter appeared in Oxford Review of Education, Vol. 13, no. 2, 1987, 129–139.

Postscript: 'Beyond Children's Needs'

'Children's needs' is a powerful rhetorical device for constructing images of childhood, prescribing for care and education, and judging the quality of adult–child relationships. While I challenge widespread, uncritical use of this way of framing childhood I do not reject the evidence that there are some universal prerequisites for children's health, care and learning an impression I unwittingly conveyed to some readers of the first edition of this book. I have argued that apparently unproblematic, taken-for-granted certainty implied in statements about the 'needs of children' does not stand up to close scrutiny. I have also been interested in the way this rhetorical device defines power relationships between experts and families, service providers and consumers, in ways that have little to do with the children themselves. Children's needs is still a widely used concept, although possibly less commonly than in the past. In this brief postscript, I will take the opportunity to draw attention to the continuing role of psychology in the reconstruction of childhood in terms other than 'children's needs'.

I first embarked on the analysis of children's needs because of frustration with the indiscrimate use of the concept in professional discourse and policy statements. My aims were pragmatic as much as they were academic. I felt that much 'children's needs' talk mystified more than it enlightened. At that time (the early 1980s) my critique of 'needs' felt like a relatively isolated, in some ways sacrilegious, challenge to dominant 'child-centred' orthodoxy. Now (in 1996) I can see it as as a small part of a widespread trend encompassing theoretical shifts in developmental psychology, sociology of childhood and women's studies, as well as policy shifts reconstructing children's rights and social

participation, against a background of post-modernist social constructionism and associated methodologies, notably discourse analysis (Potter
and Wetherell, 1987).

'Children's needs' have been constructed as part of a standardized
model in which childhood is a period of dependency, defined by protectionist adult–child relationships in which adults are dominant providers and children are passive consumers. This standardized model is
underpinned by seperation of young humanity from later life-phases,
as a distinctive status (Save the Children, 1996). Euro-American developmental psychology has provided the conceptual rationale for standardized childhoods, in ways which at best draw attention away from
the diversity of developmental pathways, and at worst pathologize
deviations. 'Child development experts' have promoted normative images of how 'child development' can best be promoted within the
specialized ecology of the conventional family or kindergarten, under
the watchful eye of mothers, nursery nurses and teachers, endowed
and/or trained in sensitivity and responsiveness. While Phoenix *et al.*
(1991), Singer (1992) and Ribbens (1994) have articulated the implicit
assumptions about what it means to be a 'good-enough' mother, sensitive to 'children's needs', Walkerdine (1984) was amongst the first to
unravel psychology's role in the promotion of a 'child-centred' pedagogy. More recently deconstruction of taken-for-granted psychological
concepts has extended to the foundational concept of 'child development' itself (Bradley, 1989; Burman, 1994; Morss, 1996; Walkerdine,
1993). Even within mainstream psychology, where most researchers
continue to endorse the basic tenets of developmentalism, there is now
much more widespread acknowledgment that children's social relationships and adaptation, and hence 'needs' are culturally as much as
biologically constituted, (for example Le Vine *et al.*, 1994; Rogoff *et al.*,
1993).

This is illustrated by the current preoccupation with studying 'development in context'. Universalist theories are gradually being eclipsed
(including much 'cross-cultural psychology' which still takes Minority
World concepts as the standard). In their place a more fully 'cultural
psychology' is emerging, nowhere more than in the field of cognitive
development. Piaget's universal, stage theories of cognitive development
have been extensively re-appraised by social constructivists who favour
a more contextual, situated view of learning and thinking (e.g., Butterworth and Light, 1992; Rogoff and Chavajay, 1995). Perret-Clermont
(1996) has even begun the fascinating task of tracing the construction
of Piaget's theories about the growth of individual reason and logic
in his own personal biography, growing up in turn-of-the-century

Neuchatel. Paradoxically, these 'contextually sensitive' constructions and reconstructions of psychology's child still have their roots very firmly in Euro-American academic traditions, albeit under the strong influence of the Soviet psychologist, Lev Vygotsky. However, there are signs that a much more thorough-going contextualism is beginning to make an impact (e.g., Nsamenang, 1992; Kagitcibasi, 1996).

This may seem a somewhat esoteric academic debate within developmental psychology. But academic developmental paradigms have everyday practical implications. For example, the National Asssociation for the Education of Young Children (NAEYC) in the USA prepared an influential set of recommendations on Developmentally-Appropriate Practice (DAP) in nurseries, kindergarten and creches (Bredekamp, 1987). It was explicitly based on the best available child development know-ledge, (notably Piagetian), and designed to offer a 'scientific' defence of informal, play based programmes for children. The starting point for DAP is the assumption that there are universal, predictable sequences of growth and change. Self-initiated and self-directed play is seen as the most effective route to learning, based on a rich resource of activ-ities and materials and supported by a skilled teacher. Even within the USA, this vision of children's developmental needs has been sharply criticized as insensitive to diversity in family experiences, parenting practices and expectations (Mallory and New, 1994). Yet the possibility of a universal agenda for childhood remains tantalisingly attractive, reflected in the extension of Euro-American child-care models to eco-nomic and cultural contexts far removed from their origin (Lamb *et al.*, 1992; Cochran, 1993). Respecting the contextual specificity of many aspects of children's needs, I have proposed marrying DAP with an equally important principle, CAP — Contextually Appropriate Practice. The emergent hybrid calls for a PACED approach to child care work — Practice Appropriate to the Context of Early Development (Woodhead, 1996). However, it would be a mistake to overestimate these trends towards context-sensitivity. They are a ripple against the tidal wave of globalization.

Aware of the hidden assumptions that surround concepts of de-velopment and need, an alternative construction of childhood seems attractive, based on the concept of 'rights'. This holds the promise of much stronger empowerment of children's status. The United Nations Convention on the Rights of the Child (1989) has now been endorsed by most of the world's nations. Indeed, along with the spread of uni-versal schooling, it is one of the most powerful globalizing influences. But even children's rights are not straightforward. There is a tension between asserting children's autonomy and rights to self-determination and asserting that they must be protected from harmful influence. For example Article 32 'recognizes *the right* of the child *to be protected* from economic exploitation and from performing any work that is likely to be hazardous or to interfere with the child's education . . . etc.' (my emphasis). Bear in mind that these are rights constructed by adults and conferred on to children. It is hard to see how the denial of the ability to make choices, in practice by prohibition from activities normally engaged in by adults, has anything to do with 'rights' at all. In some parts of the world, implementing this article is tantamount to disenfranchising children from participating in working lives on which their survival and often their family's survival depends (Boyden and Myers, 1995).

Faced with this tension between protection and participation rights, many have turned to a key provision of the Convention, which asserts that 'the best interests of the child' are a primary consideration. While the emphasis on 'the child' is important, talking in terms of the child's 'best interests' leaves the door wide open to the same kinds of multiple interpretation as applied to their 'needs'. According to one commentator '"in the best interests of the child" . . . has become one of the most unhelpful and abused phrases resorted to in order to justify all kinds of decision-making. . . . On the one hand everyone is bound to agree with it; on the other hand . . . it begs the question of what actually is the child's best interests' (Schaffer, 1990: 6). 'Interests', like 'needs' are not a quality of the child; they are a matter of cultural interpretation which will certainly be context-specific and may well vary amongst various stakeholders who believe they have the wisdom to shape children's futures. The challenge is to interpret children's rights and interests in particular economic, political, religious and cultural contexts (Alston, 1994; Freeman and Veerman, 1992). In passing we may note that children's 'rights', like their 'needs' remains a very western way of constructing child–adult relationships. This is indicated in the OAU's African Charter on the Rights and Welfare of the Child', which is framed in terms of 'responsibilities' and 'duties'. For example: 'Every child shall have responsibilities towards his (sic) family and society . . . The child . . . shall have the duty: (a) to work for the cohesion of the family, to respect his parents, superiors and elders . . .' (OAU, 1990).

Despite these difficulties within the global debate, a 'rights' perspective is serving as a powerful antidote to 'needs' in many areas of policy-making. Children's rights breaks through the web of paternalist, protectionist constructions that emphasize children as powerless dependents, separated-off from adult society and effectively excluded from participation in shaping their own destiny. This is especially true in respect of rights that empower children to participate in the process of defining their 'needs', treatment and destiny, most significantly implemented in the UK by The Children Act (1989) (Lyon and Parten, 1995), and gradually into education (Davie and Galloway, 1996). Re-evaluation of children's status extends into research too. The passivity implied in treating children as 'subjects' of research is being reconstructed by increased reference to children as 'participants'. In the field of Development Studies, participatory methods originally designed for work with rural communities (Chambers, 1995) are now enabling children to work alongside fieldworkers in constructing a representation of their social worlds (Redd Barna, 1994; Johnson *et al.*, 1995; PLA Notes, 1996). Psychology is playing a role in this newly reconstructed image of young children as active, competent contributors to the process of their own social and cognitive development (e.g., Dunn, 1988).

Insofar as the implications of reconstructed childhoods are assimilated, in ways that emphasize diversity as well as universality, rights as well as needs, and participation as as well as protection, it is all too easy to fall into the trap of believing that we have reached a final chapter in the story. That would be a mistake. Constructions of childhood have a past and a present, but they also have a future.

References

ALSTON, P. (Eds) (1994) *The Best Interests of the Child: Reconciling Culture and Human Rights*, Oxford, Clarendon Press.
BOWLBY, J. (1953) *Child Care and the Growth of Love*, Harmondsworth, Penguin.
BOWLBY, J. (1969) *Attachment and Loss, Volume 1: Attachment*, Harmondsworth, Penguin.
BOYDEN, J. and MYERS, W. (1995) *Exploring Alternative Approaches to Combatting Child Labour: Case Studies from Developing Countries*, Florence, Unicef.
BRADLEY, B. (1989) *Visions of Infancy: A Critical Introduction to Child Psychology*, Cambridge, Polity Press.
BRADSHAW, J. (1972) 'The concept of social need', *New Society*, 30 March.
BREDEKAMP, S. (Ed) (1987) *Developmentally Appropriate Practice in Early Childhood Programs Serving Children from Birth through Age 8*, Washington, DC, National Association for the Education of Young Children.
BRITISH ASSOCIATION OF SOCIAL WORKERS (undated) 'Children Under Five' [mimeo].
BROFENBRENNER, U. (1979) *The Ecology of Human Development*, Cambridge, MA, Harvard University Press.
BURMAN, E. (1994) *Deconstructing Developmental Psychology*, London, Routledge.
BUTTERWORTH, G. and LIGHT, P. (Ed) (1992) *Context and Cognition*, London, Harvester Wheatsheaf.
CHAMBERS, R. (1995) 'Paradigm shifts and the practice of participatory research and development', in NELSON, N. and WRIGHT, S. (Eds) (1995) *Power and Participatory Development*, London, Intermediate Technology Publications.

Cochran, M. (Ed) (1993) *The International Handbook of Child Day Care Policies and Programs*, Westport, CT, Greenwood Press.

Davie, R. and Galloway, D. (Eds) (1996) *Listening to Children in Education*, London, David Fulton Publishers.

Dearden, R.F. (1972) 'Needs in education', in Dearden, R.F., Hirst, P.H. and Peters, R.S. (Eds) (1972) *A Critique of Current Educational Aims*, London, Routledge.

Department of Education and Science (1972) *Education: A Framework for Expansion*, Cmnd 5174 (White Paper), London, HMSO.

Dunn, J. (1988) *The Beginning of Social Understanding*, Oxford, Blackwell.

Freeman, M. and Veerman, P. (Eds) (1992) *The Ideologies of Children's Rights*, Dordrecht, Martinus Nijhoff.

Hirst, P.H. and Peters, R.S. (1970) *The Logic of Education*, London, Routledge.

Hodges, J. and Tizard, B. (1989a) 'IQ and behavioural adjustment of ex-institutional adolescents', *Journal of Child Psychology and Psychiatry*, 30, 1, pp. 53–76.

Hodges, J. and Tizard, B. (1989b) 'Social and family relationships of ex-institutional Adolescents, *Journal of Child Psychology and Psychiatry*, 30, 1, pp. 77–98.

Hoffman, L.W. (1987) 'The value of children to parents and child-rearing patterns', in Kagitcibasi, C. (Ed) (1987) *Growth and Progress in Cross-cultural Psychology*, Berwyne, Swets North America Inc.

House of Commons (1988) 'Educational provision for the under-fives', *First Report of the Education, Science and Arts Committee*, vol 1, London, HMSO.

Johnson, V., Hill, J. and Ivan-Smith, E. (1995) *Listening to Smaller Voices: Children in an Environment of Change*, London, Action Aid.

Kagan, J., Kearsley, R.B. and Zelazo, P.R. (1978) *Infancy: In its Place in Human Development*, London, Harvard University Press.

Kagitcibasi, C. (1996) *Family and Human Development Across Cultures: A View from the Other Side*, London, Erlbaum.

Kellmer-Pringle, M. (1975) *The Needs of Children*, 2nd ed., 1980, London, Hutchinson.

Kellmer-Pringle, M. (1976) 'A policy for young children', in Reedy, S. and Woodhead, M. (Eds) (1981) *Family, Work and Education*, London, Hodder and Staughton.

Kessell, F.S. and Siegel, A.W. (Eds) (1983) *The Child and Other Cultural Inventions*, New York Praeger.

Kessen, W. (1978) 'The American child and other cultural inventions', *American Psychologist*, 34, pp. 815–20.

Korbin, J.E. (Ed) (1981) *Child Abuse and Neglect*, Berkeley, University of California Press.

Lamb, M.E., Sternberg, K.J., Hwang, C. and Broberg, A.G. (Eds) (1992) *Child Care in Context*, Hillsdale, N.J., Erlbaum.

Leach, P. (1979) *Who Cares?*, Harmondsworth, Penguin.

Le Vine, R.A., Le Vine, S., Leidermann, P.H., Brazelton, T.B., Dixon, S., Richman, A. and Keffer, C.H. (1994) *Child Care and Culture: Lessons from Africa*, Cambridge, Cambridge University Press.

Lyon, C. and Parton, N. (1995) 'Children's rights and the children act 1989', in Franklin, B. (Ed) (1995) *Children's Rights: Comparative Policy and Practice*, London, Routledge.

Mace, C.A. (1953) 'Homeostasis, needs and values', *British Journal of Psychology*, August, pp. 201–8.

Mallory, B.L. and New, R.S. (Eds) (1994) *Diversity and Developmentally Appropriate Practice*, New York, Teachers College Press.

Morss, J.R. (1996) *Growing Critical: Alternatives to Developmental Psychology*, London, Routledge.

Newson, J. and Newson, E. (1974) 'Cultural aspects of child-rearing in the English-speaking World', in Richards, M.P.M. (Ed) (1974) *The Integration of a Child into a Social World*, Cambridge, Cambridge University Press.

Nsamenang, A.B. (1992) *Human Development in Cultural Context*, London, Sage.

Organisation of African Unity (1990) 'The African Charter on the Rights and Welfare of the Child' adopted by the 26th ordinary session of the assembly of heads of state and government of the OAU, Addis Ababa, July 1990.

Osborn, A.F., Butler, N.R. and Morris, T.C. (1984) *The Social Life of Britain's Five Year Olds*, London, Routledge and Kegan Paul.

Perret-Clermont, A. (1996) 'Revisiting young Jean Piaget in Neuchatel among his partners in learning', Paper presented to *British Psychological Society Conference*, April 1996.

Phoenix, A., Woollett, A. and Lloyd, E. (1991) *Motherhood: Meanings, Practices and Ideologies*, London, Sage.

PLA Notes (1996) 'Special issue: Children's participation', *PLA Notes Number 25*, London, International Institute for Environment and Development.

Potter, J. and Wetherell, M. (1987) *Discourse and Social Psychology: Beyond Attitudes and Behaviour*, London, Sage.

Redd Barna (1994) *It is the Young Trees that make a Thick Forest*, London, International Institute for Environment and Development.

Ribbens, J. (1994) *Mothers and Their Children: Feminist Sociology of Childrearing*, London, Sage.

Richards, M.P.M. (Ed) (1974) *The Integration of a Child into a Social World*, Cambridge, Cambridge University Press.

Richards, M. and Light, P. (Eds) (1986) *Children of Social Worlds*, Cambridge, Polity Press.

Rogoff, B., Mistry, J., Goncu, A. and Mosier, C. (1993) 'Guided participation in cultural activity by toddlers and caregivers', *Monograph of the Society for Research in Child Development*, **58**, 8, No.236.

Rogoff, B. and Chavajay, P. (1995) 'What's become of research on the cultural basis of cognitive development?', *American Psychologist*, **50**, 10, pp. 859–77.

Rutter, M. (1989) 'Pathways from childhood to adult life', *Journal of Child Psychology and Psychiatry*, **30**, 1, pp.23–52.

Save the Children (1996) *Towards a Children's Agenda; New Challenges for Social Development*, London, Save the Children, UK.

Schaffer, H.R. (1977) *Mothering*, London, Open Books.

Schaffer, H.R. (1984) *The Child's Entry into a Social World*, London, Academic Press.

Schaffer, H.R. (1990) *Making Decisions about Children: Psychological Questions and Answers*, Oxford, Blackwell.

Schaffer, H.R. and Emerson, P.E. (1964) 'The development of social attachments in infancy', *Monograph of the Society for Research in Child Development*, **29**, p. 94.

Singer, E. (1992) *Childcare and the Psychology of Development*, London, Routledge.

Smith, G. (1971) 'Some research implications of the Seebohm Report', *British Journal of Sociology*, **22**, pp. 295–310.

Smith, P.K. (1979) 'How many people can a young child feel secure with?', *New Society*, 31 May.

SMITH, P.K. (1980) 'Shared care of young children: Alternative models to monotropism', *Merill -Palmer Quarterly*, **6**, pp. 371–89.

SUPER, C. and HARKNESS, S. (1983) 'The cultural construction of child development: A framework for the socialization effect', *Ethos*, **11**, pp. 221–31.

SUVANNATHAT, C., BHANTHUMNAVIN, D., BHUAPIROM, L. and KEATS, D.M. (Eds) (1985) *Handbook of Asian Child Development and Child Rearing Practices*, Bangkok, Thailand, Srinakharinwirot University, Behavioural Science Research Institute.

TAYLOR, P.W. (1959) '"Need" statements', *Analysis*, **19**, 5, pp. 106–111.

THOMAN, E.B. (1975) 'Sleep and wake behaviours in neonates: consistencies and consequences', *Merrill Palmer Quarterly*, **21**, 4, pp. 295–314.

TIZARD, B. and HODGES, J. (1978) 'The effect of early institutional rearing on the development of eight year old children', *Journal of Child Psychology and Psychiatry*, **19**, pp. 98–118.

TIZARD, B. and REES, J. (1974) 'A comparison of the effects of adoption, restoration to the natural mother and continued institutionalization on the cognitive development of four year old children', *Child Development*, **45**, pp. 92–9.

UNITED NATIONS (1959) 'Declaration of the rights of the child', in *Resolution 1386 (XIV)*, *Yearbook of the United Nations*, New York, United Nations, 20 November, p. 198.

WADSWORTH, M. (1986) 'Evidence from three birth cohort studies for long term and cross-generational effects on the development of children', in RICHARDS, M. and LIGHT, P. (Eds) (1986) *Children of Social Worlds*, Cambridge, Polity Press.

WALKERDINE, V. (1984) 'Developmental psychology and the child-centred pedagogy: The insertion of Piaget's theory into primary school practice', in HENRIQUES, J. *et al.* (Eds) (1984) *Changing the Subject; Psychology, Social Regulation and Subjectivity*, London, Methuen.

WALKERDINE, V. (1993) 'Beyond developmentalism?', *Theory and Psychology*, **3**, pp. 451–70.

WALTON, R. (1969) 'Need: A central concept', *Social Service Quarterly*, **43**, p. 1.

WARREN, N. (Ed) (1980) *Studies in Cross-cultural Psychology, Volume 2*, London, Academic Press.

WEISNER, T. and GALLIMORE, R. (1977) 'My brother's keeper: Child and sibling caretaking', *Current Anthropology*, **18**, p. 2.

WILSON, P.S. (1973) 'What is an educational need?', *Forward Trends*, **17**, 2, pp. 52–8.

WOODHEAD, M. (1988) 'When psychology informs public policy: The case of early childhood invention', *American Psychologist*, **43**, 6, pp. 443–54.

WOODHEAD, M. (1996) *In Search of the Rainbow: Pathways to Quality in Large-scale Programmes for Young Disadvantaged Children*, The Hague, Bernard van Leer Foundation.

WRINGE, C.A. (1981) *Children's Rights: A Philosophical Study*, London, Routledge and Kegan Paul.

ZUKOW, P.G. (Ed) (1989) *Sibling Interaction Across Cultures: Theoretical and Methodological Issues*, New York, Spinger-Verlag.

Chapter 4

A Voice for Children in Statistical and Social Accounting: A Plea for Children's Right to be Heard

Jens Qvortrup

Introduction

The history of western societies can be seen to involve the growth of groups or categories of persons who have obtained the right to be 'heard'. This development has been an important part of the struggle for democracy and the dismantling of different types of autocratic and paternalistic forms of domination. Nowhere have rights to have a say in one's own affairs been won without serious struggle. Without necessarily being a zero-sum game, it is evident that acquiring rights and privileges on the part of so-far suppressed people means reducing the power of hitherto superordinate groups of people. 'Worker's and 'women' are only the more conspicuous examples of collectivities who have obtained at least the formal right to defend their own interests.

History also shows that one of the problems of any liberation movement is the *naturalness* with which the subordinate groups are perceived. Claims for the extension of rights to new groups have always involved a challenge to 'common sense', to the 'ordinary man' or to the 'natural' social order. Generally, long periods pass by from the launching of a cause to the implementation of its aims. Even its formal recognition far from guarantees its effective acknowledgment in everyday life, as the case of the women's movement clearly demonstrates. To raise questions of oppression seems, however, to be a necessary precondition for solving the problem, even if for the time being it may appear politically naive.

Are children a group of people who may legitimately claim to be 'heard'? In what ways do children already have a voice in determining their own lives or in bringing their particular problems to the foreground? Many adults would say that children nowadays have much more power than they deserve or than is good for them. The image that is created is of parents, rather than of children, who suffer. It is parents who claim that they not only have much less time, money and space when they have children, and that they experience a serious encroachment in their life and career prospects because of children, but also that they have to face a 'boldness' if not 'impudence' from contemporary children. School children's audacity *vis-à-vis* their teachers is often reported, demonstrating that adults perceive a waning belief by children in their elders' authority, and a lack of appreciation of what is done for them. All this may sometimes be true when children and adults confront each other in daily life situations; seen from a societal perspective, however, it is a distorted picture.

It is not surprising that individual adults draw on their experience of children in daily life and make generalizations on this basis; neither should anyone be surprised if children object to their parents and teachers in a direct and perhaps insulting way. It may be children's only way of airing their dissatisfactions. It would, however, be misleading if we restricted our analysis of the intergenerational relations to these small-scale, interactional aspects of children's lives and their relationship to the adult world.

A nineteen-country study (the European Centre study) is attempting to widen the scope of analysis of childhood to a societal level. Its main thrust is that children are active and constructive members of society and that childhood is an integral part of society. The study is not and cannot be a truly comparative work since so little material is available on children as a social category. It has, however, in a number of topics, highlighted children's role, place and status where it has hitherto been relatively hidden[1].

It is the purpose of this chapter to make plausible the idea of letting children speak for themselves at an aggregate and a societal level. It is not a report on the European Centre study, but takes up only the perspective of the nature of children's representation. To understand such representation it must first be noted that in European societies it is generally unquestioned that children are 'dependents', and are as such best served if they subdue to adults' understanding of 'their best interests' or 'their own good'. This often leads to a 'protective exclusion' of children in real life as well as in social accounting. Protection of children is the main reason given for restricting children's freedom, and it is in turn demanded because of children's alleged lack of responsibility, capability and competence. Children are seen as having to 'mature' before they obtain freedom to act on behalf of themselves. It is adults, primarily parents, who are assigned the task to care, protect and make decisions for children. While it is of course in many ways reasonable to protect children, it must be added that protection is mostly accompanied by exclusion in one way or the other; protection may be suggested even when it is not strictly necessary for the sake of children, but rather works to protect adults or the adult social orders against disturbances from the presence of children. This is exactly the point at which protection threatens to slide into unwarranted dominance.

Conceptual and Numerical Marginalization of Children

The representation of children in statistics and social accounting may be taken, I suggest, as one such unjustified exclusion. No risks for children themselves seem to be at stake, but rather their absence seems to be simply a reflection of their status as minors in our society. Their immaturity and incompetence convey to them a lack of credibility, and even 'credibility and the right to be heard are differentially distributed through the ranks of the system'; 'in any system of ranked groups, participants take it as given that members of the highest group have the right to define the way things really are' (Becker, 1966/7: 241).

It could well be seen as disturbing to adults, as the dominant group, if a voice was given to children in public statistics and social studies. Giving children a voice as a collectivity amounts to representing them on equal terms with other groups in society. Seeing children on equal terms with adults in itself contradicts our 'adultist' imagery, exactly because it cuts across prefigured conceptions of children as subordinates.

My plea for treating children as a collectivity on equal terms with adults is not, however, as radical as it may appear at first sight. Compared with some protagonists' claim for children to have equal access to all rights which are assigned to adults, it is indeed a very modest claim. It contains no demand for dragging children out of the haven of family intimacy, nor does it in the first place question the authority of parents or other educators. No more and no less, it envisages giving a voice to children at the aggregate level, with the purpose of discovering the life conditions of children as a population group. It suggests liberating childhood from the representational straitjackets of conventional statistical categories, which at the moment represent children only indirectly. To liberate children conceptually, and thus give voice to their specific life conditions, may in the long run challenge current political thinking about children and in this way challenge our existing social order.

A few years ago, when I began to search for data on childhood, my expectations very soon became frustrated. I was naive enough to think that obtaining good, sufficient and reliable information on children was more or less a matter of routine, since interest in children, if discussions in the media were to be taken as an indicator, was so conspicuous. Very soon, however, I had to realize that children are the invisible group *par excellence* in our society. They are invisible not only in statistics, but in many other types of social acounting as well; indeed social sciences like sociology, economics and political science simply neglect children (Thorne, 1987; Alanen, 1988; Ambert, 1986; Qvortrup, 1987). This contention has been repeated by others for some years and, as evidence for it mounts, it seems beyond debate. Research about socialization and other types of individual or biographic childhood studies are abundant, but as soon as the dynamics of individual development is replaced by childhood as a factor of *societal* dynamics, systematic approaches are generally lacking.

We may care for our own individual children because we love them, and we protect them because we are concerned about their development into adults. During this century, however, quite dramatic changes have taken place, which have altered the image not only of children as individuals but of childhood as a social category. First of all, the decrease in fertility and the prolongation of longevity have turned the age structure of populations upside-down. In many countries of Europe, elderly people of 65 years and over outnumber children (birth to 15 years). Children's share of the population has in Denmark, for example, decreased from 34 per cent in 1901 to 18 per cent in 1988, while the share of the elderly has increased from 7 per cent to 15 per cent; in other words, the proportion of children has been halved, whilst that of the elderly has doubled. The trend will continue in this direction. In West Germany, for instance, children's share has already reached 15 per cent, and it is projected that in 2030 the share of the elderly will be 27 per cent.

Apart from the apocalyptic visions of the future of our societies that the ageing population engender (Debré, 1986; Teitelbaum and Winter, 1985), such figures also suggest that new analysis is needed of the position of children and the status of childhood in western society. The particular issue to which I want to draw attention is whether information about children as a population group is helpful enough to tell how they will fare as they become a lower proportion of the population relative to other age groups, and perhaps even to other social groups who make claims on societal resources.

Despite rhetoric to the effect that children are our most precious resource, which must therefore be invested disproportionately with love and money, one should not overlook the consequence of sheer numbers. There are in fact very good reasons to believe that an unrevealed interaction is taking place between generations at societal levels, taking the form of a competition between children, young people, the 'productive' ages and the elderly for our society's available resources. When children become fewer, the strength of their potential representation for those resources diminishes, because the number of adults with everyday interests in children's lives is reduced. Even when the share of women who become mothers has increased considerably, as it has in Denmark during this century, greater importance can be given to the fact that parents are having children at home over a much shorter span of their life cycle than was earlier the case. This is due to the combination of two facts characteristic of almost all modern, industrial societies, namely that most women have fewer children and that they, on average, live longer. Thus, if it is true that people's choices are heavily influenced by their everyday life situations, it seems plausible to suggest that overall economic, political and cultural interests tend to move away from children when the majority of people's immediate bonds to them weaken. In two out of three families in Denmark there are no children; thirty years ago the corresponding figure was two out of five. The demographic development thus seems to work against children — not only quantitatively, but also qualitatively. The proportion of electors who might take 'children's lives' into account is in decline. In terms of pressure groups and 'lobbyism' children also come out badly; although there are a number of voluntary associations working on behalf of children, they are comparatively small and weak. Culturally, then, the whole climate in our societies is bound to change as children in more and more Western countries are reduced as a proportion of the population.

At the general level, for example in censuses, where the whole population is counted, children are of course included. But 'the set of official data concerning children is dwindling when attention is directed to their share of social economic, territorial, and spatial resources' (Kürner and Lüscher, 1988: 23). This judgment is a characteristic one for researchers in the European Centre's childhood project. Another member of the project commented that 'the available material is poor. Children as a separate social entity hardly appear in our statistical and research documentation. All our knowledge on children and childhood seems to remain deeply and unreflectively centered around the experiences of adults, i.e., those who shaped the conceptual frameworks and methods of research' (Boh and Sadav, 1992: 10).

This economic, political and cultural displacement of children is reflected in their representation in sourcebooks which should be helpful in describing their life situations. When we find children described it is practically always done with reference to their parents' situation.

Figure 4.1 *Methodological approaches*

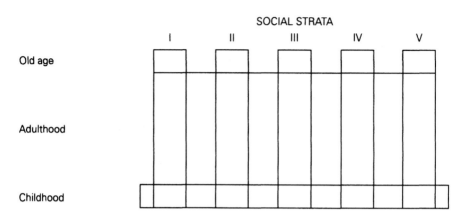

Children are ordered in accordance with *parents'* income, with (mostly) *father's* occupation, with the education of *parents*, and so on. The socio-occupational background of children, as we may call it in a generalized way, is in fact a description of their *parents'* status. This approach is not wrong in itself. It has, nonetheless, a major drawback in relation to a description of children's own life situation; namely that it splits up the population of children according to variables which are alien to their own life expressions. This can be illustrated in figure 4.1.

For the purpose of illustrating this point, it does not matter whether the terms 'socio-occupational groups' or 'social classes' are used. From the figure it is clear that children are divided between such groups or classes. It is not my idea to deny the existence or the importance of the traditionally used socio-economic factors, but in applying them we may also hide another interpretation: that there may be a reality which is *common for children* irrespective of their parents' backgrounds. This reality might furthermore be one which in principle differs from the reality of adults. This is exactly the point which is obscured by dividing children according to variables which do not directly belong to them. This state of affairs does not necessarily express any conspiratorial intentions on the part of adults. Rather it may indicate how we as adults 'naturally' think about children. Their status as 'dependents' is so naturally ingrained in adult belief systems as not to be questioned at all. It is indeed a way of depriving children of an account of themselves in their own right. Whether we do children a service in promoting such an account I shall discuss in my conclusion.

In addressing this issue, Sgritta and Saporiti (1989) have demonstrated the paucity of information about children in a number of international handbooks, such as the Demographic Yearbook, the UN Statistical Yearbook and even the annual 'State of the World's Children' from UNICEF, convincingly putting the omissions and their adultist nature in perspective. I shall not repeat what has already been said by Sgritta and Saporiti, but rather underline it by some additional evidence.

Current statistics directly oriented towards children describing their particular life situations are so far unavailable, perhaps because a demand for them has not yet been discovered[2]. If public statistics are an instrument for social reproduction (LeBras, 1979; Alonso and Starr, 1982), then the collection of data about children must also be seen in this perspective. The data found in public statistics about children are, in fact, mostly about how children as a resource are reproduced most effectively as a new generation. Available statistics concentrate on (1) the production of children, (2) expenses invested in them, and (3) their failure to meet the desired requirement.

Vital Statistics and Family Statistics

Population statistics are about fertility, mortality and migration; in other words they concern the size of the population and how it is determined by people entering it or leaving it. Besides describing the development and size of population according to age and sex, such tables are mostly concerned with factors such as birthrates, the length of marriage at child's birth, parents' age at this event, births within or outside marriage, etc. Without denying the relevance to children of fertility data, it is also worth contending that *births are not the same as children*. Births are an important event for parents, but they do not, as such, tell us anything about children. It is thus noteworthy that while there exists a huge statistical and demographic industry concerning age-specific (i.e. mother's age) birth rates, child-age-specific data are rare. We are not informed at all about 'the average ages of the mothers and the fathers of, say, the current population of 4-year-olds' as Oldman said in his draft of his Scottish national report. Since women's age at first delivery is changing, and more importantly because women give birth to fewer children, we must expect considerable changes in the average age of parents to any age-group of children.

The advantage of population statistics compared with most other statistics is that they are person-related. This means that they count each person irrespective of age, and thus also children. In principle there is no serious obstacle, neither financial nor technical, for including children in statistical calculation. Only our sociological fantasy sets the limit.

Currently available family statistics create serious problems for those who want to give proper accounts of children's lives, despite the fact that it is exactly the family which is claimed to be the most important group and place for children. Perhaps the family as 'the haven in a heartless world', its intimacy and privateness are the reason for the paucity of our knowledge. The family is ideologically constructed as an area for non-intervention, out of the reach of intruders or snoopers. Parents are seen as there to care for children and within very wide (though problematic) limits it is not the business of the state to control how this is done. Therefore family statistics provide us with one of the best examples of the general rule that *children are not the unit of observation in the production of statistics.* It is the rule that families, parents, women, marriages, households etc. are counted, but not children. This means that a number of distortions and omissions are introduced as far as children are concerned.

Perhaps the most instructive example of this relates to number of children in families. It is a repeated claim in media discussions, and indeed even among researchers, that the share of children who are single children has risen rapidly during recent decades. As a matter of fact, this is not true. The misunderstanding is based on exactly the fact that 'family' rather than 'child' is used as the unit. The difference this makes is made clear when the tables 4.1 and 4.2 are compared. Table 4.1, which has 'childfamily' as unit of observation, is often mistakenly interpreted as if 49 per cent of all children were without siblings. It is the much more tempting to do so, perhaps, since in all countries, as far as I know, only this family based information is available in public statistics.[3] Comparing Table 4.1 with Table 4.2, which counts children, we can see how dramatically exaggerated the claims about being a lone child are, if childfamily is used as the unit. Instead of calculating the number of single children to the number of childfamilies, we relate them to total number of children (i.e. we are weighing childfamilies with number of children). But even if this, which is correct in principle, is applied, the share of singles among all children is exaggerated. The reason for this is that in a snapshot of the situation, we fail to consider that some children may have siblings who have left home and others may get siblings in the future. A calculation has been made in Denmark, based on the fact that the average spacing between siblings amounts to three or four years. This means that 9-year-olds, for instance, will almost all have younger siblings, while their older sibling will still usually be living at home. Based on these statistical methods which focus on children per se, only 16 per cent of the 9-year-olds are without siblings (see Table 4.3). Data from Norway has even documented that

Table 4.1 'Childfamilies' according to number of children 0–16 (1974 and 1985)

	1974	1985
1	43	49
2	39	42
3	14	8
4+	4	1

Table 4.2 Children 0–16 according to number of siblings (1974 and 1985)

	1974	1985
0	24	30
1	44	52
2	24	15
3+	9	3

Source: Qvortrup and Christoffersen (forthcoming)

Table 4.3 Children by age and number of siblings in the family (1988)

Age	Number of siblings					Total	Number in 1000
	0	1	2	3	4+		
	- - - - - - - - - - - - - - per cent - - - - - - - - - - - - - - -						number
0	47	37	13	3	1	101	56.2
9	16	56	22	5	1	100	62.2
18	39	45	17	3	1	101	56.5

Source: Danish Central Bureau of Statistics (unpublished)

the share of 19-year-olds without siblings has decreased from 17.2 per cent in 1960 to 14.7 per cent in 1980 (Jensen, 1989: 15).

All too often — in both research and policy — it is taken for granted that children and 'childfamilies' are more or less the same unit. Only seldomly is it even discussed in reports allegedly devoted to childhood topics, whether or not children are represented in statistically valid ways. Family sociologists and women's researchers are not infrequently surprised or angered when accused of not being interested in children in their studies, when in fact they intended to take up this issue. This problem arises not because of ill will, but is rather a problem of the sociology of knowledge in the sense that adults are often intoxicated with the view of children as dependents and themselves as fair representatives of children. Adults simply 'forget' to raise other perspectives. It is more or less taken for granted that 'what is good for the family is good for the child'. This lack of thought was probably also the reason for the introduction by the Danish Central Bureau of Statistics in the 1970s of a new age limit for children. Children were to be defined as offspring who stayed at home in the parental house until the age of 26! The drawbacks of this definition have been realized, and the age limit is now changed to 18 years again. This example nevertheless illustrates well what happens when the conceptual autonomy of children and children's own life expressions are overlooked. It was 'forgotten' that included in the 26 year age limit were thousands of persons who according to the Danish constitution had reached the age of majority. It was of course — from the point of view of family statistics — reasonable to include all those who actually lived in the family. On the other hand, it completely attenuated and blurred the concept of childhood and made it very difficult to recalculate data into children's statistics. It thus seems necessary to establish a special department for children's statistics, without of course sacrificing the demand for information about the family as such.

The upheavals in family structure during the last two decades accentuate this reorientation of statistics. In particular the divorce rate, and the growth of consensual unions (rather than legal marriages), is leaving traditional categories inadequate. It leaves us, for example, with a dramatic increase in number of 'families', and in particular families without children. Family statistics have partly managed to deal with these changes, but again: where are the children? If family statistics are taken at face value it seems that it is only adults who divorce, but as we also know children are separated from one of the parents and often even from siblings. This is not reflected in statistics, which normally only count, for instance, 'divorces according to number of children'. Whilst, then, we have a divorce rate for adults, it would be desirable also to have a 'divorce rate' for children. A divorce is indeed an event which influences children's lives as much as parents'. Information from West Germany, Norway and Finland (Engelbert and Buhr, 1991; Frönes, Jensen and Solberg, 1990; Alanen and Bardy, 1990) seems to indicate that around 1 per cent of children experience a divorce of their parents per year. This figure is, of course, cumulative from year to year, including all those children who have been involved in parents' divorce. A cumulated experience from Denmark shows that not only have close to 30 per cent of all contracted marriages broken up after seventeen years, but the same share of children up to the age of 17 have been involved in parents' divorce (Christoffersen, 1987). Furthermore, children are more or less forced to accept any new living arrangement which their parents decide for them. Thus a whole new set of experiences is now a reality for a growing number of children. It is important, however, not to exaggerate the numbers involved. Figures from Nordic countries show that about 80 per cent of all children live together with both biological parents throughout their childhood. So we are talking about the remaining, but not negligible, fifth of children. Research from several countries has been conducted (Bumpass, 1984; Noordhoek, 1988; Jensen and Moen, 1989), demonstrating that the likelihood for a child coming to live with either only one parent or in some arrangement involving a step-parent, is growing.

The Welfare State and Children

In many industrial countries the welfare state is under attack. Unemployment is a serious problem; millions of people are forced to spend shorter or longer periods without work. Partly as a result of unemployment life conditions are deteriorating, poverty is increasing and huge amounts of money are paid in different forms of social assistance. How are children affected by events such as unemployment, social deprivation, and poverty?

In its 1989 issue of the annual *State of the World's Children*, UNICEF approaches the question of the connection between children's lives and the international economy. It answers the question of former Tanzanian president Julius Nyerere: 'Must we starve our children to pay our debts?' with a clear 'yes' (1989: 30). It clearly documents that the international debt crisis has become a tragedy for poor people in the developing countries, and 'it is the young child who is paying the highest of all prices, and who will bear the most recurring of all costs, for the mounting debt repayments, the drop in export earnings, the increase in food costs, the fall in family incomes, the run-down of health services, the narrowing of educational opportunities' (*ibid* 1989: 2).

The UNICEF annual is mainly about Third World countries, but could we not ask the same type of questions, namely about the effect of major economic events on children, in any society? When a parent is forced to leave the labour market, for example, his or her children are also among the victims. But we would search in vain if we tried to find information about the extent to which children are drawn into the orbit of unemployment.

The official unemployment rate in Denmark at the time of writing is about 9 per cent. As part of our ongoing research we wanted to know the corresponding figure for children, i.e., what is the share of children having unemployed parent(s)? It is not difficult to imagine how many technical problems arise in making such estimates. The estimates we have got, however, show that compared with the presently 9 per

Table 4.4 Children and adults as recipients of social welfare outside of welfare institutions (1985)

Age	Absolute	Per cent of corresponding age group
Under 7	248,354	6.0
0–18	638,366	5.3
18–65	1,171,951	2.9
Over 65	172,302	1.9
Total	1,982,619	3.2

Source: Engelbert and Buhr, (forthcoming)

cent unemployment rate for adults, the 'rate' for children is 13 per cent — meaning that among unemployed adults we find the parents of 13 per cent of all children. If we ask for the rate of previously unemployed adults, it amouts to 17 per cent. The corresponding figure for children is 23 per cent. In other words, according to these admittedly insecure estimates, more than one in every three children is or has been experiencing unemployment as a reality in their own family, compared with one in four adults (Qvortrup and Christoffersen, 1990).

As to social assistance we generally encounter the same kind of technical difficulties in sorting out children as a particular group. Exceptionally, German statistics have some figures about social assistance showing that from 1985, children have been recipients of social welfare relatively more often than adults. On average, 5.3 per cent of all minors, compared to 2.7 per cent of all adults, were paid such contributions.

Information of this type is rare, and it is badly elaborated. Research and social accounts of children with respect to the social problems of the family is mainly of three kinds. One is about psychosocial consequences for children of parents' unemployment. Even here very little room is left for children.[4] Another common topic is deviance among children related to social problems (a popular issue in statistics, where children indeed are used as unit of analysis). The third type is statistics on long-term effects, accounted for mainly by studies of intergenerational mobility (typically again, it is the single individual who is followed, whereas the *historical development of childhood* is not accounted for).

A much more conscious effort, combined with clearer theoretical guidelines, is needed if the social position of children is to be known. In most cases we do not know what happens to children as a particular social group when the economy experiences a boom or a slump. Poverty research is traditionally satisfied with putting the situation of adults and/or families in evidence. Improvements are being made in this area on an empirical basis, but without much understanding of what it means

Table 4.5   Post-tax and transfer poverty rates of all families with children and of all children

	Per cent of All childfamilies	Per cent of All children
Australia (1981)	15.0	16.9
Canada (1981)	8.6	9.6
West Germany (1981)	6.9	8.2
Sweden (1981)	4.4	5.1
United Kingdom (1979)	8.5	10.7
USA (1979)	13.8	17.1

Source: Smeeding and Torrey, (1988)

in terms of the social position of childhood in society (Abel-Smith and Townsend, 1965; Townsend, 1979; and Gustafsson, 1984).

From a statistical point of view, the United States has already a thirty year long tradition of separating out children. Throughout the whole period, 'children have made up a larger share of the poor than their share of the overall population . . . When the number of poor children reached an all time low of 9.5 million in 1973, children still represented over 41 per cent of the poor' (Committee on Ways and Means, 1985; and Sgritta and Saporiti, 1989). In Europe, however, the Luxembourg Income Study (LIS) is doing pioneering research using sophisticated methods to compare poverty in several countries. From our point of view this work has a most interesting focus on children (Smeeding and Torrey, 1988; Palmer *et al.*, 1988). LIS shows a consid-erable difference in child poverty rates among the investigated coun-tries (Australia, Canada, West Germany, Sweden, UK and USA). Equally important from a methodological, and not least from a policy point of view, is the fact that both the US statistics and the LIS data demonstrate a significant difference in poverty rates between children on the one hand, and on the other the overall population (US) or childfamilies (LIS). The importance of this observation is that it proves the indispens-ability of focusing directly on children, that is of using them as units of observation.

All countries' central statistical offices could do much more in this area to improve their routine account not only of poverty but also of income differences in general. The depiction of the 'population' in, for instance, income deciles is typically either a depiction of families (that is parents) or income earners. By definition, thus, children fall outside the system. It is however possible to include children by making the calculation on a person related basis, as it has been done recently in some countries (see Jensen and Saporritti, 1992, p. 53). The problem to be solved in this connection is that of equivalence scales, i.e., how different persons in the family are to be weighted. This is partly a

Table 4.6 Overcrowding* in Sweden, by type of community (1933)

Type of community	Per cent of dwelling units with more than specified number of persons per room			Per cent of inhabitants living in dwelling units with more than specified number of persons per room			Per cent of children in dwelling units with more than specified number of persons per room		
	1½	2	3	1½	2	3	1½	2	3
Cities over 10,000	35.8	13.4	3.3	47.2	21.8	6.4	58.9	30.2	8.3
Other urban districts	31.5	11.0	2.6	43.0	18.6	5.1	53.1	25.1	6.8
All urban districts	34.5	12.6	3.0	46.0	20.9	6.0	57.2	28.7	7.9

Note: * A kitchen was counted as half a room and a child under 15 years of age as half a person.
Source: Myrdal (1945)

technical problem (which I shall not further discuss here) but also an ideological one — 'adultist' assumptions are involved, which should be unpacked and challenged.[5] For example, why are children always represented by the *fraction* in the equation?

Are Children a Burden or an Asset?

Many years ago Alva Myrdal reported in a book about the housing situation of Swedish families. Table 4.6 is taken from her book. The construction of these statistics is an exemplary illustration of how we can do justice to children. The first section using dwelling as the unit of observation corresponds to the presentation which is (still) normally used. It showed amongst other things, that more than one third of all *dwellings* had more than 1½ persons per room. The second section informs the reader that 47 per cent of all *inhabitants* lived at that level of crowding, while almost 60 per cent *of all children* according to the last section lived in dwellings with on average more than 1½ persons per room. Since 'inhabitants' also included children, the difference between adults and children was even larger than indicated here. Myrdal commented that 'these social family studies revealed that the standard of housing, both quantitatively and qualitatively, is inversely related to size of family. The problem of overcrowding is mainly a child welfare problem' and she rightly concluded that 'children generally have a lower housing standard than adults' (Myrdal, 1945: 245). It is — after almost sixty years — sad to realize that we are unable to draw any conclusions at all about children's relative housing standard on the basis of currently available public statistics, since children are not counted as a unit of observation. As a matter of fact it would take only a little effort to make the calculations on the basis of available material in the statistical offices. In connection with the European Centre project such a calculation was made. Of course the general housing situation has improved considerably since the 1930s, but there is still a striking difference between children and adults. Only 7.7 per cent adults live in dwellings with more than 1 person per room, compared with 19.6 per cent children; at the other end of the scale, in the very spacious dwellings (0.5 or less person per room) it is only 7 per cent children compared with 40 per cent adults (Qvortrup and Christoffersen, forthcoming).

Myrdal also, perhaps inadvertently, makes the statement that 'children are the chief *cause* both of the overcrowding and of poverty itself' (1945: 245). This statement is, from perspective of childhood, highly problematic, but one which explicitly or implicitly is often a part of the discussion about families with children. It is repeated, as I show below, in 'cost of children' studies as well as in time budget studies.

In the first place nobody would disagree that children belong to the family. In public imagery a family is only a 'real' family when children are included. Nevertheless our language is full of phrases giving the impression that 'parents' and 'family' are identical. It is indeed a paradox, that on the one hand our family ideology vehemently demands children as part of the family, while on the other hand in public, and even in scientific parlance, they are seen as *causing* some of the problems faced by families.

If, as seems reasonable, we take parents and children as equally legitimate 'members' of a family it is obviously nonsense to think of any of them 'causing' reduced resources. This does not mean, however, that one cannot or should not make accounts of the actual consumption of either part. A balanced review of a family's use of resources would imply either sticking to an account of the whole family, or to account for both costs of children and costs of parents; parents' use of time for their children as well as children's use of time for their parents. Most importantly, from the children's point of view, would be to insist that not only parents, but also children have resources worthy of being counted.

Time budget study is an established discipline within sociology, but one which has always neglected children as contributors and discounted the idea of children having their 'own' time. In a well-known monumental comparative study on time use (Szalai, 1972) there is no sign at all of children doing anything useful. As a matter of fact it is difficult to cite a single major study intended to cover useful activities at home, which do not classify children other than as an 'item' alongside other items on the time budget, such as cooking, personal hygiene, transport.[6] This way of categorizing children's time is also true for many studies of women, the purpose of which have been to demonstrate the imbalance between wife's and husband's participation. It is only a recent idea that children's own time should be counted and included *sui generis*, and a few interesting studies can be cited to that effect (Medrich, 1982; Solberg and Vestby, 1987; Andersen, 1989). There is a large difference in the results these studies have yielded, for instance, about the extent of children's participation in house work. This may be due to different realities, or to lack of methodological experience in this new field. When, however, all children's activities are counted, schooling, homework, more or less organized leisure time activities and gainful work outside the home, no one doubts that children have their very own, and often very full, time schedule. To family sociology, which has almost totally overlooked children as active people in their own right, this may cause surprise. It is one task of the incipient sociology of childhood to provide further evidence on this topic.

As with time budget studies, children are also objectified in 'cost of children studies'. They are turned into items on *parents'* budgets, and are thus made into expensive objects, similar to the dwelling, the car and domestic appliances. While it may of course be of some importance for prospective parents to learn about changes in the economy of their family when it is being extended by a new member, it is certainly not conducive for a positive attitude towards children as human beings to see them reduced to cost factors. The question is, therefore, how to improve our knowledge about the family economy without such normative and ideological reification of children. It is of course a fact that the family economy deteriorates when more persons must be sustained by the same income. But the notion of children *causing* the misery is a solution which is not likely to alleviate the problem, since it only seems to nurture the idea that either children are guilty because they consume, or parents are guilty because they have been heedless enough to beget children. In both cases the problem is reduced to a familial problem without taking structural and historical considerations into account.

One possible solution seems to be to think in terms of the economic role of children as a population group having a place in the long term economic development. Thus, they contribute whilst still children to the economy in terms of their school work, which is a kind of accumulation of knowledge indispensible for society. There is no theoretical argument which can plausibly suggest that children are of less importance than in previous eras, when they were generally regarded as assets (Qvortrup, 1987: 19–20). An improvement in our theorizing of children's economic role would therefore mean, for instance, expanding human capital theories to include a notion of the contributions which children themselves make. For the moment there are no signs at all of this happening, perhaps because it is part of a network of statistical practices which exclude or reify children.

Conclusion

If we seriously mean to improve life conditions for children we must, as a minimum precondition, establish reporting systems in which they are heard themselves as well as reported on by others. This is a very modest demand of, or on behalf of, a population group which at a societal level is mute and is being kept mute by adults, the dominant group.

In this chapter I have given a sketch of some ways in which children are represented in public statistics and social accounting. A much more systematic and encompassing treatment of the topic is needed, but enough has been said to establish a misrepresentation of children and childhood social life as such. In the European Centre project, which has been referred to, much more evidence will be presented, and what was said by one participant was characteristic of the nature of information in all countries. 'Data on children served by public programs . . . are typically fragmented, incomplete, locally based, and administratively-driven. National statistics do exist, but the definitions and categories applied to the children served differ between programs and policy sectors' (Heyns, 1988: 5). Children are, in other words, in most important aspects of their own life situation not focused upon directly; they are most often represented by other agencies which means, at the same time, other interests.

It may, however, be questioned whether it is to the advantage of children to be accounted for as a particular social grouping. Is it not enough to use the family as our unit of observation, since practically all children belong to a family? Are we not, by focusing directly on children, sacrificing the traditional social class perspectives, and in this way excluding questions of deprivation and inequality?

There is in my view no reason to believe that we have to circumvent a classical class perspective by illuminating more particular interests. It is without doubt important to be aware of the danger and the experiences from women's studies clearly demonstrate this predicament, but few would deny the gains won by such research in focusing directly on women. The examples mentioned above have served to make plausible the parallel advantages of focusing directly on children. It is in my view a way of depriving children of the right to be 'heard', if we fail to account for the impact specifically on children of important events, whether at the familial or the societal level.

Policy makers as well as researchers will have to make up their own minds. It is perfectly legitimate to be interested in children's families, but we must be conscious of the fact that a child's family is not the same as a child, still less to be identified with 'childhood'. We need information at all these levels. We must understand that the interests of adults, even when parents, are not always identical with those of children. The demand for more kindergartens, for instance, is unequivocally understood as a positive child family policy by parents who both want to work. Can we be so sure that it is also a positive children's policy, and would a serious examination of children's interests in this respect not be dangerous to parents' interests? The guilt feelings which we all have as parents when leaving our children in the morning prove that this question cannot so easily be discarded as reactionary.

I do not want to create the impression that parents are a 'problem'. Parents are in many respects as much victims as children, and there can be no doubt that the state must more actively assume responsibility for the welfare and well being of its child population. The ingrained and inherited way of accounting for children as appendixes to the family hides many of the realities of children's own lives behind the veil of the family institution. Opening up the secrets of family life and laying bare the life conditions of children as a collectivity and at an aggregate level might be a key for improving children's own life situations as well as alleviating parents' lives with children. So far, however, little of this has been attempted.

Notes

1 The forthcoming material from the project 'Childhood as a Social Phenomenon' will be published 1990–94 and will consists of partly eighteen booklets (sixteen National Reports, an Introduction to the series, and a Statistical Appendix), and partly of a concluding analytical volume (Childhood Matters, Avebury, 1994). The project is part of the Childhood Programme of the European Centre for Social Welfare Policy and Research, Vienna.

2 Some statistical offices have during the last decade edited special issues about children *Die Situation der Kinder der Bundesrepublik Deutschland*, Wiesbaden, 1979; Arvid Hansen og Arne Andersen, *Barns levekår*, Oslo 1984; *Barns levnadsvillkor*, Rapport 62, Stockholm 1989.

3 As a result of discussions with members of the European Centre project, the statistical office of Denmark in 1990 began currently to produce this kind of child-
   oriented statistic.
4 See Olsén, 1982, pp. 103–6; and Halvorsen, Brekken og Fugeli, 1986, pp. 110–11,
   where briefly the 'relation to families and children' is mentioned.
5 We talk about 'adultist' ideology when children are discriminated against in ways
   which are unconscious and 'natural' and therefore unchallenged. Parallel concepts
   in other areas are the 'natural' supremacy of for instance 'the white race' or 'the
   male sex'.
6 See also Lupri, 1983.

Postscript: Six Years Later

Apart from a few corrections to references, the chapter is unchanged
since it was written for the first edition. If it were to be written today
the tone in it would be different. The frustration and complaints about
the lack of data would not be so prevalent, although, at the time, this
was for very good reasons. However, the main argument — that children are seen as dependents — still holds water. What has been a positive change over this short period, though, is a better appreciation of
the need for change. In addition, the climate for doing research in
childhood has improved considerably, as is mentioned in the editors'
preface.

This is true also for the topic addressed in this chapter. However,
as far as the collection of childhood-directed statistics is concerned, one
would probably find that in most nations' statistical offices, no change
has taken place — in part because the new winds have so far not come
to them. On the other hand, one can see that specific statistical reports
about children have been published in quite a few countries while in
other countries special sections about children have been inserted into
current statistical series.

It is my personal experience also that statistical offices are interested, when they are told about what has not been done and what can
be done about children. Thus, within the framework of the Nordic
Council of Ministers, the Nordic Statistical Office invited members of
the European Centre project as experts and a so called 'technical report'
about the prospects of making childhood statistics was produced. Now
Denmark, Finland, Norway and Sweden all have special statistical publications about children; children are represented as units of observation on a few selected issues in current statistics and special files or
registers have been set up.

Also in other countries publications on children's statistics are available, for instance in Israel, Canada and the UK; in the USA Hernandez

(1993) has published a very important book, *America's Children*, which has consequently set a high standard in making children count; finally, the European project concluded its series with a statistical appendix, which sought to demonstrate how statistics on children could be improved (Jensen and Saporiti, 1992).

However, even if this movement in a positive direction is to be welcomed, one also has to admit that much more remains to be done; not only is it merely a few countries which have begun to systematically count children, but also there is still much to be desired in the way it is being done. In many of the new children's statistical reports the temptation to deal mainly with questions such as deviance or, more generally, those of children at risk is apparently not to be resisted. In addition the traditional trend to put the family at the centre is seemingly hard to overcome (Social Focus, 1994). Although a report such as the Danish one (Tal om børn, 1996) exemplified a very good report, the editor — the Ministry of Social Affairs — hampered the endeavour in its press release through resorting to a family perspective.

As mentioned above, the chapter stands as it was written; let me however conclude with an interesting example from the UK demonstrating how careful one has to be in interpretation. The UK publication on children (*Social Focus*) gives a figure for the number of children killed in road traffic accidents and was able to demonstrate a very satisfying decrease from around 1000 in 1970 to little more than 300 in 1992 (*Social Focus*, 1994, p. 52). This is likely to be interpreted as a sign of protective measures towards children, one of the classical concerns of any country's child policies. However, at the same time, a study was made in 1990 in Britain which was a replication of one done in 1971. Among others, this survey asked children aged 7–11 about whether they were allowed to 1) cross the road alone, 2) walk to parks on their own and 3) take the bus without being accompanied by adults. The astonishing result was that the percentage of children who were permitted to do these activities had decreased dramatically, respectively from seventy-two in 1971 to fifty in 1990; sixty-three to thirty-seven; and forty-eight to fifteen (Hillman, 1990, p. 131 and 44). One can therefore only conclude that one of the reasons for the welcome decrease in road deaths was partly paid for by children themselves in that they were kept indoors. This example shows, therefore, how important it is to be careful in interpreting data and to see events within the broader perspective. Statistics is an important, necessary, indeed indispensable research instrument to give expression to children's life conditions; politically it has even a strategic importance in that it is easily understood and grasped; on the other hand, it represents only a small part of the different sources of information which are needed to encompass the life worlds of children. Though the risk is always there for over interpreting aggregate statistic, used with care, it remains a helpful tool.

References

ABEL-SMITH, B. and TOWNSEND, P. (1965) *The Poor and the Poorest*, London, Bell and Sons.

ALANEN, L. (1988) 'Rethinking Childhood', *Acta Sociologica*, **31**, 1, pp. 53–67.

ALANEN, L. and BARDY, M. (1990) *Childhood as a Social Phenomenon: Country report from Finland*, Vienna, European Centre.

ALONSO, W. and STARR, P. (1982) 'The Political Economy of National Statistics', *Items* (Social Science Research Council), **36**, 3, September, pp. 29–35.

AMBERT, A.-M. (1986) 'The place of children in North American sociology', in *Sociological Studies of Child Development*, ADLER P.A. and ADLER, P. Greenwich, CT, JAI Press.

ANDERSEN, D. (1989) *Børns tidsforbrug*, Copenhagen, Socialforskingsinstituttet.

BECKER, H.S. (1966/67) 'Whose side are we on?', *Social Problems*, **14**, pp. 239–47.

BOH, K. and CEVNIGOJ SADAV, N. (1992) *Childhood as a Social Phenomenon*, National Report from Yugoslavia, Vienna, European Centre.

BUMPASS, L. (1984) 'Children and marital disruption: A replication and update', *Demography*, **21**, 1, February, pp. 71–82.

CHRISTOFFERSEN, M. (1987) *Familien under Forandring?* Copenhagen, Social-forskningsinstituttet.

CHRISTOFFERSEN, M. (1990) 'Børn og arbejdsløhed', *Samfurdsøkonomen*, No. 1.

COMMITTEE ON WAYS AND MEANS (1985) *Children in Poverty*, US House of Representatives, 22 May.

DEBRÉ, M. (1986) 'Michel Debré on French population policy', *Population and Development Review*, **12**, 3 September, pp. 606–8.

ENGELBERT, A. and BUHR, P. (forthcoming 1990) *Childhood as a Social Phenomenon*, Country Report from Federal Republic of Germany, Vienna, European Centre.

FRÖNES, I., JENSEN, A.-M. and SOLBERG, A. (forthcoming 1990) *Childhood as a Social Phenomenon*, Country Report from Norway, Vienna, European Centre.

GUSTAVSSON, B. (1984) *En Bok om Fattigdom*, Lund, Studentlitteratur.

HALVORSEN, K., BREKKEN, O. and FUGELLI, P. (1986) *Arbejdsøs i Velferdsstaten og Velferdsføger av å Være uten Lønnet Arbeid*, Oslo, Universitetsforlaget.

HERNANDEZ, D.J. (1993) *America's Children: Resources from Family, Government and the Economy*, New York, Russell Sage Foundation.

HEYNS, B. (1990) *Childhood as a Social Phenomenon*, Report from the United States of America, National, Vienna, European Centre.

HILLMAN, M., ADAMS, J. and WHITELEGG, J. (1990) *One False Move . . . A Study of Children's Independent Mobility*, London, Policy Studies Institute.

JENSEN, A.-M. (1989) 'Tre menn og en baby?', in QVORTRUP, J. (Ed) *Børn i Statistikken*, Seminarrapport, Esbjerg, Sydjysk Universitetscenter og Nordisk Ministerråd.

JENSEN, A.-M. and SAPORITI, A. (1992) *Do Children Count?: Childhood as a Social Phenomenon*, A Statistical Compendium, Vienna, European Centre.

Jens Qvortrup

Jensen, A.-M. and Moen, B. (1989) 'Far og Mor — Søster og Bror', *Tidsskrift for Samfunnsforskning*, **30**, 4–5, pp. 161–71.

Kürner, A. and Lüscher, K. (1988) *Childhood as a Social Phenomenon*, Country Report from Switzerland, Vienna, European Centre.

LeBras, H. (1979) *Children and Family: Demographic Development in the OECD Countries*, Paris, OECD.

Lupri, E. (Ed) (1983) *The Changing Position of Women in Family and Society: A Cross National Comparison*, Leiden, E.J. Brill.

Medrich, E.A. *et al.* (1982) *The Serious Business of Growing Up: A Study of Children's Lives Outside School*, Berkeley, University of California Press.

Myrdal, A. (1945) *Nation and Family*, London, Kegan Paul.

Noordhoek, J. (1988) 'Family and household composition during the life course: The viewpoint of the child', Danish National Bureau of Statistics.

Oldman, D. (1991) *Childhood as a Social Phenomenon*, National Report from Scotland, Vienna, European Centre.

Olsén, P. (1982) *Arbejdsløshedens Socialpsykologi*, Copenhagen, Dansk Psykologisk Forlag.

Palmer, J. *et al.* (Ed) (1988) *The Vulnerable*, Washington, DC, Urban Institute Press.

Qvortrup, J. (1987) 'Introduction to sociology of childhood', *International Journal of Sociology*, **17**, 3, Fall, pp. 3–37.

Qvortrup, J. and Christoffersen, M. (1990) *Childhood as a Social Phenomenon*, National Report from Denmark, Vienna, European Centre.

Sgritta, G.B. and Saporiti, A. (1989) 'Myth and reality in the discovery and representation of childhood', in Close, P. (Ed) *Family Divisions and Inequalities in Modern Society*, London, Macmillan.

Smeeding, T.T. and Torrey, B.B. (1988) 'Poor children rich countries', *Science*, **242**, 11 November, pp. 873–77.

Social Focus on Children (1994) Central Statistical Office, London, HMSO.

Solberg, A. and Vestby, G.M. (1987) *Barns Arbeidsliv*, Oslo, NIBR.

Szalai, A. (Ed) (1972) *The Use of Time: Daily Activities of Urban and Suburban Populations in Twelve Countries*, The Hague and Paris, Mouton.

Tal om børn (1996) Det Tværministerielle Børneudvalg, Copenhagen.

Teitelbaum, M.S. and Winter, J.M. (1985) *The Fear of Population Decline*, San Diego, Academic Press.

Thorne, B. (1987) 'Revisioning women and social change: Where are the children?', *Gender and Society*, pp. 85–109.

Townsend, P. (1979) *Poverty in the United Kingdom*, Harmondsworth, Penguin.

UNICEF, (1989) *The State of the World's Children 1989*, Oxford, Oxford University Press.

Chapter 5

It's a Small World: Disneyland, the Family and the Multiple Re-representations of American Childhood

Pauline Hunt and Ronald Frankenberg

Here you leave today and enter the world of yesterday, tomorrow and fantasy (Sign over the entrance to Main Street USA, Disneyland, Anaheim, California).

The wild and the sublime sun of the originals has set, or is at least veiled, even in those presentations which connect the popular with the cheaply saleable instead of with popular energy and ancient popular imagination . . . long active in dance, fairytale and brooding reflection (Ernst Bloch, *The Principle of Hope*: 911).

Introduction

Disney's own introduction is to be found on a plaque at Disneyland:

To all who come to this happy place: Welcome. Disneyland is your land. Here age relives fond memories of the past . . . and here youth may savour the challenge and promise of the future. Disneyland is dedicated to the ideals, the dreams and the hard facts that have created America . . . with the hope that it will be a source of joy and inspiration to all the world (Bailey, 1982: 209).

Keeping a central course from the entrance of the Disneyland theme park and across Fantasyland, visitors reach a huge toy-town clock set in a castle. They board one of the family-size passenger boats in the castle moat and are carried on a world tour through symbolic national settings inhabited by mechanical models of children in stereotyped adult folk costumes. This is 'It's a Small World', one of the most popular

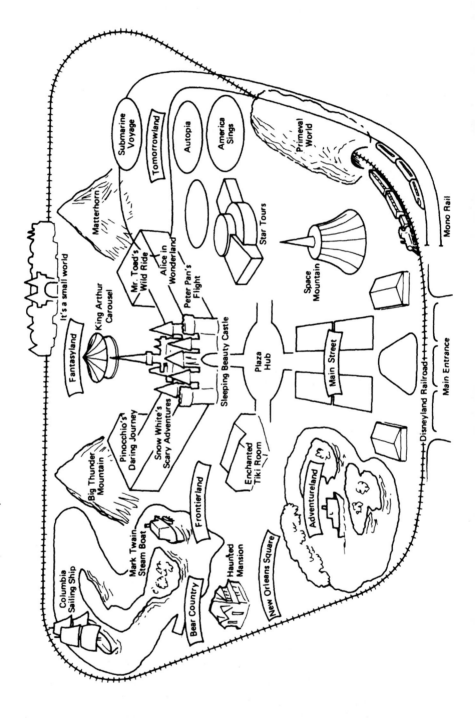

Figure 5.1 Simplified map of Disneyland

rides in Disneyland, and one of the few with external sponsorship. As they drift through this toy representation of a world tour, they hear, as if from the mouths of the mechanical children, the same song in many different languages:

> It's a world of laughter, a world of tears:
> It's a world of hopes and a world of fears.
>
> There's so much that we share,
> That it's time we're aware,
> It's a small world after all.
>
> There is just one moon and one golden sun,
> And a smile means friendship to everyone,
> Though the mountains divide,
> And the oceans are wide,
> It's a small world after all.
> (© 1987 Bank of America Corporation)

The sense of togetherness and unity in a bright secure, wholesome and unambiguous world of playtime expressed in this attraction epitomizes Disneyland as a whole; its sponsorship by the Bank of America is an ironic reminder of the park's history and its unashamed allegiance to capitalist and American ideals.

Disneyland, the first of several such institutions, is at Anaheim in Orange County, Southern California, adjoining the city of Los Angeles and within easy reach of Hollywood. It was the brainchild of the creative film maker Walt Disney who first outlined his idea for a theme park in August 1948. His financially astute brother Roy did not originally warm to the idea, reminding Walt of the immense debt they had already incurred with the Bank of America (Thomas 1980: 226). By the early 1950s:

> Walt realized that he would have to provide his own financing, since Roy maintained his opposition. To Lilly's [Mrs Disney's] dismay he began borrowing on his life insurance; before he finished, he was $100,000 in debt (Thomas, 1980: 251).

Plans for Disneyland were drawn in September 1953 and excavations for the pleasure park began in August 1954. Disneyland was first opened to the public in July 1955. It is now big business and attracts peak daily attendances of between 60,000 and 65,000 people on weekends in the Christmas and New Year period, and drops as low as 10,000 to 20,000 on weekdays in late January to March. Attendance fluctuates according to season and weather, weekday or weekend, holiday or workday between these limits, (Birnbaum, 1989: 12).

Many visitors arrive (as we did), by Monorail from the Disneyland Hotel, or by bus from other hotels, and have paid the entrance fees for a day, several days, or a week, as part of their holiday package. Those arriving directly at the main entrance pay $21.50 for each adult ticket and $16.50 for each child between the ages of 3 and 12. We were accompanied by two children and therefore would have paid a total of $228 dollars for our two daily visits had it not been compounded with our return airfares from San Francisco and family room at the hotel. Our privileges did not extend to the special evening opening for a New Year's Eve Party for which there were no children's concessions, costing $132.00 for the four of us.

The area around Disneyland, once made up of orange groves, which Disney would have bought if he could have raised the money, has, as he feared, become an unplanned, and not very attractive, resort with many hotels and tourist attractions, including Knott's Berry Farm, a much less grand amusement park with music, concerts and sports facilities, Universal Studios tours in nearby Hollywood, and the Queen Mary and the Spruce Goose in Long Beach. Visitors from outside Southern California sometimes take a short package holiday, as we did, in Orange County and intersperse their two or three visits to Disneyland with visits to the smaller, less expensive attractions. We did not, in fact, see everything in Disneyland in our three days; although we were able to revisit attractions in relatively privileged and uncrowded conditions from eight in the evening on New Year's Eve until three a.m. on New Year's Day, we by no means felt that we had exhausted its attractions.

Visiting Disneyland is not inexpensive but once through the entrance, all the rides and spectacles have been paid for; one is free to select adventures without the delay and hassle of queuing for tickets and having them checked before boarding a ride. Since parents have also paid to participate, they can, if they wish and have the courage, do so with their children and need not wait around, bored and weary, awaiting the return of their excited offspring, as often happens in similar entertainments. Disney himself spoke of having experienced such dismal waits in run-down amusement parks, and although he was wont to squat down to obtain a child's eye view of his park (Thomas, 1980: 281), he was determined to provide a place of entertainment for all age groups. Thus within the overall pattern of Disneyland, the rides in Tomorrowland are designed to appeal to young adults' hopes for the future world (or worlds) which will be different and yet essentially similar (an idea carried much further at the Epcot Center at Disneyworld in Florida); Frontierland and Main Street USA provide older adults with a nostalgic trip back through time with period buildings and sailing vessels which are scaled down in size but sufficiently detailed to provide a charming illusion of yesteryear (see Schechner, 1985 for the complexities of would-be authentic restoration).

The whole park is pleasantly landscaped. The visitors, or 'guests' in Disney parlance, follow curving paths through well-kept gardens; since several rides take place on water, they can enjoy being transported silently and gently from one scene to the next. Even though our visits to Disneyland took place during the peak attendance period, Christmas vacation, so expertly and efficiently are the queues managed, arranged like mazes doubling back on themselves to supply new vistas and a sense of progress, that we never experienced the large crowd as a serious impediment to our enjoyment. One could not but admire the efficiency of an organization which could comfortably accommodate such large numbers of people.

> If it is a ride they [the patrons] will discover that the vehicle, instead of having one or two entrances, has one for each row of seats and that the rows exactly match the number of exits from the waiting maze. An attendant gives you a firm hand into the vehicle, which helps prevent accidents, seems a polite thing to to do and, incidentally, speeds the loading process. The whole thing is a marvel of technology applied to mass psychology. People simply feel better if the line they are in is short and constantly moving (Schickel, 1986: 321).

We subject Disneyland to a critical appraisal in this paper, but it should be said at the outset that we (and our children) found the 'field-work' involved thoroughly enjoyable. It is a fantasy-wrapped amusement park, which the skills of a film-maker have served to make intrinsically interesting and entertaining. As Christopher Finch writes:

> What makes Disneyland radically different from other amusement parks is the fact that it is designed as a movie lot. The skills that go into building film sets are the same skills that went into Main Street and Frontierland (Finch, 1988: 151).

Similarly, the rides themselves incorporate the images and animation expertise associated with Disney. The rides in Sleeping Beauty Castle (named after Disney's technologically most advanced and least popular film) reproduce models and images from cartoon films which are familiar world-wide; clever visual devices used in other rides make them seem like trips through films. The unfolding experience staged in the Haunted Mansion ride is a good example of this feeling. Finch writes of this ride:

> Each car is on a swivel so that it can be turned, by electronic signals, to face just what the designer wants it to face at any particular moment. In this sense, then, it is used exactly like a movie camera. The rider is travelling through a programmed show which unfolds in time. The choice of where to look is not his to make — it has already been made by the designer, who determines what will be seen, just as a director determines what the movie patron will see. This degree of control is, of course, limited to certain rides, but everything in the parks is touched by the motion-picture expertise of the Disney organization (1988: 155).

Unlike in a film, however, the visitor can — and perhaps on the second go will — look round, which adds to the pleasure of submitting to deception, the joy of seeing partly how the illusion is created, which is denied to all but the most sophisticated moviegoers.

Thus an entertaining spectacle is provided for all age groups, strictly separate from the world of work and reality. Disneyland projects itself as a playground stocked with pleasing but undemanding playthings. Perhaps it is this association with play that prompts Schickel to link Disneyland so firmly with childhood that he writes of its creator,

> Disneyland could have been created only by a man-child who never tired of toys or shed the belief that animals and insects have human attributes. . . . He had the courage to proclaim the childlike quality of his imagination for all the world to see, and that, frankly, was more than his audience ever did. They hide their happiness over the opportunity he provided for controlled regression behind middle-class styles and attitudes and thus avoid damaging admissions about the true nature of the Disneyland experience (Schickel, 1986: 329–30).

This last point is addressed to those who have poured scorn on Disneyland and those who enjoy it, for accepting tawdry substitutes for real experience. The critics perhaps betray the sense of their own superiority, as if most people actually had the opportunity of exploring Amazonian jungles or climbing the real Matterhorn. In Disneyland the general public is offered both the lighthearted opportunity to pretend and at the same time to wonder at the ingenuity of the special effects involved in achieving the pretence. Here the semblance of a world tour and of crossing time barriers are available for those who are willing, at least partially, to suspend disbelief and to play along.

An existential longing may be embedded in people's enthusiasm for Disneyland. Few have the means to engage in worldwide travel, and no one, however rich and free, can see *everything* at first hand. Modern life tantalizes by communicating the existence of many inaccessible worlds and turns the passage of time into a roll call of lost opportunities. David Lodge in his novel, *Nice Work*, expresses it through the mouth of his awakening, apparently successful businessman:

> When he came back from the bar with their drinks, he said, 'I've never bought draught bitter for a woman before.'
>
> 'Then you must have had a very limited experience of life,' she said, smiling.
>
> 'You're dead right,' he replied, without returning the smile. 'Cheers.' He took a long swallow of his pint. 'Some times when I'm lying awake in the small hours, instead of counting sheep. I count the things I've never done.'
>
> 'Like what?'
>
> 'I've never skied, I've never surfed. I've never learned to play a musical instrument, or speak a foreign language, or sail a boat, or ride a horse. I've never climbed a mountain or pitched a tent or caught a fish. I've never seen Niagara Falls or been up the Eiffel Tower or visited the Pyramids. I've never . . . I could go on and on.' He had been about to say, *I've never slept with a woman other than my wife*, but thought better of it.
>
> 'There's still time.'
>
> 'No, it's too late. All I'm fit for is work. It's the only thing I'm any good at.'
>
> 'Well, that's something. To have a job you like and be good at it.'
>
> 'Yes, it's something' he agreed, thinking that in the small hours it didn't seem enough; but he didn't say that aloud either (Lodge, 1989: 255).

John Berger puts this contradiction of capitalism in more theoretical and universal terms, when he writes:

> . . . the seer, when human, is conscious of what his eye cannot and will never see because of time and distance. The visible both includes him (because he sees) and excludes him (because he is not omnipresent). The visible consists for him of the seen which, even when it is threatening, confirms his existence,

and of the unseen which defies that existence. The desire *to have seen* — the ocean, the desert, the aurora borealis — has a deep ontological basis (1984: 50).

In Disneyland, insofar as the visitor suspends adult disbelief, the world is her or his oyster. Yet the regression called for is perhaps infinite. A deep nostalgia for one's own past is engendered because one cannot fully enter into the pretence. Rebecca, our 6-year-old daughter, sighed as she left Disneyland. 'I wish I were still a baby! I wish I were younger!' Would she then have experienced it as totally real? We think not. Even for a toddler, a longing for a past-that-never-was is likely to be created. The complicated dialectic of the experience for many is illustrated by an American academic friend who recounted spontaneously, on hearing the title of this paper, how the intention to visit Disneyland some years ago awakened in her the guilty consciousness that her 2-year-old son was, contrary to cultural norms, still at the breast. She resolved that the visit would also mark the end of this situation. The toddler was therefore persuaded to end the drawn-out pleasures of breastfeeding apparently in return for the visit to Disneyland. For him as for many others, Disneyland is intricately interwoven with elusive memories of a golden era, an example of how Disneyland both serves and is used to re-enforce conventional values and practices. (A general discussion of the treatment and suppression of Oedipal themes in traditional stories adapted for the Disney oeuvre as a whole has to await a later paper; on the originals see Bettelheim, 1978)

Pilgrimage to and within the Magic Circle

Disney went to great lengths to separate his park from the surrounding area and to establish a clear boundary where the park begins and ends.

> He threw an earthen bank fifteen feet high around it so that nothing of *its* surroundings could be seen from inside; he spent fourteen thousand dollars removing telephone poles from sight and burying the lines (Schickel, 1986: 326).

Disneyland is bordered by a circular railroad. Visitors step off the train and descend within the park or step across it from the car park or bus terminus into a realm of images and sensations representing both idealized childhood and conventional family relationships. Within its magic circle (described elsewhere as 'ritual space', Moore, 1980) time and space are absent or irrelevant; the class, language and ethnic differences of the United States and its attendant world appear transcended in already shared, and now materialized, solidified and confirmed, cultural experience. There is special currency available, to be spent within its confines or more often to be carried away as souvenirs. Regular customers are even issued with 'passports' rather than season tickets.

The longer journey from the outside time-regulated world to the fairy-ring threshold of Disneyland is almost always collective. You take your children or grandchildren or you are taken by your parents or grandparents in family or hire cars. Young adults come with their peers in coach-borne parties from school, college, or youth group; or as romantic couples hitch-hiking, by Greyhound or in old jalopies in a brief but perhaps highly significant symbolic stage in the progression from dating, courting, betrothal, and marriage to family formation. You expect to be amazed but not surprised, for you go with expectations. You have seen the films, are familiar with the cartoon characters, and know that their trials and tribulations are humourous, and will eventually resolve into happy endings. You expect (and know that an omnipresent but unobtrusive management intends) a similar ending from the thrills and spills of their own visit.

You have come like a pilgrim to participate in the clean and wholesome fun of Disney, following in the footsteps of the millions of visitors who have preceded you. Unlike pilgrims in older conventional modes visitors are not reminded of past lapses by present symbolic suffering (even standing in line is made relatively painless) or necessarily returned to time and social relationships with a new sense of reality. Turner and Turner (1978: 250–55) call structural breaks (giving birth, sickness, festival, serious disputes) in long periods of accepted structure (marriage, school, work, family) 'communitas experiences'. During such experiences, described in their secular form as 'liminoid episodes', people, they claim, relate to each other directly rather than as incumbents of social roles. This anti-structural experience may cause people to return to their structured interactions with different conceptions, leading either to reconciliation or to the emergence of new social groupings. In the pilgrimage to Disneyland, the progression is from fantasy, through fantasy and to fantasy and reconfirms and strengthens commitments to status quo, conventional family practices and to courtship progression. The mixing of visitors and the shared participation of the rides (see Caillois, 1961) in conditions cut off from paidwork-associated roles and social positions reinforces both the club-like atmosphere deliberately fostered within the park and domestic, private sphere, relationships.

A Quality Club

The Walt Disney Company set out to make a profit but also to portray themselves as the vendors of good-value family entertainment, eschewing sex and violent horror in their films, and establishing a reputation for quality both in the superb craft skills of their animation and later in the facilities and products available in Disneyland. They were successful on all counts.

> Walt insisted on fine furnishing for the restaurants even though they would be serving reasonably priced meals. He believed that if a family sat under a $50,000 chandelier and ate good food at a fair price, the experience would add to their enjoyment of the park (Thomas, 1980: 276).

In sharp contrast to the disposable plastic dross and sordid litter of many mass entertainment outlets, Disneyland is almost ostentatiously clean and litter-free, with china crockery and metal cutlery, clean lavatories and well-appointed restaurants. A numerous hierarchy of litter-removers, culminate in the highly visible, neatly uniformed pooper-scooper-bearing pages attending Cinderella's carriage horses in the daily Grand Parades. The time and class intervals implied in the Londoners' proverb 'After the Lord Mayor's Show comes the dustcart' are here characteristically eliminated. Every aspect of the park is kept well groomed:

> Every night every street and walkway is thoroughly hosed down and crews armed with putty knives get down on hands and knees to scrape up carelessly discarded chewing gum. Even the targets in the shooting galleries dulled by the previous days shots are repainted. Every year some 800,000 plants are replaced because Disney refused to put up signs asking his 'guests' not to trample them. All of this . . . adds immeasurably to the appeal of the place and undoubtedly contributes to the astonishing fact that 50 per cent of the people who enter the gates are returnees (Schickel, 1986: 317).

Disney, after a brush with a discourteous guard, decided that his creation would have to train its own security force, taught to treat visitors as guests, if sometimes wayward ones, and to remember 'We're selling happiness' (Thomas, 1980: 307). Nowadays all employees are trained in the 'University of Disneyland' to become 'people specialists'.

> All are carefully schooled in good grooming and good manners, as defined by local custom, and crammed full of the facts, figures

and folksy anecdotes that comprise the lore of the place. Some measure of the prevailing institutional tone may be gathered from the the university's text book: 'We love to entertain Kings and Queens, but the vital thing to remember is this: Every guest receives the VIP treatment.' Or, 'Disneyland is a first name place. The only "Mr" here is Mr Toad . . . at Disneyland we get tired but never bored, and even if it is a rough day, we appear happy' (Schickel, 1986: 318).

The cleanliness, courtesy and quality of the product on offer in Disneyland, combined with the well-heeled yet relaxed posture of the guests creates a universalizing particularity, a club-like atmosphere. Except on New Year's Eve, and even then in a restrained (and alcohol-free) way, exuberance is expressed only on the rides and not between them. Style of dress is respectable leisure rather than outrageously casual. ('No shoes, no shirt: no service,' as it is put elsewhere in California.) As with any club, togetherness is based on establishing who does and who does not gain access to membership. The relatively high price of entrance excludes one unwelcome section, the unsuccessful poor. The omnipresent security, although courteous and unobtrusive, excludes other unwelcome outsiders, the improperly dressed, the crazy, the drug user and the disruptive or even the noticeably drunk.

Disneyland, therefore, provides good clean fun for good clean families. Trash, literally, and in terms of undesirable people, is excluded. The millions of people who have been able to visit Disneyland have been treated as guests. Not only does this policy pay in financial terms, it also engenders a feeling of equality. As guests, visitors are seen to have made it, not only financially, but as well-adjusted and respectable members of society.

Images in Action: Inaction Before Images

Adult visitors relive a sanitized childhood where they can enjoy rides in a safe and protected environment. Prudence, insurance companies and United States liability laws demand that pregnant women, people with heart conditions, back problems and the unduly nervous should be advised to forgo some of the more exciting rides (even where, such is the correctly perceived power of the fantastic imagination, the motion of the ride is merely simulated and can be avoided merely by shutting one's eyes). Unusually for Disneyland, this advice is presented through the written word and in English alone on poster-sized printed notices, rather than through the pictorial image. The written word is otherwise only present in suitably symbolic styles in the small and almost unperceived bookshop, the programme guide, the titles of features, and the price tags and statutory descriptions of commodities. This is not merely a latent concession to the foreign tourist or to the many Californians who are more at home in Spanish or an Asian language. Disneyland operates through controlled imaging aimed at controlling controlled imaginations. Its images, however complex the network of representation and illusion involved, are clear cut and self explanatory living up to Disney's own continuing advice: '"Make it read!" meaning, making the action distinct and recognizable. No contradictions, no ambiguities' (Thomas, 1980: xv).

The all-encompassing imagery is reinforced by the clear-cut layout of the park and the reliance on one main entrance. Visitors know where they are geographically and intellectually. The rides and spectacles appear to be full of surprises but the visitor is able without hesitation to interpret them. The fun is reassuring and undemanding; it is very difficult to lose status by either missing the point or feeling excluded. In this respect, at least, Disneyland and the fast-food chain, McDonalds, share a family likeness; the less salubrious surroundings of the latter contain a parallel reassurance in that packaged meals take the mystique out of ordering and the throwaway containers and utensils remove the anxieties from imperfectly grasped table etiquette (Law, 1984, 186). Such clear-cut dining-out etiquette may well be appreciated by young couples out dating, and by very young children who find it easier to consume food that can be picked up in their hands (Charles and Kerr, 1988: 91). Its direct equivalents in Disneyland are the appropriate snack foodstands in the various areas.

At Disneyland the illusion of time re-presented within a framework outside of time itself is reinforced by the unchanging nature of exhibits once they are established: yet another level of nostalgia is experienced by parents and even some grandparents introducing children to sights like the Enchanted Tiki Room that they themselves experienced in their own childhood. This room was the Park's first use of the now commonplace electronically controlled moving and speaking models. Audiences are entertained in a supposedly Polynesian environment surrounded by talking plants and birds which sing and tell jokes. Main Street USA with its apparently old-fashioned stores is nevertheless stocked with up-to-date Disney merchandise, which thereby has imparted to it a timeless flavour and an identification with the memory of a romanticized, idyllic past. It leads directly to Sleeping Beauty Castle at the entrance to Fantasyland. Here is the ideological and geographical centre of Disneyland.

The castle houses the rides based on the Disney versions of Pinocchio, Snow White, Peter Pan, Toad of Toad Hall and Alice in Wonderland. These literary fantasy figures were first reinterpreted in animated cartoons and here reappear as images and three dimensional models re-representing the cartoon representations. Such illusions based on illusions are protectively distanced from reality, enabling us to enjoy, without engagement in real danger, the excitement. Elsewhere in the park we can smile complacently at the snapping teeth of model wild animals in Adventureland's jungle cruise. We participate in the park, not as genuine participants in dramas that require from us responses that generate consequences we will have to live with, but merely as passive spectators. Our only genuine participatory act is to pay our entrance fee and pass through the gates and then, in British parlance, to join the queue; in American, to stand in line. We do not even commit our own resources since the entrance charge is all-inclusive and real time has ceased to exist. Once that choice is made, our reactions are conditioned by the subtle pre-determined meanderings of the queue which make it seem shorter, the style of the vehicle which we eventually reach, and which conveys us at a speed and with pauses, if any, chosen for us at an appropriate distance (determined by the organizers) from the spectacle. (Disney wanted to let people wander through in their own time but was discouraged by his advisers in order to avoid costly and alienating bottlenecks.) Ours is but to laugh at the jokes and to marvel at the genuine technical achievements of modellers and engineers. We too are reduced to the 'ideal' child-like condition of being acted upon rather than acting. The excitements of reading (or of being read to) have truly been doubly translated and betrayed.

The characters in the various rides in Sleeping Beauty Castle are all subject to frightening but not totally destructive adventures which happen to them when they are separated from or separate themselves from traditional family situations. They are punished, if at all, for naughtiness, normal acts out of context or carried to excess rather than for sin. Similarly, elsewhere in Disneyland these adventures are mimicked by transformed neighbourhood park pleasures; slides, swings and roundabouts carried to extremes of speed and bumpiness and in fantasy surroundings. Participating children and youth enjoy the illusion of living dangerously while anticipating happy landings and reunion with older and very young, less hardy family members. Happy endings are also achieved for the fantasy figures when the representation ends with a tableau of their safe return to their families (Alice, Pinocchio or Wendy) or when family life is about to be romantically established (Snow White and Sleeping Beauty with their respective Princes). All is well once more within the protective embrace of the family freed from enemies within like inimical stepmothers or defiantly outside like Fire-eater the Showman.

The Fantasization of Commodities

Opportunities to buy abound. Disneyland stores provide theme-related merchandise in the different sections of the park; fur hats, 'skulls', spears and the like in Adventureland, photographs and space novelties in Tomorrowland. Dry goods in general are readily available, especially in Main Street USA. Soft toys and models of Disney cartoon characters are on sale everywhere and images of the most popular attach Disney identity to toys, stationery, clothing and other novelty items. These brand images reinforce the club identity of Disney. Disneyland itself is not exclusive except in the senses already outlined. It is even inclusive in that purchases worn in line at airport check-in counters, or back home, provide for its continuation through shared conversation about separate but shared experiences. This is as true for the travelled primary school children of middle-class England and other parts of the world as it is for the dinner parties and the self-consciously role-distancing common room chat of US universities (cf. Law, 1984: 185).

The general utilization of popular characters from children's entertainment is, of course, although originally pioneered by Disney, now a well-established sales technique. Successful toys, films or television programmes can generate images which are then attached to a wide range of franchised products which may, in the long run, be the major source of both profit and ideological influence. The popular mass-selling toy 'My Little Pony', for example, has spawned images on video, film, in comic books, on pencils and pens, pencil-cases, rulers, notebooks and activity books, on lunch boxes, purses, jewellery and much more. The parents of a child enthusiastic about 'My Little Pony' reinforce the enthusiasm by regularly adding to the child's collection. The fantasy forms of make believe stimulated by these items become entangled with personal history through the material-object reinforced memory of birthday and (a case in point from an age where commercial enterprise knew its place) *un*birthday presents (Carroll, 1872, itself the source inspiration for a Disney film and a Disneyland ride). Special outings to Disney films, available in cinemas during school holidays, but available in full length only in national TV film festivals, link the child's self-identity not only with the product and all its simple symbolism but also with relationships within the family itself. These cover the whole gamut of family experiences from sibling rivalry to the competitive strivings of estranged spouses, as well as the 'normal' interplay of shared household life.

Sales techniques based on identification with cartoon characters or named toys are effective since once the basis for a collection has been acquired, by purchase or gift, a foundation exists which induces buyers to add to it continuously on future occasions; such techniques, however, paradoxically limit the choice of both commodities and lifestyles. In the market for children's possessions, choices are between prepackaged styles of childhood fantasy and self-identification. Cartoon films provided the Disney organization with a medium for the establishment of a product-friendly disposition which they have skilfully utilized. In Disneyland, as in most airports and hotels, the products available are firmly restricted to the entertainment and 'luxury' side of consumption. The tedium of regular shopping, getting in groceries, finding shoes, socks and underwear to fit the family, replacing light bulbs, toilet rolls, medicines, nappies and the like, is absent. Necessary and duty-bound shopping which takes up the outside paid employment time of workaday women and men is replaced with time out of time for Disneyland shoppers, as well as those on the rides.

All Play and No Work Makes ... ?

Disneyland is about play, not work; visible work is confined to such as the seven dwarfs and Geppetto, apart from the quick glimpses of rushing litter collectors and cafeteria waitresses. Obviously exacting work is continually performed by those employed behind the scenes to provide and preserve its fantasy illusions. Consider, for example, the effort entailed in repeating, endlessly and without alteration, the patter and jokes employed on the Submarine Voyage, the Jungle Cruise or the Storyland canal trip, without skimping on the dialogue, hurrying, taking short cuts en route or allowing personal boredom or cynicism to show through. However wearisome the spectacle may become, those personnel, unshielded by costume or occasional taped voiceover, must in this context behave with smiling courtesy like the hostess at a party, making everything seem deceptively easy and undemanding. The frisson enjoyed by recognizing the contradiction between character played and character playing identified by writers on drama and at other more uniquely focused theme parks (Schechner, 1885: 89–90) is here deliberately eschewed. The park fosters a sharp dichotomy between work and play. The visitors, young and old, come to have fun. They are on vacation. The daily world of school, office and domestic toil (as well as deep emotional experience or its dramatic catharsis) is kept out of sight and out of mind. It is to help to achieve this that the real work of social construction of place and time in Disneyland as venue for such leisure and escape is kept as unobtrusive as possible. It is supposed to be play time for all: visitors must not be disturbed by realizing it is work time for some. Like the fantasy family it fosters, all play together; the work and sacrifice that make this possible is concealed.

In the traditional, ethnocentric, white urban middle-class view (see Prout and James, this volume), childhood is seen as a period of preparation and socialization, relatively free from the responsibilities and the work-related pressures of adult life. It is the time when the 'real' self is supposedly on the tip of their own tongues, only they do not yet know what they taste like (Bloch, 1986: 927). Even in Bachelard's (1969) formulation, childhood is a time for daydreams, when boredom is a virtue. In Britain and the United States children legitimately and regularly engage in what is called play, in contrast with the work punctuated by leisure pursuits which is said to typify adult life. In Disneyland, adults also are allowed to re-experience an ideological reconstruction of partially remembered childhood where idling time away in play is legitimated. The consciously nostalgic features of the park set the scene of such a personal trip back into an illusory and *cute* era of childhood. Perhaps in Disneyland, the Peter Pan and Wendy ride over the rooftops of London to Never-Neverland reflects this most closely as, does Disney's film masterwork, *Mary Poppins*. The essential pathos of Disneyland, Disneyworld and the mature Disney oeuvre in general, is that no one who can appreciate an image is too young to feel nostalgia for an unreal past free from work, from frustration and from time itself. This is not however even the felt, let alone verbalized, romanticism of Wordsworth's

> There was a time when meadow, grove, and stream,
> The earth, and every common sight,
>   To me did seem
>   Apparelled in celestial light,
> The glory and the freshness of a dream.

In Disneyland even nature is miniaturized and beautifully but carefully ordered. Freedom from toil is placed outside of time and space and allied to freedom from power and control. The memory of this supposed freedom is preserved only in commoditized, manufactured souvenirs; materialized memories, truncated symbols which at once prompt recollection and falsify and sentimentalize it.

The entry into this playland is thoroughly processed and packaged. Visitors flow collectively down Main Street, USA and through the park. They wait in lines that double back on themselves, giving a sense of progress and of continually renewing views of people and things. In Fantasyland, the people in the lines are entertained by catchy tunes from the soundtracks of the appropriate Disney films. When their turn comes, as we have described, they ride in boats, wagons, cars, trains and the like in which they are without autonomy or power to change direction for themselves. They are channeled through the experience. There are no simple climbing frames or other playground-type facilities, so ubiquitous in other US parks which children utilize with their own meaning, at their own pace, and to a great extent, in their own way. Here forms of play are, for both economic and ideological reasons, inseparably combined. Served up prepackaged, timed, priced and valued.

Time Out

It is possible that in modern urban and suburban US middle-class society a subtle and complex change is taking place concerning the adult approach to children's time. In the first place, there is increasing pressure that children should show, as early as possible, their commitment to adult individualist enterprise values and, like the film portrayal of the young Thomas Edison (and indeed like Walt Disney himself) and like Peanuts characters before them, branch out into their own paper round or other entrepreneurial activity, for example Lucy's 'Psychiatric Help' stand. Second, while school is not paid work, its role as preparation for work is becoming intensified; teachers are more anxious than ever about homework and out-of-school supplementary learning, while parents are concerned with grades and 'foreign' competition at home and abroad. If this is true, the trip to Disneyland, often in Southern California a reward for school-time virtue, represents time off and even nostalgia for their own always-already absent childish past, for children as well as for adults. A good time can be had because all the visitors, courting couples, parents and their children are out of time: out of the routine, demands and conflicts of the daily timetable. What goes on here is not really serious; it does not count in the workaday world. At the same time, like other leisure activities, it carries a more or less concealed philosophical socialization for the family and for the ethnocentric white Anglo-Saxon tradition which masquerades as American values. Disneyland provides the residual dying embers under the mythical melting pot. Perhaps Disney, in addition to this, really has managed to sell a brief happiness: although if this passive form of pleasure, squeezed into the margins of life, is to count as happiness it implies a low-level of gratification, unity and even contentment elsewhere. In the words of George Eliot in her novel *Felix Holt*: 'One way of getting an idea of our fellow-countrymen's miseries is to go and look at their pleasures' (1977: 373).

The adventures of Disneyland are packaged and stage-managed illusions that take place in an undemanding and reassuring setting. Here in the company of other relatively prosperous, well-adjusted, adequately conformist members of society a pleasurable sense of belonging is engendered (!). In the Plaza Inn Restaurant, the silent Disney characters in costume mingle with the crowd and pose for photographs with the visitors. They sit with them at the tables and engage in elaborately extravagant mime and gestures which attract the attention of bystanders. A few individual visitors sit, usually temporarily, alone on the sidelines, waiting for their companions to finish their rides and return. The costume-wearers turn towards and include these individuals making it difficult to achieve isolation in this world of pre-programmed, prepackaged togetherness. The Disney Corporation's worldwide activities have made the world small; in Disneyland they have also made a small world in other senses. The potential challenge posed by youthful and other cultural imaginations of beneficial anarchy is tamed and regulated and only then, and that temporarily, joined in pseudonirvanic togetherness by the romanticized, sentimentalized, nostalgic myths of their progenitors. Unlike the parties characterized by Goffman (1961), or the structured anti-structural communitas of the pilgrimages chronicled by Turner and Turner (1978) this is no status blood bath; no waves of contradictory (e)motion rock the boats which circumnavigate this small world to the genuine delight of parties of customers of Disney and the Bank of America.

References

BACHELARD, G. (1969) *The Poetics of Space*, Boston, Beacon Press.
BAILEY, A. (Ed) (1982) *Walt Disney's World of Fantasy*, New Jersey, Cartwell Books Inc.
BENJAMIN, W. (1936) (1970) 'The work of art in the age of mechanical reproduction', in *Illuminations*, London, Jonathan Cape, pp. 219–53.
BERGER, J. (1984) *And Our Faces, My Heart, Brief as Photos*, London, Writers and Readers.
BETTELHEIM, B. (1978) *The Uses of Enchantment: The Meaning and Importance of Fairy Tales*, Harmondsworth, Penguin Books.
BIRNBAUM, S. (Ed) (1989) *Disneyland: The Official Guide*, Anaheim, Mifflin and Hearst Professional Magazines Inc.

Bloch, E. (1959) (1986) *The Principle of Hope*, Oxford, Basil Blackwell.

Caillois, R. (1961) *Man, Play and Games*, New York, Free Press.

Charles, N. and Kerr, M. (1988) *Women, Food and Families*, Manchester, Manchester University Press.

Carroll, L. (1865) *Alice in Wonderland*, London, Macmillan.

Dorfman, A. and Mattelart, A. (1975) *How to Read Donald Duck*, New York, International General Editions.

Eliot, G. (1866) (1977) *Felix Holt: The Radical*, London, Penguin Books.

Finch, C. (1988) *The Art of Walt Disney*, London, Bison Books Ltd.

Goffman, E. (1961) *Encounters: Two Studies in the Sociology of Interaction*, Indianapolis, Bobbs-Merrill.

Law, J. (1984) 'How much of society can the sociologist digest at one sitting?: The "macro" and the "micro" revisited for the case of fast food', *Studies in Symbolic Interaction*, **5**, pp. 171–96.

Lodge, D. (1989) *Nice Work*, London, Penguin books.

Moore, A. (1980) 'Walt Disney world: Bounded ritual space and the playful pilgrimage center', *Anthropological Quarterly*, **53**, 4, pp. 207–18.

Schechner, R. (1985) *Between Theater and Anthropology*, Philadelphia, University of Pennsylvania.

Schickel, R. (1986) *The Disney Version*, London, Pavilion Books Ltd.

Thomas, B. (1980) *Walt Disney*, New York, Pocket Books.

Turner, V. and Turner, E. (1978) *Image and Pilgrimage in Christian Culture*, Oxford, Basil Blackwell.

Wordsworth, W. (1807) 'Ode: Intimations of immortality from recollections of early childhood', reprinted in Smith, D.N. (1983) *Wordsworth: Poetry and Prose*, Oxford, Clarendon Press.

Chapter 6

Negotiating Childhood: Changing Constructions of Age for Norwegian Children

Anne Solberg

Introduction

The starting point for the new paradigm of the sociology of childhood is that childhood is a social construction. This suggests that conceptions of childhood — what it is like or should be like to be a child — is part of culture and, as such, transforms through time and space. This article aims to unpack some of the elements of one such construction through exploring the changing nature of Norwegian childhood. Using empirical studies of child roles in the family, I shall explore the different ways in which children contribute to household management and to the division of labour in the home and suggest that through these children are themselves actively involved in constructing the new perceptions of childhood in Norwegian culture.

My main interest is in the processes through which childhood is constructed and, to this end, I explore how particular Norwegian families with school aged children 'decide' what it means to be a child in their family. Obviously this is not a matter which families decide independently, since family life is itself structured by the many material and cultural forces which define the general features of childhood in contemporary Norway. But, as I shall show, to some extent the shaping of particular childhoods *is* the family's task, particularly in relation to ideas of age and conceptions of dependence. It is the organization of daily life, the dividing up of tasks between family members, and the laying down of rules of conduct that implicitly determines what it means to be a child.

The ways in which the family shapes the content of childhood are both subtle and varied but, in general, it can be argued, it is through the interaction of parents and children that its form most clearly emerges. This takes place through both verbal and nonverbal exchanges, through direct interaction as well as the establishment of rules, or the adopting of positions about, for example, doing (or not doing) the dishes. In this paper, I use the term 'negotiate' to cover all these different kinds of utterances and communications. The negotiating partners of greatest interest here are children and their parents.

Negotiations about what childhood means in any particular family may take place on many different levels. At one level, the family members may negotiate (both verbally and nonverbally) about specific practical matters: how long the children can manage on their own during the day or how much the children should participate in household tasks. These discussions take place explicitly and information can be obtained about such issues by talking to parents and children directly. They can be asked to detail the ways in which decisions are reached about the organization of everyday domestic life. In this instance it is crucial to pay special attention to the position of children and to try to discover what aims and strategies children have, or have not, in the negotiating process.

At another level, however, family members negotiate the meaning of childhood more abstractly through reference to conceptions of 'age' and age-related activities. Discussions of this kind do seldom take place explicitly. Children and parents may make statements about, for example, what rights and duties can be expected from a 10-year-old. Mostly, however, such negotiations about age take place implicitly and to gain access to this kind of knowledge about the meaning of childhood I have had to read between the lines of the more explicit discussions. I have had to grasp what has been inferred about the organization of everyday activities in order to get a hold on the metadiscussion which goes on between parents and their children about what childhood should be like and about the meanings attached to 'age'.

The two negotiating parties do not of course have the same social rank. Parents have authority and power to punish and reward their children. Children do not have the corresponding means at their disposal. But by using the term 'negotiate' I wish to emphasize the fact that although in many ways children's position is a weak one, they do not passively adapt themselves to what their elders say and do. In everyday life, as I shall show, children have and make use of a considerable freedom of action. They are in a position to influence the outcome of the negotiating process in directions which they perceive to be favourable to themselves.

Such an approach may seem to indicate that the negotiation process which takes place within the family *precedes* perceptions of age. However, no causal relationship is intended. Rather I wish to emphasize its dialectical nature. For parents, their conceptions of what age means set the limits within which they permit negotiations to take place; these limits are therefore expressive of those conceptions. But, through the very process of negotiating, these 'prior' conceptions of age may be modified and the limits altered. Conceptually, children may therefore 'grow' or 'shrink' in age as negotiations take place. In much the same way children's own conceptions of age are subject to change over time in and through the negotiating process.

Data and Methods

This article is based on several studies conducted during the last ten years, all of them concerning the everyday life of Norwegian children; especially the kind of work they are engaged in, inside and outside their household. My point of departure in the first of these studies, (a field study in a fishing community in the northern part of Norway), was an observation previously unknown to me, namely that children of school-age were part of the local labour force (Solberg, 1979). Since the 'discovery' that children worked was done in a rather special local framework, I asked myself if I had been studying a niche, a throwback from the past. Did work also belong to modern childhood? To get an answer to this question, the next study concerned the extent and distribution of different kinds of work, both work in the market and outside of it. 800 schoolchildren (aged 10–12 years) from all over the country filled in a questionnaire covering eighty specifically definable tasks, from making sandwiches for school to feeding calves (Solberg and Vestby, 1987). In the third study the definition of work was extended to include also what may be called 'invisible' work: for example negotiations about managing singlehandedly or sharing work (Wadel, 1973; 1984). In this study, named the Family Study, qualitative interviews were used to collect data on everyday routines in ten families living in two different parts of Oslo (Solberg and Danielsen, 1988). Mothers, fathers and children (12 years of age) were interviewed separately.

I have seen children's work as a topic of interest in itself. Since the work of children in western modernized societies has been almost totally neglected in both social science and public debate, my studies have led to 'discoveries' of something unknown. My interest in children's work has, however, also had another justification. Working in my own culture and by and large sharing the same world views as my informants, getting the necessary distance to be reflexive can be problematic. In this respect it was useful to approach the subject of childhood in an unusual way. In Norway, as in many other western industrialized cultures, the idea of combining children and work is relatively unusual. Concepts of work are more usually discussed in relation to concepts of adulthood, while concepts of childhood traditionally have belonged to the realms of play and socialization. Studying children and their work allows me, as I shall show, to break out of the traditional concept of what children are, what children can do and what 'age' itself means.

The Framing of Contemporary Norwegian Childhood

Before turning to the analysis of family negotiations it may be useful to pay some attention to the frames within which this interaction takes place. Of special interest to us here is the increasing participation of women in the labour force. The increase has taken place during the last decade in Norway as well as in most western industrialized societies (Frønes, Jensen and Solberg, 1990). This has changed the role of women in household management and, as we shall see, has created new possibilities for the role of children. Since 1972 the amount of Norwegian women in the workforce has increased from about 50 to 70 per cent (Moen, 1987). A large proportion of these women work part-time. But during the 1980s the proportion of women working less than twenty hours a week has decreased, from one-third in 1980 to one-fourth in 1987. Indeed, 50 per cent of employed women are now working thirty-five hours or more per week. There is therefore a growing share of mothers in the female labour force and it seems that the age of their children has but a small effect on employment rates. For example, about 80 per cent of women whose youngest child was aged between 7 and 11 years, were employed. The number of full-time housewives has decreased correspondingly; in the age group 25–54 years the percentage fell from about 45 per cent in 1972 to 15 per cent in 1986.

Even though studies of domestic labour sharing prove that mothers remain the main contributors and thus may still be termed housewives, the amount of time they actually spend at home has decreased (NOS A 692, 1975; NOS B 378, 1983). Until the late 1970s the usual term used in Norway for a full-time housewife, '*hjemmeværende husmor*', was, directly translated, a 'homestaying housewife'. Today this term has an antiquated ring, since most houses of families with older children remain empty of adults for much of the day. The increase in female labour force participation has not, however, been followed by an increase in daily school length for children. In fact the opposite seems to have happened.[1] For children aged 10–12 years, time spent in school in

Norway is currently between four and six hours a day, and daycare facilities for school children arranged by the authorities are almost nonexistent.

This situation constitutes an important background for political claims for better day-care facilities and extended schooldays on behalf of the youngest schoolchildren, as well as for shortening the daily working hours of adults, so that parents' and children's time schedules can be more synchronized. The number of families involving adults outside the family for daycare help with children decreases according to the age of the child. Only 15 per cent of children aged 7–9 years old have any daycare arrangement after the schoolday is over and, for children of 8–9 years old the percentage is about 10. Approximately 30 per cent of the children aged 7–9 with both parents working full time are cared for regularly by others (SA 53, 1984). From the age of 10 years old probably very few Norwegian families have adult daycare assistance.

From these figures we cannot draw conclusions about the welfare of the children involved or how parents feel about leaving their children. We have some clues, however, indicating that the picture given by the statistics not only reflects how the families arrange their everyday life, but also to some extent what they feel to be a decent way of arranging it. Some qualitative studies show that the question of children's independence (here concerning how long children can manage on their own during the day) has been an important negotiating topic in the families during the first years of school. At the age of 10 years, however, this question seems to have come to a solution in most families. The parents in the Family Study reported that they were quite content with their children being without adult supervision and felt their children could handle the situation very well (Solberg and Danielsen, 1988). The children themselves seem to have been rather active in negotiating their own independence in this area by gradually making less use of the daycare that was arranged for them by their parents. Ongoing research about the everyday life of children in the first schoolyears show that they both want to and are able to take care of themselves for longer and longer periods (Guldbrandsen, 1989).

Compared to other countries, the Norwegian attitude to children may appear indifferent and sloppy. Taking Britain as a contrast, people in general would conceive 10 years as a rather young age for children to be left alone (Editorial comment). A strong argument against the Norwegian pattern would be that being alone at such an age may involve many dangers. But the two countries differ, for example, in the degree of urbanization: compared to central parts of Britain, Norway can be seen as a collection of villages. I do not wish to elaborate this point here but would, instead, emphasize the different conceptions of childhood reflected in these contrasting views.

The general conception of school children as being able to spend some time without adult supervision is not a new one in Norwegian society, and should not be too closely connected to the increase in women's labour force participation. It is deeply rooted in Norwegian culture that children, when not busy with duties like school work and household work, should be outdoors playing with their friends (Frønes, 1989). Although the housewives of the 1950s and 60s were accessible to their children since they stayed in the home, this does not mean that mothers and their children necessarily spent much time together. Rather it seems that a large part of children's lives in the previous generation took place out of sight of their mothers, as it does today (Lian, Solberg and Vestby, 1989). What has happened is that children and mothers have changed places: the children have invaded the home as the mothers have invaded the labour market. It can be seen as a lucky coincidence that homes became vacant for much of the day at the same time as children's outside playgrounds became less attractive or even disappeared due to increased urbanization.

Children's Role in the Division of Labour at Home

As suggested above, the changed female role has resulted in changes in household management. Women spend less time at home and, consequently, have less time left for housework. But they still bear the main responsibility, carrying out four times as much housework as men (SA 51, 1983). However, this picture of the division of labour within the home derived from Norwegian official statistics, which shows only the adult contribution, is rather incomplete. The result from our questionnaire study of children's work shows that in Norwegian families with children, the household work is not shared only between the parents (Solberg and Vestby, 1987; Solberg, 1987). Our material does not offer the possibility of a direct comparison between adults and children, as we lack information about the amount of domestic work carried out by the parents of 'our' children. Applying the results of the Norwegian Time Budget Study (NOS A 692, 1975; NOS B 378, 1983) however, may give us a picture of the working position of the two generations which can be informative for our discussion of negotiations in the family set out below.[2]

The proportions of children and adults having carried out various household activities during a given day are found to be surprisingly

Anne Solberg

Table 6.1 The proportions of children and adults having carried out housework during a given day (per cent)

	Children	Adults
Preparing food	71	63
Washing dishes	38	52
Vacuum/cleaning	49	51

Source: Solberg and Vestby (1987)

Table 6.2 Time spent on housework by children and adults (hours per week)

	Children	Adults
Food making	1.8	4.2
Washing dishes	0.9	2.1
Vacuum/cleaning	2.7	4.2
Total	5.4	10.5

Source: Solberg and Vestby (1987)

similar (Table 6.1). The divergence is greater in the amount of time spent (Table 6.2). Still the figures show clearly that children of 10–12 years of age are partners in dividing up the housework. In families with several children of 'working' age, the total work time spent by children may be considerable. Another qualification of children strengthens their position even further. Their extensive presence at home makes them available for performing tasks which do not necessarily need high time investments, but have to be done at special points in time. School children expand the 'opening hours' of the home, being there to take phone messages and to let in the plumber (Shangar-Handelman and Belkin, 1984). They may put the potatoes on to boil or pick up a younger brother or sister from the neighbouring daycare centre. In the tight time schedule of a modern family, with both parents working outside the home, these timebound contributions are particularly appreciated.

Analyzing the gender differences demonstrates that the traditional division of labour between men and women also applies for children. The distinction is, however, markedly less among children than among adults, which indicates that there is no automatic transfer of sex-related roles from adults to children (Tables 6.3 and 6.4). Women contribute the most, but the children's contribution is significant, especially the daughters'.

Getting men to take over a larger share of domestic work has been considered of paramount importance in offering women the opportunity to increase their participation in the labour force. The feminist discussion about the division of domestic labour is based upon the

132

Table 6.3 The proportions of women, girls, boys and men having carried out housework during a given day (per cent)

	Women	Girls	Boys	Men
Food making	90	75	66	43
Washing dishes	78	45	30	30
Vacuum/cleaning	82	53	46	30

Source: Solberg and Vestby (1987)

Table 6.4 Time spent on housework by women, girls, boys and men (hours per week)

	Women	Girls	Boys	Men
Food making	7.7	1.9	1.6	1.4
Washing dishes	4.2	1.0	0.7	0.7
Vacuum/cleaning	7.0	3.3	2.0	1.4
Total	18.9	6.2	4.3	3.5

Source: Solberg and Vestby (1987)

assumption that the husband is his wife's sole collaborator. The results above, however, indicate that older children, and particularly the girls, may be more important collaborators with their mothers than are the fathers. This is substantiated by the fact that children to some degree adjust themselves to the occupational role of their mothers. Children of women in full time employment did more housework than did the children of part-timers or full-time housewives. The amount of work carried out by men is not correspondingly influenced by the job situation of the women.

Changes in adult time use on housework from 1971–72 to 1980–81 show that women's time used on housework has decreased, without any corresponding increase by men (NOS A 692, 1975; NOS B 378, 1983). It is supposed that a simplification in the way the house is managed has been going on, possibly combined with a lowering of standards (Grønmo and Lingsom, 1982). My own suggestion, not necessarily in opposition to the previous one, is that children during this period have increased their contribution. That the children's contribution to household work to some extent complements the contribution of their mothers supports this assumption.

Does Working Make You 'Grow'?

The figures referred to above, placing children in the division of labour at home, show that children's capacity to work is large. Withholding it

Anne Solberg

Figure 6.1   Shows relationship between amount of domestic work carried out by children and amount of time spent by parents at home

		Amount of domestic work carried out by children	
		Large	Small
	Large	Carl Carlsen	Bente Brun
Amount of parental time in the home			
	Small	Anne Andersen	No Cases

could obviously, in some families, have negative consequences for the running of the household in general and for the mother's situation in particular. This indicates a certain negotiating power among children, but how is this possible strength perceived by parents and children themselves? What is the connection between the working role of the child and the role of the child at large? Does contributing to the household work increase the child's independence and autonomy in general? Does the child 'grow' while working? And, on the contrary, does the nonworking child remain 'little'? The family study indicates a connection between work and autonomy (Solberg and Danielsen, 1988). There are instances, however, where children do a lot of work but are still perceived as 'small' by their parents and themselves. The probability of children having an autonomous position in the family seems to be greater if they not only do a lot of work at home, but also if they are alone in the house a lot of the time and do much of the work without their parents present.

A four cell table may give a simplified picture of this. A large amount of work combined with parents seldom at home is associated with high independence; while small amount of work combined with parents often at home is associated with a lower degree of independence. There are, however, positions in between: large amount of work combined with parents often at home and small amount of work combined with parents not often at home. In the following I will illustrate three of these positions, giving voice to the children themselves — see Figure 6.1 — but the fourth alternative (small amount of work combined with parents seldom at home) is not exemplified since empirical cases are lacking.

In the examples which follow, Anne Andersen illustrates the first position. She regards her role in the family as being to a large extent the same, in principle, as that of her parents. For her the very fact of belonging to a family implies rather extensive obligations and rights.

Bente, on the other hand, looks upon her role in the family as unique in relation to the adults. Obligations and rights are to a large degree age specific. In the Brun family the role of the child is regarded very much as a recipient's role. The third example illustrates the point that there is no causal relationship between children's participation in work and their autonomy in the family. Although Carl's contribution to the housework is significant this does not seem to help him 'grow' in the Carlsen family.[3]

The Andersen family is the one in our sample which has made the greatest effort to practice equal rights and duties for adults and children. Like her mother, father and older sister, Anne decides how to spend her own time and takes on a quarter of the housework. She cleans the whole house every fourth week, and prepares the family dinner twice a week. Anne regards this equality between the sexes and ages as both practical and reasonable. It is a matter of course to Anne that each member of the family prepares his or her own sandwiches to take to school or to work. She has done this ever since she started school. In another family Anne knows, the mother makes the sandwiches for the whole family, even for the father, who is 38 years old. Anne thinks this is ridiculous. If she forgets to make her sandwiches one day, she is the one to suffer. This is no more than reasonable, in her opinion. She also thinks that it is obvious that all four should share the housework. No-one in her home likes cleaning the house, so it is only fair to share the burden as equally as possible.

Anne likes to concentrate the work. It is better to make a concentrated effort than to carry out small tasks all the time. The whole house is cleaned every Saturday. When Anne has taken her turn, it is good to think that there is a whole month before the next time. Anne decides herself how to do the work. She cannot remember ever having been criticized for not cleaning the house properly. However, for a period she did get complaints about her dinners. This was because she made the same meal every time her turn came round. Now she tries to make her dinners more varied.

It is important to Anne that the rest of the family notice what she does in the home. When she has prepared the dinner, she likes to receive praise and it irritates her if the others are late. The Andersen family has agreed to a system of rewards, with which Anne is very satisfied. The children have an opportunity to receive more money from their parents than their fixed monthly allowance. Anne's mother and father have a book in which they write 'plus' if there is something which they think deserves extra reward or 'minus' if there is something with which they are dissatisfied. As a rule the book contains mostly 'pluses'. It functions almost like a bank book; Anne and her sister can ask to take out the extra money whenever they want.

The Andersen family has also, to some extent, introduced equal status regarding money. The two girls receive 500 kroner a month to buy clothes and other things they need. This independence is very important to Anne. Before, her mother bought things which Anne did not really like. Now she can buy what she likes herself. Sometimes she asks her mother for advice, but does not always follow it. Anne's mother and father have never criticized what she has bought, which makes her feel proud.

The Brun family is a contrast to the Andersen's. Bente and her brother have very different obligations and rights than their parents. In this family, the housework is a task for an adult, and the adult is the mother. She is not only responsible for most of the housework, she also makes sure that everyone does what they are supposed to do, and at the right time. This has always been the situation for Bente and she takes it as a matter of course.

Bente's breakfast and supper are prepared for her and her sandwiches placed in her satchel before she goes to school. Some of her classmates, who have the same arrangement at home, complain from time to time when they get sandwiches they do not fancy. This is no problem in Bente's case. Her mother knows what she likes and she gets the fillings she wants. She also gets what she likes for dinner. Her mother and father are fond of fish but the children do not like fish, so their mother makes something different for Bente and her brother. The children are used to this special treatment. Bente is also used to being able to fetch clean clothes from the cupboard and to the house being clean and tidy without any effort on her part. Her mother does everything in this respect. But although Bente is used to receiving services from her mother, she is aware of the work this involves. She spends a lot of time together with her mother and knows all about her various duties. She also likes to help, but this is very seldom necessary. Her mother manages everything so well on her own.

There are very few obligations connected to Bente's role in the family, and few rights. Bente does not receive any fixed allowance but gets money whenever she needs it. Her mother is the one who decides about that. It is also her mother who administers the household and this involves deciding about the use of the living space. Bente's mother does not like having Bente's friends in the sitting room. This does not worry Bente. She has no particular wish to play with her friends in the sitting room. They either play outside or go to a club. In one restricted area, Bente has definite obligations and rights. She has her own room which she cleans and keeps tidy. Here she can decide for herself, though admittedly within certain limits set by her mother. Here she can invite her friends, as long as they do not make too much mess. Bente likes listening to music and she knows that her mother likes her to do this with her friends.

Anne stands out as a 'big' 12-year-old. Her family does not give much consideration to age in connection with everyday tasks. Bente gives the impression of being 'little'. In her family, age is a very relevant factor for what tasks each person carries out. Anne seems 'big' because of all the work she does and because she manages her own money. However, her parents' conception of Anne's social age is probably important for how this child role has developed. We can say that Anne works because she is 'big', but becomes 'bigger' as she works. In the same way, we see that Bente seems 'little' because she contributes so little towards the general running of the household. And the creation of this role is connected to her parents' conception of her social age. She contributes little because she is 'little', and confirms this by her 'childish' behaviour.

The third example, the Carlsen family, illustrates that the connection discussed above between social age and work participation is not a necessary one. Carl and his mother share the household duties, but not like the Andersens. Mrs Carlsen is the one is charge of the housework. Carl's only fixed duty is to keep his room tidy. Mother does, however, frequently ask him to run errands to the grocery store, the chemist or the post office. When cleaning the house she usually asks him to do the vacuuming. If he has nothing else to do, Carl likes to be asked, especially when it is about errands and he can use his bicycle. He gets a lot of praise and feels that he is a 'good boy'. But at other times he has entirely different plans, which are disrupted by his mother's requests.

At times Anne and Carl spend approximately the same amount of time on housework in the course of a week but there are important distinctions between the parts each plays in household management. Anne works independently and, although her mother does monitor the results, it is rarely whilst the actual work is in progress. Carl works under the leadership and supervision of his mother. He gives his mother a helping hand and it is his mother who decides when and what he is to do.

The two mothers perceive their 12-year-olds differently: Mrs Andersen regards her daughter as 'older' than Mrs Carlsen regards her son. One cause of this discrepancy in age may be that they offer their two children different degrees of responsibility. On seeing them carry out the responsibility given to them, the mothers' conception of age is further strengthened. In the Andersen family Anne 'grows' through her tasks. Mrs Andersen, seeing the result of her daughter's work — the cleaned floors and cooked meals — sees a responsible subject behind. Carl remains 'little' despite his work, because Mrs Carlsen sees a 'helper' behind it, a person who can manage to do certain well defined tasks but who does not have any responsibility for organizing or completing large tasks.

The cases above illustrate some of the changes which have taken place in the child's social role in the wake of the altered position of women in Norwegian society. It is my contention that the new role of the child (exemplified by Anne) is inextricably linked to the role of the modern woman and that it is a role in which the child is perceived as more equal and more 'grown up' than was the case in the housewife managed family. This is expressed both in the role they play in the division of labour at home and, as we shall now turn to, the ways in which the children take possession of the house.

Children as the New Homestayers

Changes in women's position in the labour force have, as previously mentioned, resulted in family dwellings where no adults are present for much of the day. The 'homestaying' housewives who previously were 'in charge' of the household for the entire day, are now staying outside this arena for extended periods of time. Here I will pay attention to the significance of this change in the women's position for the social age of children. Based on the findings of the Family Study (Solberg and Danielsen, 1988), I will argue that by letting their children manage on their own for periods of the day, parents will probably change their conception of their children, seeing them as more capable and independent than before. The children themselves, on the other hand, seem to have new spaces for action by being left alone, giving them new opportunities to appear able and independent. The family home is largely the children's domain whilst their parents are working. The children are often the last to leave home in the morning and the first to return in the afternoon. In many respects, therefore, one might say that they have taken over the position of 'homestayers' which belonged to the housewives of previous generations.

As already suggested some housework may have been transferred from the women to the children in the wake of the increased female labour force participation. Using the term 'homestayer', however, does not imply seeing the children as small housewives in a broad sense.

What I want to underline is that children have taken possession of the house in the time when it is vacated by the adults. Even if they use some of the time for housework and school homework, the 'homestaying' position gives the children a large amount of self-determination as well as determination over the dwelling. How they make the most of these opportunities will be the topic of this section.

The parents and their children were interviewed separately and naturally made points on different topics. The children told about their own everyday lives, how they organize themselves and who they spend their time with. The parents occupy a relatively limited place in this picture. The parents, on the other hand, emphasized their own efforts in connection with their children, first and foremost their role in upbringing as educators. These stories are not contradictory; rather they reflect different perspectives from which the children's everyday life can be considered: the perspective of the child and of the adult.

In general, parents of these 12-year-olds regarded the present period of family life as being relatively free of problems, compared with the previous phase when their children were small and what they expected of the prospective teenager phase. Many things that earlier required an effort on the parent's part now take place 'by themselves'. For example, they can cope with most of the everyday chores which, as smaller children, they had needed help with; they can take care of their personal hygiene, dress themselves and prepare their own food when hungry. They can also organize the greater part of their everyday lives: they make appointments with their friends and shop for presents when invited to birthday parties; they remember their school assignments and relay messages to parents from the school. They are able to tell the time and to be punctual. The parents praised their children for being so independent and it was easy to gain the impression that much of an adult's work in connection with these children has 'disappeared' compared to the time when they were small. During the interviews with the children, however, another way of expressing it seemed more obvious to me: the work has not disappeared; rather a major part of it has been taken over by the children themselves.

The children who had access to a vacant house often expressed the opinion that they preferred that place to spend their free time with friends after school. The reasons for this seemed to be that being indoors offers scope for a variety of activities. There is ample space to socialize freely with their friends. Besides, the home contains a lot of the equipment which children enjoy using; for example, the tape recorder, television and video recorder, as well as the telephone, are popular mediums of entertainment and interaction. The supply of freely available food is also considered to be another important resource offered by the home.

Some of the children who had experience to compare having an adult in the house during the day with 'ruling' the house by themselves, expressed the opinion that they saw important advantages resulting from the lack of adult supervision. In one family the mother began working from home for a period of time, after having worked for several years outside the home. Her two daughters, aged 12 and 13 years of age, experienced this change as a restriction on their field of activity and found that they had lost something of great value when this possibility ceased to exist. They expressed concern that they were no longer as able to bring friends home, since their mother was disturbed by the noise. Nor did they feel quite as free to prepare the snacks which they liked (for example, milkshakes) but which they knew fell short of their mother's nutritional standards.

At issue here then are questions of control: control of time and space. The house represents an important asset for children in this respect. Knowing the time when mother or father is due home enables the children to prepare to 'hand it over' to them. This sometimes means stopping doing things they know their parents would not appreciate and covering up any traces of these activities before their return. Although the parents felt proud of their independent children, experiencing your own children making it totally clear to you that they do not welcome your company, may be a little difficult to face. One of the fathers, a few days in advance of our interview, wanted to go home an hour earlier than usual in order to be a 'good father'. He was not met by enthusiasm for this, something which made him feel a bit disappointed.

The transmission of tasks from parents to their children implies changes in their respective social roles, but children have also changed the way they perform the 'homestaying role' in the very act of taking it over. This alteration has been achieved through processes of negotiation of a different kind. Discussions about how the children's time after school should be arranged, to make sure the children had a good time without breaking too many family rules, are, in these families, to a large extent a theme of the past. In the initial period of children being alone in the house, the parents aimed at trying to minimize the effects of their absence from the home through endeavouring to transmit their own standards for everyday life to their children. The new homestayers, on the other hand, were eager to get permission and advice from the more experienced: for example, on how to make a cake. For this the telephone was a frequently used channel of communication.

Even if negotiations between children and their parents about these practical matters has gradually decreased in all the families, this does not mean that they have come to a fully negotiated agreement about them. Rather they seem to have a 'working agreement' between them. The parents who feel reasonably assured that their children manage quite well on their own feel content with a low interference in 'internal matters'. The children, on the other hand, are well informed about the rules of the family but their own ways of arranging matters may, nevertheless, be different from the ways their parents do it or would prefer their children to do it. At the age of 12 they are wise enough not to ask for permission too much.

The temporal and spatial distance between the children and their parents enables these different standards to coexist without too much conflict. Both parents and children have an interest in maintaining this distance. Independent mothers need independent children and issues of control and supervision are time-consuming for both. When the standards clash — for example, if the mother insists on rubber boots while the 12-year-old prefers trainers — it takes time to come to a decision. When mother and father are not at home, the children do not need to take part in these kinds of negotiations and may develop their own standards and rhythm of living, following it without too much interruption or intervention.

In negotiating the use of domestic space, children increase their social age. The negotiation of age is, however, hidden since they use the house in ways in which their parents are not aware of. The relatively autonomous life led by many children has had, I would suggest, an impact on many parents' conceptions of their children's age and of their dependency. Parents are pleased to see their children looking after themselves and this has consequences for the role of children in the family beyond the time when children are by themselves in the house. Even though the children may assume a more subordinate role on their parents' return, this role is probably less 'childish' than that of those children whose mothers are full-time housewives. When parents of the new 'homestayers' see their children carry out the responsibilities placed upon them, they experience their children to be 'growing' older socially with respect to their biological 'age'.

Researchers as Negotiators

In this chapter I have shown some of the ways in which research can highlight differences in the social construction of childhood through exploring in detail the meanings which are negotiated within the family about the nature of childhood. In conclusion I want to suggest that the process of research may itself also contribute to the social construction of childhood. Attention should be given to the ways in which this is done.

Much social research denies children any voice at all and is highly adult centred. Official statistics often restrict their information to adult activities or concerns, ignoring children's contributions (see Jens Qvortrup, this volume). The feminist perspective has also done little to challenge the marginalization of children from much social science research. Having women's experiences and activities as their point of departure, children are more often described as the receivers of women's work and attention (see, for example, Oakley, 1974). Feminist research has uncovered the work of women and has, for example, revealed that the amount of housework is extensive when compared to men's work. But while uncovering women's work, women's research has effectively covered up the work of children.

Although the social sciences have reflected public concern about the effect of altered female roles on children, on the family and on women themselves, their involvement in research into these areas has primarily been focused on families with young children. The construction of children here is on being small and dependent, as problems for parents seeking care for them. Alternatively, by focusing on children as a problem in terms of the provision of nursery or day care facilities, attention has been placed on families with young children. Other family phases which might yield alternative constructions of childhood have been neglected and children are generally portrayed as small, weak and dependent. Other accounts of childhood, which are framed by social policy concerns, similarly render children small and helpless. Attention is paid to children as victims of adult misbehaviour, of child abuse within the family or, at the societal level, of the lack of justice to children.

In contrast, there is a growing body of writings about childhood which construct children as capable agents of their own lives and which argue they should be considered as such in the field of sociology (Alanen, 1988; Thorne, 1987). The present article is an answer to this challenge. I make three explicit arguments: children belong to the division of labour at home; they do this to a large extent as the independent collaborators of their mothers; and they take possession of the home for part of the day. In my account children are responsible, independent and 'big'; to some extent they are adultlike.

I know some readers will react negatively to the analysis I have presented, especially to the positive value I implicitly attach to the autonomy and independence of modern children. I am not only arguing that my construction of childhood is true to reality, but that this construction is advantageous for the children who shape and are shaped by it. One type of objection might be political. Some may be afraid that the picture of children given here might be used in public debate as an argument for cutting down, rather than increasing, public expenditure on children and families with children, with the most obvious example being day care facilities after school. Another kind of objection might be inspired more by developmental psychology. According to this view, every child has a right to be a child. This implies that adults have an obligation to protect their children against responsibilities which are too heavy at their stage of maturity. Lastly, a sceptical attitude towards the picture of childhood I have painted may be based on a feeling of being hurt, of adults (especially parents) being given a too peripheral place in children's lives.

It should be a matter of course to social scientists that social reality is conceived differently depending on the position of the actor. My answer to the objections above is that what I have done is to present a picture of children's life as seen from the children's point of view. If this picture looks unfamiliar, it is because most of us are unfamiliar with the world as children perceive it. I shall conclude with a last example. Looking at it from their own point of view, adults sadly describe a home with no adults present as being 'empty'. Coming home with their friends, children are pleased to find it vacated.

Notes

I am grateful to Dag Album for inspiration and support during the work for this article.

1 In Oslo, the daily school hours have decreased during the last decades. A pupil in 1987 spent sixteen hours a week in the first year of school, seventeen hours the next year and so on, up to twenty-seven hours a week in his/her sixth schoolyear. This adds up to 138 'weekly-hours'. In 1959 the sum of weekly hours from first to seventh grade was 156 (Frønes, Jensen and Solberg, 1990).
2 There are of course problems connected to comparing results obtained from two different studies in which different methods of data collection are applied. We cannot tell exactly how much difference the dissimilarity in measuring methods makes but assume it to be small enough for a valid comparison.
3 This paper does not focus specifically on the relationship between gender and the division of labour which is discussed more fully elsewhere (see Solberg and Danielsen, 1988).

Anne Solberg

References

ALANEN, L. (1988) 'Growing up in the modern family: Rethinking socialization, the family and childhood, *Acta Sociologica*, **31**, pp. 53–68.

FRØNES, I. (1989) *Den Norske Barndommen*, Oslo, Cappelen.

FRØNES, I., JENSEN, A. and SOLBERG, A. (1990) *Childhood as a Social Phenomenon: Implications for Future Social Policy*, Vienna, Eurosocial Report no. 36/1.

GRØNMO, S. and LINGSOM, S. (1982) Sexual Differences in Household Work: Patterns of Time Use Change in Norway, Paper presented at the 10th World Congress of Sociology, Mexico City.

GULDBRANDSEN, M. (1989) Personal communication of research presented at the seminar 'Hverdagslivets pedagogikk', University of Oslo.

LIAN, R., SOLBERG, A. and VESTBY, G.M. (1989) Changes in Children's Everyday Life in the Postwar Period, Unpublished notes from the project, NIBR.

MOEN, B. (1987) *When the Unusual Becomes the Rule: A Brief Survey of Certain Socio-demographic Trends in Norway and Their Consequences*, Oslo, Central Bureau of Statistics.

NOS A 692 (1975) *Norwegian Official Statistics, The Time Budget Survey 1971–72*, Oslo, Central Bureau of Statistics.

NOS B 378 (1983) *Norwegian Official Statistics, The Time Budget Survey 1980–1*, Oslo, Central Bureau of Statistics.

OAKLEY, A. (1974) *The Sociology of Housework*, New York, Pantheon Books.

SA 51 (1983) *Statistical Analysis, Social Survey*, Oslo, Central Bureau of Statistics.

SA 53 (1984) *Statistical Analysis, Children's Level of Living*, Oslo, Central Bureau of Statistics.

SHANGAR-HANDELMAN, L. and BELKIN, R. (1984) 'They won't stay home forever; Patterns of home space allocation', *Urban Anthropology*, **13**, 1, pp. 117–144.

SOLBERG, A. (1979) 'Vilkàr for barnearbeid', *Tidsskrift for Samfunnsforskning*, **20**, pp. 494–508.

SOLBERG, A. (1987) 'Barn arbeider, hvorfor ser vi det ikke?', *Sosiologi Idag*, **1**, pp. 25–39. (Based on an article, 'The working life of children', Report No. 15, pp. 1069–78, Trondheim, Norwegian Centre of Child Research.

SOLBERG, A. and DANIEISEN, K. (1988) 'Dagliglivets organisering i barnefamilier', *NIBR-Report*, **22**.

SOLBERG, A. and VESTBY, G.M. (1987) 'Barns arbeidsliv', *NIBR-Report*, **3**.

THORNE, B. (1987) 'Revisioning women and social change: Where are the children?' *Gender and Society*, **1**, 1, pp. 85–109.

WADEL, C. (1973) *Now, Whose Fault Is That?: The Struggle for Self-esteem in the Face of Chronic Unemployment*, Toronto, Toronto University Press.

WADEL, C. (1984) *Det Skjulte Arbeid*, Oslo, Universitetsforlaget.

Chapter 7

Street Children:
Deconstructing a Construct

Benno Glauser

Introduction

The subject matter for this chapter arose from what seemed to be just a practical problem of my ongoing research into 'children of the street' in Asunción, the capital city of Paraguay. The need to know more about the situation, characteristics, feelings and problems in the everyday life of street children arose from an increasing urge to take action on their behalf. The number of street children in Asunción had started to grow noticeably in the early 1980s and, in 1983, my wife and I and several friends began our research, which set the base for an educational programme aimed at street children. Starting in 1985 this still continues.[1] Our research also led to the publication of a book which dealt mainly with children working in the streets who live with their families (Espinola, Glauser *et al.*, 1987). Later difficulties in the educational programme, particularly with those children who also live rather than just work in the streets, made a second phase of research centred on their specificities necessary. Within the framework, then, of a personal, rather informal research project I shall piece together, from practical as well as theoretical sources, the current state of knowledge about street children drawing on the wide range of action which exists — be it practical grassroot level work with street children, advocacy work on their behalf or the definition of global policies in response to the problem which their existence raises.

'Children of the street' is the term which grassroots level social workers, non-governmental organizations, international agencies like UNICEF and also social researchers use when, within the broader category of 'street children', they want to refer to children who live on the street, as opposed to ones who work on the street but return home after work. Obviously in any social research a clear definition of the subject is necessary and, in my own case, I had intended that the definition should allow a clear separation between the subject group and the rest of the 'street children'. Moreover, as my research was to deal with reality rather than second-hand accounts about children of the street, the definition had to enable me to distinguish between them and the rest when I encountered them in everyday life. I needed, therefore, to be able to state their differentiating characteristics. This is where the problems began.

A Problem with Reality

While I seemed to know intuitively which street children were, and which were not, 'children of the street' when meeting them, in the course of my daily work I found myself having difficulties explaining the generation of the categories. Was this a general problem of the concept of 'children of the street', or was it just to do with the way I had understood and applied it? Everyday observation continued to confront me with children in new and different situations and, after coming to terms with my anger about my apparent incapacity to apply what had seemed to be a clear definition, I began to appreciate the creative side of my confusion. I became curious about what else I might come across.

In the first place, I felt obliged to question what the standard concepts which I had tried to use really refer to. 'Street children' is the generic term used to refer to a group of children with a special relationship to the street. The frequency of its use seems to suggest that such a group exists as a homogenous phenomenon in reality. Often, however, two differentiating subcategories are used to divide the group into 'children in the street' and 'children of the street'. The former refers to children who just use the street as their workplace, and the latter to children who also live in the street. Although the two categories do have the term 'street' in common, the street also acts as a differentiating element between them. This differentiation is made according to the type of relationship which exists between 'the child' and 'the street' as well as between 'the child' and 'his/her family'. 'Living at home with one's family and working in the street' is opposed to 'living in the street away from one's family', suggesting a basic, but implicit, dichotomy between 'home' and/or 'family' and 'street'. This differentiation contains many hidden assumptions about the meaning attached to the idea of 'the family', 'the child', 'the home' and 'the street' which, as I argue below, must be unpacked and explored to help overcome conceptual problems. Indeed, it was precisely some of these assumptions which had, as I shall show, led to difficulties with my research. To whom, amongst the children I met on the streets of Asunción, did the concepts children 'in' and 'of' the street apply?

First, there are many children whose situation does not fit easily into either category. For example, there are the children who spend the night on the street for reasons of convenience related to their jobs: there may be less competition and better business at night. For example, some of the boys who shine shoes at the central bus station of Asunción prefer working at night as long distance buses, leaving around midnight, means that an important number of passengers are waiting there during the early evening. Many of these may be potential customers. Also there is considerably less competition and therefore better business for the shoe shiners at night as there are fewer of them, since many parents do not allow their children out to work late at night. For others there are no late bus connections home or no early connections from home. Some of these children work all night whilst others get a few hours sleep wherever they can; some return home in the morning to get some sleep; others only go home every two or three days, spending the other nights together with the children who do not go home on any regular basis at all.

Some stay in the street during the week and go back home for the weekend; others do it the other way around; and still others stay on the streets for the warm nights of the summers, but tend to go home again when the nights get cooler. During the Paraguayan summer, November to March, high night temperatures not only make it easy but almost necessary to sleep outside whilst winter brings sudden periods of cold weather. Accordingly, the number of children who stay away from home at night and sleep in the streets increases in summer and decreases again in winter. There is, therefore, a great variety in the ways in which these children make use of the street. Whilst there is no doubt that many of these children are at risk of staying away from home for good, many others have led this way of life for long periods without their family ties loosening. At the start of my work I had thought of all those children described above as belonging to the category 'children in the street', as they in principle lived at home, but it soon became clear to me that this was inadequate for they share much of the life of the 'children of the street'. They spend the nights anywhere in the streets, stay up late, get little sleep, are exposed to police abuses and maltreatment and are sometimes considered by passersby as abandoned, homeless, tramps, thieves or juvenile delinquents. On the other hand some of the 'children of the street' would also spend periods of time back home. I was therefore left asking: from what point on did a child become 'of the street' rather than just 'in the street'?

The second difficulty arose when I realized that many of those I had been counting as 'children of the street' did not in fact live continuously on the street as is always assumed. They might spend days, weeks and sometimes even months at a time living within institutional homes or shelters, before returning to the street. Were these children still 'children of the street' when they had stayed off the street for six months? Other children might spend weeks or months off the street either with their families or close relatives in an attempt to re-establish themselves. Or they may live with somebody else who takes temporary charge of them out of compassion or for some other reason. Such an example would be that of a car thief who on several occasions during 1988 succeeded in convincing two or three children of the street, who had temporarily established themselves in an institutional shelter, to leave their institution and to travel with him to a town on the Brazilian border. There he gave them shelter and made them take part in car thefts — he needed children as partners as they draw less suspicion and are able to get their hands and bodies into small openings. This 'business partnership' lasted for two or three weeks at a time. Other examples are those of artisans who offer one or more children food and a place to sleep at their house in return for temporary work. Another is the young prostitute Maria, who offered a boy called 'Sucio' (his gang-name which means 'dirty') to live with her in her small rented room. She started to maintain him in exchange for the 14-year-old's affection which was obviously vital to her. Children of the street may also spend shorter or longer terms in jail between periods on the street. The one factor common to them all is that eventually they return to the street.

The third difficulty presented itself when I discovered that there were other children who live on the street, or resort to it in ways comparable to those classified as 'children of the street', but who were, however, generally considered to belong to other, separate parts of our local reality. Among them, for example, is a child prostitute who spends most of her time, including the night, on the street. She does not return home for long periods during which time she sleeps at the bar, where she also helps out, or at a friend's place. Also regarded as not really 'children of the street', despite their comparable lifestyle are the different types of runaway children: runaways from home; child soldiers who have deserted the army[2] and runaways from homes where poor families often place their children as unpaid household help in exchange for bed and board. Within the same group are those children who rather casually, as it appears, decide to stay away from home at some stage. For example, Ignacio and Ramiro are brothers who, up to February 1989, lived with their parents, small peasant farmers, in the countryside about 110 miles from Asunción. From there they would travel together to the capital once a week in order to sell medicinal plants they had brought with them. One day they decided to stay instead of going home. Like most of the runaways (or 'stayaways') they are, as they say, sleeping in the street 'for the time being'. In many cases children like them would return home after some adventurous days and nights in town but some others might stay. Most of these children would not fit the standard image of 'children of the street' employed by international agencies, policy makers and social workers. What amount of time and under what conditions would these children have to live in the streets in order to be considered 'children of the street'?

Having met up with such practical difficulties I turned for help to some of the available writings on the subject: scientific papers, articles and books as well as newspaper reports from different countries and unpublished programme-related policy papers. Here I found, instead of clarification, parallel sets of confusion (Yopo, 1989). A great number of sources, even though they may use subcategories like children 'in' and 'of' the street, do not go into further and more exact definitions and continue to refer to both as 'street children' (UNICEF, 1986: 15–16). Apart from a resulting lack of precision when talking about social reality, this absence of well defined differences between subcategories has consequences for people's views of the problem. Its magnitude can be seen in the wild numbers given for street children with no clear indication of exactly which kinds of children were counted. Another consequence is the fact that some of the terms applied to some of the street children — like the term 'abandoned children' — extend themselves to the totality of street children and ends up giving a distorted and misleading image of the reality of street children (Ennew, 1986).

Some authors are conscious that there is a problem with concepts and definitions, but do not make any alternative proposals (Anti-Slavery Society, 1985: 4; Goode, 1987). Others do attempt new definitions, but even the more useful of these lack precision and can add to the confusion when applied in practice (UNICEF, 1986). For example, UNICEF mentions a category: 'children without family contact'. 'It includes orphans, runaways, refugees and displaced persons.' It states that 'abandonment is deeply felt by the child' and concludes that 'street children in this situation might be described as being "children of the street"' (*ibid*: 15). Although this definition is open to be applied to different types of street children, its defining terms lack precision ('deeply felt abandonment') or do not apply in reality (most children of the street do maintain family contacts.). The same must be said of the definition given by the INTER-NGO programme: 'street children are those for whom the street . . . more than their family has become their real home, a situation in which there is no protection, supervision or direction from responsible adults' (*ibid*: 15). There are authors who, instead of using definitions, resort to descriptions, either of different types or situations of street children, or who refer to the entire subject-universe as a 'continuum' ranging from the child who just works for a few hours a day on the street to the one living there permanently and to the juvenile delinquent (Goode, 1987). Still others simply refer to the subject by using the popular names which are common knowledge in their given local community without any further explanation.

Another problem is that the same terms are used internationally even though definitions and circumstances may vary from one local community, country or continent to another and that they may be using different terms of reference. Possibly as a function of 'different social attitudes to gender roles', African approaches focus differently and more emphatically on the presence and role of girls within the street children context, than has been traditionally the case in Latin America (Anti-Slavery Society, 1985: 14). Western industrial countries, on the other hand, refer to the problem in terms of 'runaways', 'young homeless' or 'juvenile street gangs' (*ibid*). Indian cities, finally, have whole families living in the street as is beginning to occur in Brazilian cities too: their children are also to be considered 'children of the street', although in a way rather different from that discussed so far.

My practical difficulties had therefore led me to discover that the terms and concepts used about street children were not only imprecise but also that they lacked operational value. The same terms were used in different parts of the world to refer to very different types and situations of children. This means that when talking about street children we may do so without having a clear idea about what we are talking and, in addition, we take the risk of mutual misunderstanding. In spite of this the terms and concepts mentioned above seen to have a surprisingly general acceptance. Clearly from a methodological and scientific point of view this is of course unacceptable. But it is even less acceptable that international organizations, policy makers, social institutions and individuals who feel entitled to intervene in the lives of children with problems, do so on the basis of obviously unclear and arbitrary knowledge about the reality of these children's lives. The result of this may, very probably, be harmful to children: it is obvious, for example, that a child with serious problems might be deprived of vital institutional care, protection and help only because s/he is conceptually left out of the definition which labels children deserving of care within a given society. Being let undefined or even nameless may well mean being invisible to society.

The Need to Deconstruct

People do not form the concepts which they use but rather apply those currently hegemonic within their society. Those with social power (which may have a variety of sources) can therefore define the reality of others by shaping and constraining the ways in which it is possible to talk and think about issues in society. This does not mean that hegemony flows automatically to the politically and socially powerful. It is always contingent upon the balance of forces in an ideological struggle. Nevertheless some individuals and groups have the power to make themselves heard whilst others find this more difficult. Very little, for example, has been heard about street children from the 'popular' classes which form the majority of the population in Third World societies. Equally there is very little knowledge about the way the children who are themselves directly affected by serious problems of life and survival think about their situation. The dominant ways of speaking about street children are discourses 'about others'; about lives, problems and situations which are not lived or shared but merely observed externally by the speaking subjects.

Thus the importance of 'deconstructing' lies in trying to find out what lies behind and at the origin of the concepts currently dominant. It means trying to answer questions such as: to what do the terms used refer; how were they generated; in response to what problems and issues did they arise; and whose interests and needs do they serve? If we fail to deconstruct concepts, especially dominant ones, then we risk being determined by and dependent upon others. In this sense deconstruction is necessary not simply in the quest for better knowledge. It is also necessary as a liberation from the influence and reach of unwanted power. In the Third World this is especially important because present life-threatening dependencies express themselves and act through the concepts and discourses which define 'reality'.

An Attempt to Deconstruct 'Street Children'

When the term 'street children' is used, the first aspect which draws our attention is the conjunction between 'street' and 'children'. It would seem therefore that a concept like 'street children' becomes necessary in response to the desire to speak about children who fall outside the frame of what is considered 'normal'. As long as children just circulate or play in the streets, or use them in other ways also considered 'normal', there is no need for a new category. After all, children can also be found using fields, lofts and gardens without there being any apparent need to coin terms such as 'field children', 'loft children' or 'garden children'. The need for a name seems to arise therefore when the situation departs from current social norms and, with respect to street children, two aspects must be distinguished. In the first place, concern arises from the fact that their situation is considered inadequate in their own interests and second, concern responds to this inadequacy in regard to the interests of society at large.

Street children's own interests are at stake, for example, when the use they make of the street puts them in danger. This in fact applies to most situations they find themselves in when working or living in the streets. The children who work as windshield washers in Asunción, amidst queues of heavy traffic waiting at traffic lights, are in an obviously dangerous situation, as are those who sleep in markets or on doorsteps unprotected from all kinds of possible abuses. Equally, the fact that they work or live without being accompanied by their parents is also viewed as inadequate and contrary to their interests since the prevailing view in most cultures is that a child ought to grow up with his or her natal family, i.e., in the presence of at least one of his/her parents. Even when physically separated from the family, a child is supposed to be under the supervision and protection of a responsible adult or group of adults. The term 'street children', then, seems to point to a group of children who are found outside situations considered adequate to them, and the coining of the term responds to the need to take action on their behalf.

However, their existence is also a concern in the interests of the society. The use street children make of the street differs from what is normal, usual and acceptable: instead of using the street as a channel through which one circulates in order to get from one point to another, they stay on the street to work, eat, sleep and roam about. This use of the street contradicts not only dominant ideas about situations suitable for children to grow up in, but also ideas about the purpose of the street or any public space seen from the point of view of adult and class needs and uses as Ward (1977) has shown. Furthermore they are usually perceived as a physical menace, as they roam the shopping districts and the residential neighbourhoods of towns, either by themselves or in gangs. Their behaviour, especially the violence and aggressiveness of the ones living in the streets and the fact that many of them survive by any means — ranging from petty theft to assaults — is obviously seen as a danger by the public who fear for their integrity, tranquility, security and property. The concern with street children in particular seems to arise, therefore, not only because they may suffer, be at risk or be on the edge of survival but, I would suggest, because they disrupt the tranquility, stability and normality of society. Their behaviour on the street may seem aggressive on an individual level but their very existence 'in the open' and visible to everybody, outside what is thought of as normal, questions social and cultural patterns. This is ultimately what is at issue. Street children represent deviations from normal standards and it is they who, in a way which cannot be ignored, confront and touch society's dominant sector's views and lives and interfere or threaten to interfere with its major interests. It becomes clear, therefore, that society as such has a practical need to conceptualize this phenomenon in order to both express public concern and take action.

Even though we might be inclined to think that the dominant sector's prevailing concern aims not at the preservation of its own interests but at that of the children, evidence expressed in the mass media suggests the contrary: there is pressure to see street children disappear from the streets, but little concern about where they should go to or what could happen to them afterwards.[3] The fact that societies have normally found no need to distinguish between different subcategories of street children and are content to use an unclear and ambiguous concept also leads to the suspicion that their main concern did not start with the children themselves. (If it were otherwise surely they would have been analyzed according to the complexity and variety of their situations?) On the contrary, I would argue that they were concerned with the public space involved, 'the street', as well as with the daily visible presence of deviant children, permanent and sometimes harassing reminders that all is not normal.

The strong relationship between the concept of street children and the normative interests and concerns of society becomes even clearer when we consider the arbitrary way in which children deserving care, like street children, are being selected and earmarked for priority action, whilst other children, also deserving care, are unconsciously or not left aside. There are, for example, many children who live in conditions similar to those of street children but who do not receive the same amount of attention. It would seem that it is not enough for a child to be away from his or her natal family, without the supervision and support thought necessary for the transition to adulthood, or to be living, working and sleeping on the street. Those children or categories of children who are ignored (or for whom much less concern is shown) are those whose social situation does not contravene ideas of normality, who are not as visible as street children or who do not impinge uncomfortably on sections of the population. Indeed sometimes the very opposite is the case: children working as unpaid domestic servants or child prostitutes assure the needs and comforts of adults, and society may have little interest in thinking about them in terms of a concern deserving category. In addition to this, they may be hidden, as is the case of child soldiers, children working in factories or children living in permanent institutional care. It is, therefore, the concern not for children's but society's needs which has given importance to the concept and to the category of 'street children' and, as the problem they constitute grows in scale, has caused them to become the focus for a growing amount of theoretical and practical attention, ranging from research, representations of their situation in mass media, to national and international policy and projects.

So far, I have dealt with the role the concept of 'street children' plays at the level of society as seen through public opinion, the way society is represented or reflects itself in mass media and, to some extent, in the expressions of a given community. In what follows I shall now explore the way the concept has been taken up by grassroot level social workers, project activists and policy makers (experts of international organizations etc.). I shall not, however, refer to politicians or governmental authorities, as I consider that they tend to follow the ways the two above mentioned groups conceptualize phenomena like 'street children.'

Social workers and project activists, who, at least in Latin America, include also the numerous middle- and upper-class ladies' charity commissions, have increasingly taken over societal concern for street children and implemented action on their behalf. While many of their actions provide for *individual* street children those human bonds of recognition and affection that they so badly lack, I would nevertheless suggest that they attend the activists' own interests in the first place. They tend to benefit the activist's personal goals, pretensions, and satisfactions, which are often related to the need to purge a sense of social guilt or to find a field of application of 'good ideas' about what should be done for the needy, more than they benefit the children they work with. For this, 'street children' are a particularly handy target as they are permanently present as a visible issue of concern which does not seem to need any further legitimation. Also, because they are an urban phenomenon, they are within easy reach of the activists, most of whom live in the cities. Finally, the 'street children's' concrete, tangible problems appeal to people's needs to be protective and encourages an easier type of action on symptoms rather than on the deeper problems and causes. In this way, 'street children' help to fulfil an urge to help without requiring a deeper involvement in political action or a more profound analysis of social conditions. This is why there is hardly any questioning, at this level, of the way the target category of action has been conceptualized, selected and delimited with regard to others.[4]

For the same reason, the undifferentiated concept of 'street children' has suited and still suits the predominant approaches to the issue taken by project activists and policy makers. Only gradually and fairly recently has there been a tendency to introduce at this level, as opposed to the level of society in general, the distinction between 'children in the street' and 'children of the street'. It is possible that this distinction is the result of a more adequate understanding of the context within which street children work and live but this, in itself, is not necessarily motivated by a desire to respond better to the children's interests. Rather, pragmatic social interests taken up by activists and policy makers may suggest the introduction of the distinction. On the one hand, the growing numbers of 'street children' may oblige agencies to introduce more discriminating criteria for the application of their limited resources and aid. On the other, there may also be an increasing need for different responses to different types of street children, and therefore for an articulation of the differences in subcategories. Indeed, this articulation sustains the activists' work options. For example, when they decided to direct their efforts more towards children working in the streets whose characteristics are such that more effective and successful action can be achieved. Indeed, children working in the streets are easier to handle since they are generally more tranquil and orderly, more inclined to behave well and to submit themselves to methodical work procedures. They are also more willing to be organized into self-sustained groups, an option which represents a growing interest among the more progressive activists. In this sense children living in the street have been in some cases consciously excluded from project action[5] and the questionable notion of 'irretrievable' has been introduced in policy discussions to be applied to some or all of the 'children of the street'.[6]

Policy makers, on the other hand, who are faced with growing numbers of 'children of the street', without being able to propose successful policies of control, direct their attention also to the subcategory of children working in the street. They fit better with the social norms and expectations that everyone should be productive, and there is a growing tendency to legitimate child labour on the streets as an adjustment to the obvious impossibility of its eradication in a context of growing poverty and unemployment for adults.[7] Conversely, the 'children of the street' also risk being increasingly considered as beyond hope or 'lost' by policy makers.

In both cases — grassroot level activists and policy makers — the differentiation does not respond equally to criteria of concern for both categories, but rather to a need to be coherent within the prevailing social framework of norms and to be effective in action, even at the price of segregation, for at least one part of the 'street children' population. Thus it seems that social norms and needs, especially the need to prevent disruption of normality and dominant interests, have a strong bearing and influence on the formation of the concept of 'street children'. In the same way, it is the needs of activists and policy makers which induce and maybe determine the creation of its subcategories whose roots, therefore, are not in the reality of the lives of street children but rather in the social and political responses to them. A reconstruction of the concepts involved may therefore not only make them more applicable to reality but may also contribute to a greater awareness of the influences involved and hence to the possibility of favouring children's needs and interests over others.

An Alternative Reconstruction

Since it was a confrontation with reality that prompted my questioning of exiting concepts, then elements of this social reality would seem to be the essential building blocks for the construction of new and more adequate concepts. Below I list some of the main conclusions — several of which have already been touched on above — which I have drawn from responsive observation during the last six years of working on the streets of Asunción with children:

(a) The 'street' has different meanings for different sections of the urban population. As Ward (1977) has also shown, poor shanty town dwellers and others who lack living space use the street for different purposes than the rest of the urban population.

(b) Children who just work in the street make different use of it than those children who live there. For the latter, more than a channel of circulation and a working place, it is a place where they stay and resort to, a place to build up social relations.

(c) Children living in the street are in an unstable situation, with a tendency to sudden changes. Most of them do not live there permanently and continuously; they try and find a stable way of life in a situation away from the street. Usually, however, they do not succeed.

(d) Growing up with his or her own family is crucial for the social-ization and developmental processes of a child, at least from the perspective of the role of the family in Latin America and maybe in Third World countries in general, which may differ from the way the family's role is now understood in industri-alized societies. Growing up, at least from a certain age on, out-side his or her natal family has serious negative effects for a child. Unlike industrialized societies, Third World societies do not provide formal substitutes for the family's functions but 'abandon' the child to a jungle-like, socially disorganized, aggressive sphere where there is no coherent value system and where he or she finds no clear limits or orientations for his or her actions.

(e) Most children who lose the vital ties with their families do so by force of circumstance which 'drive them away', make them break contact or prompt the family to give up educational efforts. These factors are the result of the combination of a num-ber of conditions and circumstances affecting their lives as well as the life of their families and communities, and range from economic conditions which break up families to the incapac-ity to face new types of crises to which traditional ways of life have no adequate responses.

The model formed by these elements can be visualized in the form of a triangle (see Figure 7.1) divided into an upper and lower realm by an imaginary and mobile line which I call a threshold. The children in the lower realm lead a daily life in close relationship with their natal families. In these circumstances the nearer surroundings of the family home, such as the close neighbourhood and the street in front of their houses, are predominant features in the children's lives and their grow-ing up is likely to be assisted and protected by the proximity of their family. For these children 'the street' is the street in front of their home. As such it is part of their home since, even from a young age, daily life in poor neighbourhoods occurs on the street in front of the home because of the extreme lack of space within the house. 'The street', this time thought of as the streets of the wider neighbourhood or town, may for some of these children also be the public space where they work, either on their own or with their families, and from where they return

Figure 7.1

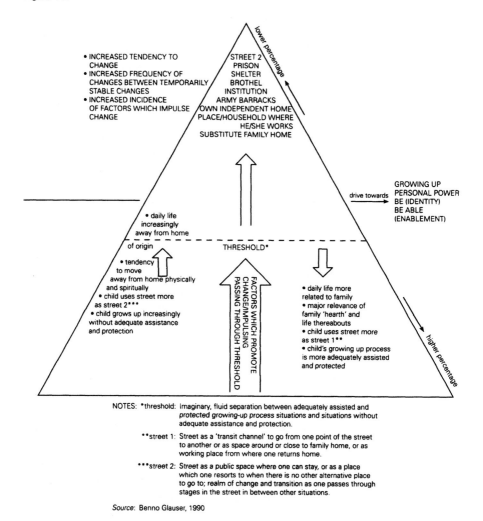

NOTES: *threshold: Imaginary, fluid separation between adequately assisted and
protected growing-up process situations and situations without
adequate assistance and protection.

**street 1: Street as a 'transit channel' to go from one point of the street
to another or as space around or close to family home, or as
working place from where one returns home.

***street 2: Street as a public space where one can stay, or as a place
which one resorts to when there is no other alternative place
to go to; realm of change and transition as one passes through
stages in the street in between other situations.

Source: Benno Glauser, 1990

home. It is also for them a channel through which one goes from one
place in the street to another. Within this lower realm of the triangle are
found most of the children thought of as normal and as growing up
adequately. This group includes most rural children, the majority of
children living in poor urban neighbourhoods, and children who live
and work on the streets with their families. Last but not least it includes
those who live at home but who work in the street — the group who
make up the majority of those referred to as 'street children' in the
conventional terms which have been criticized above.

   In the upper realm of the triangle are the children who, for various reasons, stay away from their families. Their socialization occurs away from the family and in most cases they lack the assistance and protection needed for growing up. For some of these children 'the street' has more the character of a public space where one can also stay. For many of them 'the street' is a place of last resort, when there is literally nowhere else to go, or a transition place used during the shift from one temporary life-style to another. Included in this group are children who grow up in orphanages and similar institutions or who spend periods of time in shelters provided by projects and agencies for street children. In the specific Paraguayan context, it also includes children who have been placed as household helps in other families, child soldiers, child and adolescent prostitutes, children who are or have been in prison, children and adolescents living independently from various activities qualified by society as delinquent or criminal, and runaways.

Children from the upper realm of the triangle are very unlikely to move below the threshold, even though many try to do so by re-establishing themselves with their families. On the other hand, children from the lower portion may cross the threshold into the upper section at some stage, usually being 'driven' upwards through circumstances which result in them abandoning or being given up on by their families. These circumstances may vary from one social context to another but they are usually determined by factors such as the following: by their parents' lack of understanding of the street work situation and their view that the child, when s/he fails to meet their difficult expectations — namely, to be their child but also to work as regularly and responsibly as an adult — is simply disobedient, leading to menaces, blackmailing, physical punishment or even maltreatment of the child; by the fact that the family is confronted with new types of crisis situations for which their culture, which belongs to another time and another setting, does not provide any useful answers; by the physical disintegration of the family and the 'hearth', as economic pressures oblige its members to subordinate family needs and conviviality to whatever work opportunities there are available, even at bad hours or far away; by the physical destruction of a community and its loss of cultural roots; by problems arising from the family's characteristics or history, such as one-parent families or the presence of a step-father; or by a child drifting away from home because more and more time is spent at work in order to contribute to the family's income. Thus we may visualize a spiral up and down movement within the triangle but with a tendency to go upwards. Crossing the threshold seldom occurs because of a sudden, conscious decision but is usually the outcome of a long process during which families, including children, struggle to maintain themselves. Often those involved are not even fully conscious of the direction that events are taking.

A child who crosses the threshold will, in most cases, have moved away from the companionship and care of the family. More often than not s/he does so by opting to live on the street along with other children. In some cases children try and become established with a substitute family (sometimes their kin and sometimes a shelter or an institution) before they stay on the street more continuously. But, basically, crossing the threshold marks the beginning of a life characterized by increasing instability. Most of the children do seek a stable alternative to their family but these are not usually successful. As time goes, by the intervals between stable periods become longer and more frequent. The street becomes the only resort for periods in-between time spent in institutions, prisons, own family's home during unsuccessful attempts to become re-established, or other substitute homes. Socialization, apprenticeship for life and the development of affectionate relationships occur according to the constraints and possibilities of the situations in which the children find themselves. Often these situations set children onto trajectories which may prove to be quite irreversible.[8] Finally, the general lack of stability also means increased exposure and lack of defence against factors which impel constant change.

The upper realm will move the child into the vicinity of other children and youths who, having been separated for different reasons from the families, share the same lack of adequate companionship in their process of growing up. Some of them may live in more stable ways, but they are at least at risk of becoming unstable; a few of them may resort to the street or even end up living there more permanently. In the Paraguayan context, for example, there are child deserters, runaways from family homes where they have been placed to work, child and adolescent prostitutes, members of independently-living gangs of adolescents, all of whom may occasionally share the life in the street and who become frequent contacts for the children who stay in the street more permanently.

It should be noted that, as well as dynamic movement up and down the spirals within the triangle, there is also movement through time. In this sense, the triangle is not static, but moves along a time axis as the children involved progress towards adulthood by physical development, increasing personal power, identity and enablement (to be and to be able). By proposing this triangular model, I am far from trying to advocate a generalized and universal model for analysis, but rather the concrete analysis of social situations by the use of alternative models. It is therefore important to bear the limits of the model in mind.

It may prove to provide useful new insights, hints and questioning along the process of its construction and interpretation, but it may also be necessary to supersede it in order to advance further. In the present case, the model permits the visualization, among others, of the following insights:

(a) It seems important to overcome the concept of 'street children' in general, as representing a homogeneous group of problem children with the same essential characteristics.

(b) What has been called so far 'children in the street' and 'children of the street' are not subcategories of one and the same global generic category, but have to be viewed as being well apart.

(c) Accordingly, responses to either group in terms of policy decisions or actions should be different.

(d) Both groups, children working and children 'living' in the street, have their own separate context they share with other groups of children with similar essential characteristics, making them deserving of care but which, up till now, have been kept invisible or have been ignored by society. It is important to rescue these other groups and to take action on their behalf alongside the ongoing actions on behalf of children working or 'living' in the street.

(e) The socialization of children living in the street does not just occur among themselves, but includes other children or adolescents in the vicinity, the potential importance of whom the present model suggests. Thus existing relationships with young prostitutes or young delinquents may be of more than just accidental nature and may be of vital relevance.

(f) Finally, the model provides a way to understand problem children which is dynamic and rooted in the processes which shape their lives, processes which imply growing up but also the changing conditions of life during childhood.

Notes

1 In 1987, the programme was institutionalized under the name of *Callescuela* (meaning 'street school' or 'the street as a school').

2 Traditionally from the age of approximately 12 years old, male children of poor families in Paraguay may be enrolled by their parents in the army, although the regulatory age for military service is considerably higher. It is a way to reduce the number of mouths to be fed, assuring that the child's needs are met by others.

The army as an alternative to overcome problems of social indigence and survival also reflects the lack of corresponding care facilities or state mechanisms in Paraguay.

3 Paper given by Jose Atilio Alvarez, undersecretary for minors of the Argentinian government on the 11.10.89 at the 'First Latin American Workshop on Public Policies with Regard to Street Children', in Sao Paulo, Brazil.

4 Those who have worked actively within the context of such action may find examples of what is being said here in their own experience: especially in the ways suitable target groups for action are looked for and found, or given priority over others, without there being any rational analysis or decision taken to endorse the selection.

5 This is the case of, for example, projects in Lima (Peru) as well as Asunción (Paraguay).

6 The notion of 'irretrievable' was, for instance, introduced at a workshop on street children organized by the Paraguayan state authority in October 1989, to refer to individual 'children of the street' who had proved particularly difficult to come to terms with. Although several workshop participants expressed their disagreement with this concept, most of them are likely to apply it, at least implicitly, within their own action. Indeed, most projects working directly with street children draw, at some point, a limit concerning the extent of their action; children beyond this limit are excluded from the benefits of the project. Sometimes there are other institutions who take care of them but, generally, there exists a number of children living in the streets who do not fit the project requirements or are not able to respond to what the project wants them to be or to do. They may not actually be called 'irretrievable' but they are viewed or treated as such.

7 This tendency shows, among others, in policy discussions at the level of international agencies concerned with the matter.

8 Too little research has been conducted so far on the adult life of former children living in the street, but available evidence suggests that socialization in the street creates a type of affective relation and familiarity which, being different from the one occurring in the natal family, prompts the former 'child of the street' to return as an adult to street related surroundings, particularly in moments of personal crisis.

Postscript

In the six years which have passed since I first wrote the present chapter, the situation of children in all societies has evolved considerably. Likewise, the ways children are viewed and dealt with have changed. However, street children — children living in the streets, children working in the streets, children who spend much of their time in public spaces — have neither decreased in number nor disappeared.

Meanwhile, the term 'street children' appears as a part of a broader context, related to the steady emergence of future mega-cities of both the North and the South, and their social environment. Increasingly this broader context becomes more important than any of its components, and the ways of conceptually grasping reality change. 'Street children' appear in policy papers and in social programming almost like a unifying label for actions whose focus, in fact, reaches far beyond, to extend and include street economy and questions of productivity, the extended family, neighbourhood and community, the school system, legal norms, socialization in the street etc.

Thus, this chapter's substantive focus on issues of definition — what counts as a 'street child' — may have lost some of its relevance. Recognition of these definitional problems, and the ways of dealing with them, have themselves evolved. What remains relevant, however, are the deeper concerns which form the background to the debate identified in this chapter: concerns about how such concepts emerge and are formed, with the effect of controlling and manipulating societies in favour of dominant interests by, among other things, excluding or concealing parts of the social reality.

As author of the chapter I have evolved and changed as well during the last six years: today, taking a broader perspective, I would want to understand in much more detail how a given society 'sees', i.e., detects, isolates and subsequently 'names' specific sub-groups as its parts, and especially what this society then does or doesn't do with regard to these parts. What do such groups or sub-groups, like street children, represent and mean to the society as a whole? By interpreting the meaning of such disavowed parts or groups, like street children, and the function they fulfill for the entire society, how could a society subsequently change itself as a whole, rather than pretending to change those parts? Might growing up in the streets, rather than just being a negative experience for children, also show new and potentially positive ways, and even provide a new paradigm, for children's lives and growing up in disintegrating societies? Obviously, such questions stretch beyond the limit of this postscript but they do point the way forward for new research and analysis.

Finally, on a more personal note, I should like to share the impression I got when looking back at my chapter from my present standpoint. Driven by an urge to contribute to concrete action, the text of 1990 reflects a confident, almost omnipotent attitude, based on the belief that any problem can be tackled or solved, and that 'we are in charge'. Today, I find myself with a more modest approach: I would like to understand first what is happening and from there find my place and discover what to do. Being part of my society I am also a part of its problems. Future social action could well mean becoming active also and primarily with regard to oneself, both individually and collectively.

Benno Glauser

References

ANTI-SLAVERY SOCIETY FOR THE PROTECTION OF HUMAN RIGHTS (1985) Children in Especially Difficult Circumstances/Street Children — An Annotated Bibliography, London, unpublished.

ENNEW, J. (1986) 'Children of the street', *The New Internationalist*, **164**, pp. 10–11.

ESPINOLA, B., GLAUSER, B. *et al.* (1987) *In the Streets: Working Street Children in Asunción*, Bogota, UNICEF/Methodological Series.

GOODE, J. (1987) *Gaminismo: The Changing Nature of the Street Child Phenomenon in Columbia*, USFI Reports, No. 28.

UNICEF (1986) *Exploitation of Working Children and Street Children*, E/ICEF/CRP, 3.

WARD, C. (1977) *The Child in the City*, London, The Architectural Press Ltd.

YOPO, B. (1989) 'Derechos humanos y niños abandonados', in *Revista Chilena de Derechos Humanos*, **10**, pp. 6–15.

164

Chapter 8

Who Are You Kidding?
Children, Power, and the
Struggle Against Sexual Abuse

Jenny Kitzinger

Introduction

The child sits limp and despairing — her face hidden in her hands; the young girl clutches her blanket — the figure of a man lurks in the shadows; an infant cowers in the corner of his play pen, a blank-eyed Victorian china doll lies cracked and discarded on the floor. These are the images which appear in the publicity about, and campaigns against, child sexual abuse. They are used by people who are outraged by the abuse of children and are seeking to prevent it. While the images of alluring Lolitas and lying little minxes used by the *apologists* for sexual abuse have been widely criticized, less attention has been paid to the type of images described above and it is these images, those emerging from the campaigns *against* sexual abuse, that are explored in this chapter.

The debates around child sexual abuse draw on multi-stranded discourses about sexuality, the family, gender, class and race (Parton and Parton, 1988; Campbell, 1988). In addition, these debates are embedded within, and draw upon, a variety of discourses about childhood, for child sexual abuse is presented as, above all, a crime against childhood. It is the victim's youth that lends this form of assault its poignancy and it is that youth which is emphasized in the accompanying publicity. Documentation of specific cases in the press dwell on child-specific attributes such as the victim's favourite plastic purse with the rainbow handles, her pony tail, Paddington Bear watch and sailor suit dress (*The Sun* 10.12.86; *Today* 2.6.87; *The Mirror* 9.12.86). Textual references are made to picnics, Wendy houses and visits to the sea-side while the background music used in television discussion of this issue draw on a 'childish' repertoire of clockwork musical boxes and songs such as 'The Teddy Bears' Picnic' (Cook, 1987; *Testimony of a Child Debate*, 1989).

All these visual, written, and aural cues accentuate the fact that the victim is a child — and, ultimately, that childhood itself is at issue. 'Kevin's 8, but for him childhood's over' reads the headline of the National Children's Home advertisement — 'Kevin's been raped'. Childhood then is not defined by age but by some set of qualities or experiences which are incompatible with being assaulted. The images of unhappy and frightened children (usually white) represent, not individuals, but a concept. The image of the solitary black child would represent a different concept — racism means that while a white child can represent 'Childhood' the black child is only used to represent *black* childhood, or 'The Third World' or 'Foreign' or 'Starvation'.[1] The concern is, therefore, not just about the assault on an individual child but with the attack upon, and defence of, childhood itself (that institution and ideal which exists independently from, and sometimes in spite of, actual flesh and blood children). Indeed, the sexual abuse of a child is often referred to as the 'theft' or 'violation' of childhood (e.g., Barr, 1986; *The Sun*, 13.12.86; Bradbury, 1986).

In this chapter I draw on media coverage, leaflets, education videos, books, academic articles and survivors' personal testimonies to explore how childhood is constructed and reconstructed within the contemporary 'pro-child' debates and how these constructions affect our understandings of child sexual abuse as 'a problem' and our visions of 'a solution'. The first part of the chapter documents, and challenges, the discourses of childhood innocence, passivity and innate vulnerability. The second part introduces and questions one of the main *alternative* set of discourses — the discourse of empowerment in which children are viewed as socialized into victimhood and capable of escaping it.[2] All these mainstream approaches to child sexual abuse are, I argue, full of tensions and contradictions resulting from their failure to question the social construction of childhood itself, or fundamentally, to challenge children's oppression. Finally, I suggest ways in which we could begin to develop a radical, social constructionist approach to the struggle against, and prevention of, sexual exploitation.

Childhood Innocence

Implicit in the presentation of sexual abuse as the 'violation of childhood' is an assertion of what childhood 'really' is, or should be. The experience of abuse is contrasted with the 'authentic experience of childhood': a carefree time of play; an asexual and peaceful existence within the protective bosom of the family.[3] The quality of childhood

Figure 8.1 The term 'ponytailed victim', rather like the phrase 'gymslip mum' serves to draw together and exploit the contrast between traditional understandings of childhood on the one hand (as signified by ponytails and gym-slips) and sex and violence on the other.

Ponytailed 'victim' accuses doctor on sex charges

Source: The Daily Mirror, 9 December 1986

Figure 8.2 This favoured 'Babes in the Wood' headline was used in 1986 when two 10-year-olds were abducted and murdered and again in 1988 when a 14-year-old was raped on her way to see a pantomime of that name.

Source: Daily Record 8 January 1988, and Mirror 11 October 1986

that is most surely 'stolen' by abuse is 'innocence'. Books and articles about this topic have titles such as: 'Shattered Innocence' (Kohn, 1987), *The Betrayal of Innocence* (Forward and Buck, 1981) and *The Death of Innocence* (Janus, 1981). Child sexual abuse is 'prototypical innocence as a foil for grandiose corruption, and, simply — a battle between good and evil . . .' (Summit, 1986, xi). Indeed, 'robbing children of their innocence', has become a synonym (and euphemism) for sexual assault (*The Sun*, 13.12.86).

Asserting that abuse is never the child's fault, declaring her innocent, is a necessary challenge to the long tradition of victim-blaming, which views abused children as active participants or even 'aggressors' (Nelson, 1987: 38–45). The notion of 'lost innocence' also 'rings true' for many adult survivors who feel guilty and ashamed; 'reclaiming' that innocence can be a potent symbol of healing (Bass and Thornton, 1983: 201). However, what is happening now is not simply a challenging of guilt. It is a fetishistic glorification of the 'innate innocence' of childhood, and, indeed, a rhetoric which implies that sexual abuse stains that innocence.

Using this concept of innocence to incite public revulsion against sexual abuse is problematic for three main reasons. First, the notion of childhood innocence is itself a source of titillation for abusers. A glance at pornography leaves little doubt that innocence is a sexual commodity. 'Kiddie porn' magazines specifically set out to highlight the purity of their child models (Rush, 1980: 164). Advertising makes use of images of young girls made up to look like Marilyn Monroe with slogans such as 'Innocence is sexier than you think' (Rush, 1980: 125), and the fashion industry cashes in with baby-doll nightdresses for adult women and, for girls, T-shirts emblazoned with the words 'Forbidden Fruit'. If defiling the pure and deflowering the virgin is supposed to be erotic, then focusing on children's presumed innocence only reinforces their desirability as sexual objects. As one child abuser wrote: 'It was so exciting, she was so young, so pure and clean' (*The Star*, 4.12.86).

Second, innocence is a double-edged sword in the fight against sexual abuse because it stigmatizes the 'knowing' child. The romanticization of childhood innocence excludes those who do not conform to the ideal. Innocence is used to imply asexuality, 'pre-sexual personhood' (Hancock and Mains, 1987: 32), or a limited and discrete 'childlike' sensuality. This penalizes the child who sexually responds to the abuse or who appears flirtatious and sexually aware. If the violation of innocence is the criterion against which the act of sexual abuse is judged then violating a 'knowing' child becomes a lesser offence than violating an 'innocent' child. It is this notion which allows an abuser to defend himself on the grounds that his victim was 'no angel', citing as evidence, that the girl drinks, smokes and often fails to do her homework on time (*Daily Mail*, 14.12.85). Without her innocence the child has lost the magic cloak supposed to make her impervious to harm. Thus, as Sgroi (1982: 114) suggests, 'the sexually victimized child may be viewed neither as a child nor as an adult but rather as a piece of "damaged goods" lacking the attributes of both childhood and adult . . . sexually victimized children may become "walking invitations"'. Indeed, a child who is known to be a victim of sexual abuse is often the target of further exploitation: 'Publicly deflowered as she is, she is regarded as no longer deserving respect or protection' (Summit and Kryso, 1978: 244).

The third, and most fundamental, reason why it is counterproductive to use 'innocence' in the fight against child sexual abuse is that it is an ideology used to deny children access to knowledge and power and hence actually increases their vulnerability to abuse. The twin concepts of innocence and ignorance are vehicles for adult double-standards: a child is ignorant if she doesn't know what adults want her to know, but innocent if she doesn't know what adults don't want her to know. Those adults who champion 'childhood' use innocence as an excuse to exclude children from 'the adult world' and indeed, to isolate them from other children's experiences. In the name of innocence adults repress children's own expressions of sexuality, such as masturbation (Stainton-Rogers, 1989), deny children control over their own bodies (e.g., the Gillick campaign to prevent girls under 16 gaining access to contraception) and seek to protect them from 'corrupting influences' (e.g., Section 28 in the UK which prohibits the promotion of positive images of homosexuality)[4]. Highlighting child sexual abuse is even, in itself, seen to debase childhood and destroy 'the age of innocence' (*News on Sunday*, 3.5.87). Indeed, it is the notion of innocence which prevents some people from telling children about incest (*Independent*, 28.4.87) because they do not want to 'corrupt the few years of innocence that should be every child's right' (Brown, 1986).

The Passive Victim

Complementing the image of the *innocent* victim is that of the *passive* victim. Instead of presenting the child as an active 'participant' in the 'relationship' (as described in the old 'anti-child' research on child abuse e.g., Bender and Blau, 1937) the bulk of the recent 'pro-child' publicity shows the child as a helpless victim of adult sexual demands. The abused child is represented by a despairing and pathetic figure mutely appealing to the adult viewer for help or, sometimes, simply by a limp rag doll. She is described as a 'silent sufferer of victimization' but rarely allowed to speak about her own actions as opposed to the acts committed against her. Child survivors remain faceless and inaudible; their struggles to resist and endure abuse remain largely uncharted and unheard.

Many abused children, like adults in similar situations, not surprisingly, become resigned and listless in the face of overwhelming odds. The dramatic imbalance in power and socially sanctioned routine subordination of children means that they are often malleable 'objects of victimization'. Many, however, at least at some stage, rebel against what is happening to them. Some try (and a few succeed in) physically defending themselves with their teeth and nails, knives and hammers (Gordon, 1988: 213; Russell, 1986: 126). However, rather than (or as well as) engaging in the unequal struggle of direct physical combat, children employ the strategies of the most oppressed, dispossessed and victimized: joking and gossip, passive resistance and underground rebellion. My own research involving interviews with adult survivors suggests that, although such tactics are rarely recognized by adults, children seek to evade abuse with all the resources they have of cunning, manipulativeness, energy, anger and fear.[5]

Survivors describe how, as children, they induced nose bleeds, held their breath until they fainted, or had various 'accidents' to ensure they could not be sent off on their access visit with daddy or be left alone with the abusive babysitter. They also tried barricading their bedrooms, fleeing and hiding. Kate ran away to London on five different occasions and Lorna started going to church to avoid being called to her father's bed on Sunday mornings; one girl encircled her bed with squeaky toys (to ensure the abuser could not creep up on her while she slept); another enlisted her own bodyguard by taking her dog to bed (the dog would growl and lunge at her father when he approached) (Armstrong, 1987: 169). Joanne found a different kind of 'minder' when, at 15, she started to go out with 'the local thug'. 'I chose him specifically as a way of keeping my dad off,' she told me, 'my dad was quite a pathetic man and I knew as soon as he met this boy, that he was scared of him. So I went out with him, as a way of keeping my dad at bay.'

Whether overtly, or covertly, children often gain comfort, information, and assistance from each other rather than from adults. Lynda's sister always hugged and soothed her after their uncle's assaults; Vida's best friend gave her the courage to phone Childline; Diane and her sister sustained each other with 'jokes' about killing their father and

Figure 8.3   Book cover for Dangerous Families: Assessment and Treatment of Child Abuse

Source: Dale, Davies, Morrison and Wakers, 1986

Rowena's brother helped her to rig up a shotgun against their step-father designed to fire when he opened the bedroom door. It was Hilda's sister who warned her about their uncle and Hilda's friend who then slept with her, thus successfully preempting an assault.

Victimized children also plead and bargain with their abusers or try to repel them by making themselves 'unattractive' — strapping down developing breasts, cutting off their hair, or hiding inside an armour of bulky jumpers in all weathers. Samantha refused to wash, deliberately making herself physically disgusting: 'I told myself that if I was dirty and smelly no one would want to have sex with me.' Another girl, identifying being female with being vulnerable, rejected all the para-phernalia of femininity. 'He said I was ugly and just like a boy, and why didn't I ever wear pretty dresses, and make-up like other girls, and he bought me perfume and I broke the bottle. I would wear bovver boots, and always wear trousers. I really hated him then and he knew it.'

If the abuse is unavoidable some children try to make it less in-vasive by segregating it from their day to day lives. 'I blanked it [the abuse] off when I was at school', says Lisa, whose abusive step-father worked away from home during the week: 'It just wasn't there, it was only sometimes that I would remember. But I didn't normally, I mean it [the abuse] was usually only on Fridays, when he came home, but all the other days of the week I don't think I ever let myself remember really'. Other children withhold any physical or mental participation. One 16 year-old describes, with some satisfaction, how she discovered the art of 'blanking out':

> One day, I was about eight, he was making me dress up in my mother's clothes — suspenders, bra and everything. He was looking at me in these clothes. I was thinking about school. Then all of a sudden, I got this great slap around my face — he says 'are you listening to me?' That is when I realized that I could take my mind somewhere else and it was really good because I thought 'ooh, great, I don't have to be here.' [. . .] It felt kind of freeing because before I had been suffering [. . .] but now I could take my mind somewhere else and please him, give him what he wanted but just shut everything off and not be hurt.

Another woman, who at first sexually responded to her uncle's manipulation of her genitals, learnt to hold herself rigid during assaults: 'When he touched me I used to be really stiff, obviously I'd let him do it, but that didn't mean I had to take any type of part in it. I just felt like a doll'. Passivity, being as lifeless as 'a doll', is here chosen as a form of resistance — refusing to be involved.

Alternatively, submission to sex may be used as a bargaining point by children seeking rewards of 'affection', 'the right to stay up late' or 'a bit more freedom than my brothers'. Such 'privileges' make children feel implicated in their own violation but, for some, these pay offs are 'better than nothing'. As Imogen comments:

> In some families I think kids are pretty desperate for the attention they need to grow and live and if they have to trade a bit of pain for it, or a bit of sex for it, then they will do that. And there is a bit of me that says good luck to them. I am *glad* that I was the one in my family who managed to get something. The fact that I was entitled to an awful lot more is neither here nor there because there was no more available.

Children also try to limit the degree of physical invasion — learning to fake pleasure or quickly stimulate their abusers to orgasm so as to curtail the abuse and, perhaps, avoid the soreness and pain of persistent rubbing or penetration. 'I satisfied him and allowed him to satisfy himself without totally surrendering my body to him' writes Charlotte Vale Allen, explaining how she consistently avoided vaginal intercourse with her father, 'No matter what happened I was determined never to let him do that to me. I clung to my virginity — technical scrap of membrane — with passionate tenacity' (Allen, 1980: 110).

Children are constantly acting to preempt, evade, or modify sexual violence. However, 'adult-centric' discourses ignore such strategies: children are not seen as agents in their own lives. They are only visible as they relate (literally or theoretically) to 'the adult world'.[6] Working with children is a relatively low status activity and researchers who listen to children and take them seriously as 'objects' of study *in their own right* have sometimes found their work ridiculed and 'rubbished' by association with their 'childish' subjects. Researchers who have challenged 'common sense' interpretations of children's behaviour, as Mandell does in her work on children's negotiation of meaning, have even been accused of 'anthropomorphising' children (cited in Waksler, 1986: 72). Such refusal to accept children as fully human and such negation of their ideas and strategies not only ignores children's *individual* acts of resistance but obscures relations *between* children and thus the importance of young people's alliances with one another as a resource against adult violence. Children's successful defences rarely come to public/adult attention — they do not appear in the statistics, a preempted potential assault is a 'non-event'. When they 'fail' however their struggles also go unrecognized. The survival strategies described above are, in the mainstream literature, labelled 'symptoms' of abuse or listed as a catalogue of sickness illustrating the terrible consequences of incest. Activities that could be recognized as attempts to resist, or cope with abuse are, instead, labelled 'post-traumatic stress syndrome' or cited as evidence of deep psychic scarring. Such disease terminology obscures the child actively negotiating her way through the dangers of childhood. She is recast as a submissive object of victimization even by the process of intervention and treatment.[7]

Protecting the Weak

The logical extension of the image of the innately passive child and the refusal to recognize children's resistance strategies is to rely totally on adult protection to prevent, or interrupt, abuse. We are told that *all* children are at risk — the victim of sexual exploitation 'could come from anywhere — even next door . . . it could be anybody's little girl or boy' (Cook, 1987). Significantly, this is not matched by a similar focus on the abuser — we are not warned that the abuser could come from anywhere, 'even next door to you . . . it could be anyone's father, husband or son'. Focusing on children's weakness and 'incapacity', the call is for increased surveillance, we are urged to guard 'our' children closely and avoid letting them out alone or at night.

Such siege mentality places a huge strain on parents, and particularly mothers. Just as the Health Education Authority advertisement showed a busy mother 'allowing' her child to run out under a car, it is women who bear the greatest burden of chaperoning duties. Those who are unable to buy into the individualistic option of childcare substitution are censured for not being available to their children twenty-four hours a day. During a series of child murders in Atlanta, the press demanded 'Where were these children's mothers?' (Cooper, 1986: 40) and when a child was abducted while on her way to a bus stop her mother was blamed for not accompanying her: 'At times, the anger seemed more directed against her than at the murderer' (Elliott, M., 1988: 25). Indeed, helpful hints on how to combat child sexual abuse include the suggestion that mothers of pre-school children should not go out to work at all (Kelly, R, 1988) and mothers of incest survivors are blamed for being unavailable to their children through illness, death, or because they were out at Bingo, doing the shopping or had 'abdicated' child care responsibilities to their husbands. As one lawyer defending an alleged child abuser pointed out — the mother must take some responsibility because: 'This woman repeatedly went out to the grocery store leaving this child alone with her father'! (quoted in MacFarlane, 1988).

The fate of women and children are intimately intertwined — not only because women (and men) spend many years *being* children but because women take primary responsibility for all types of child-care. We can not construct and reconstruct childhood without construct-ing and reconstructing what it means to be a mother (or a teacher, or a health visitor and all the other, predominantly female, child care 'vocations').

In addition to the burdens it places on women, the protectionist approach encourages children to live in fear. At its most extreme it reflects a 'lock up your daughters' philosophy which, ironically (given that much abuse takes place within the home), increases children's isolation within the family by encouraging them to keep all other adults (literally) at arms' length; it also implies the need for increased parental control (Barrett and Coward, 1985: 23).

Protection, then, is neither a long term, nor even a short term, 'solution' to the exploitation of children. Such paternalistic approaches can, in fact, act *against* children's interests. Reforms which impose restrictions on children — 'for their own good' are routinely turned against the very people they are meant to protect (Takanishi, 1978). The focus on children's innate vulnerability (as a biological fact unmedi-ated by the world they live in) is an ideology of control which diverts attention away from the socially constructed oppression of young people. Children in western society are kept dependent for much longer than is considered necessary in other societies (Jackson, 1982). Currently, in the UK, this dependence is being lengthened and intensified by Con-servative government policies in housing, health care, employment, taxation and education which increase parental responsibility for, and rights over, their daughters and sons. It is now harder for a young person to leave home and exist independently from her or his family (Shelter, 1989) and parents' increasing control over, for instance, chil-dren's sex education is, potentially, in direct conflict with their protec-tion from sexual exploitation (Dingwall, 1987).

Attributing sexual violence to a decline of traditional values, and, specifically, to 'The Decay of Childhood' (Seabrook, 1987), some pro-tectionists call for the 'preservation' of childhood. In this way, child-hood is treated rather like a rare animal threatened with extinction. Just as early attempts to preserve endangered species relied on locking up specimens in zoos (rather than intervening against the 'man-made' at-tacks on their environment) so this child protection approach attempts to 'preserve childhood' by confining children behind bars. However, it is precisely this kind of 'protection' which leaves many survivors feeling trapped and imprisoned. As children they desperately longed to escape the restrictions of childhood: 'I used to sit at the window watching people walk along the street and think — one day I'll be out there.

When I'm grown up I can get my own place, I can close the door, go to bed when I want, get up when I want, do what I want and, of course, IT won't happen anymore'.

The conflict between survivors who identify the barriers surrounding childhood as *restrictive* and those who see them as *protective* is perhaps best illustrated by their contrasting use of the imagery of bars. Adult and child survivors use prison-like bars in their pictures: the child is caged or chained, houses are drawn without doors or windows (Bacon and Richardson, 1989). By contrast, the child protection literature uses play-pen bars to symbolize safety and security (*Times* 17.12.87, and 18.12.87). Under the protectionist philosophy, childhood is a sanctuary to be lovingly preserved; little consideration is given to the implications for the children (or women) whose lives are increasingly confined, still less attention is paid to challenging the forces which make those bars 'necessary'. Such unreflective images of childhood are, however, being challenged by more hopeful developments in the area of child sexual abuse 'prevention'. I shall now go on to look at these developments and, in particular, at the notion of empowerment.

Adult Awareness and Child Assertiveness

Traditionally, attempts to prevent abuse have been in the form of veiled warnings to children about not taking sweets from strangers or not walking home from school on their own. Today, while some warnings (notably the government-led campaigns) still follow the old 'Say No to Strangers' line, more innovative and radical programs have also appeared. These programs (many of which developed out of grass roots feminists' initiatives) vary in imagination, in degree of sophistication and in specific political perspective, but broadly they are all trying to assist children to identify abuse and obtain help.

The images of childhood presented by these programs are in striking contrast to the images of the innocent and passive child in need of protection.[8] Indeed, many activists in this area start by problematizing such adult attitudes toward children. Adults are, they argue, too ready to dismiss what children say as lies or fantasies or to belittle children's resistance, anger and grief with a terminology reserved for 'child-like' behaviour: 'tantrums', 'home sickness', 'day dreaming' or 'sulking'. The abused child is often simply labelled 'naughty', 'clingy' or 'delinquent'. Her attempts to defend herself against adult demands are 'impudent', 'sullen' or 'uppity'. Her protests reduced to mere sound — 'whining'. 'We are too accustomed to regarding children as an irritation, a noisy, messy nuisance,' declares one NSPCC officer 'If we continue to believe children should be seen and not heard, their silence protects the molester' (quoted in Rantzen, 1986).

Books and leaflets aim to alert adults to the effect that our routine exercise of power may have on children's self-confidence. Demanding unquestioning obedience from children ('Do as you're told, it's for your own good.' 'Because I say so.') is seen to create vulnerability (Adams and Fay, 1981). They challenge us to re-assess our own use of authority as parents, strangers, friends, and teachers. 'You can't teach children they are responsible for certain areas of their life,' points out one headmistress (talking about the Kidscape child safety program) 'and then expect them to sit in a classroom and force-feed them with information they are not encouraged to discuss or query. The compliant, conforming child becomes one who is at risk' (quoted in Aziz, 1987).

Taking on board their own challenge to conventional attitudes toward children, these prevention programs employ child-centred and child-sensitive methods of teaching that emphasize involving, rather than lecturing, children. The workers try to use media familiar to young people — enlisting glove-puppets and colouring books (and TV characters such as Miss Piggy, Batman, the Fonz and Yogi Bear) to introduce the topic in an accessible and non-intimidating way. Rejecting the idea that 'childhood innocence' precludes giving children information, these programs build on children's existing knowledge about bullying and unfairness, 'nice surprises' and 'nasty secrets' and encourage children to trust their own instincts (Finkelhor, 1986: 228–229; Elliott, M., 1988: 25).

Through listening to children, and incorporating their feedback, these programs can also constantly evolve. For instance, some educators now reject the terms 'good' and 'bad' touch (with their suggestions, for the child, of being 'naughty' and being punished) in favour of 'Yes' and 'No' touch or the 'Uh Oh!' feeling (with their emphasis on the child's own reactions and possible actions). Most of these programs have, however, had a lot to learn about the different media, concepts and terminology relevant to the majority of children who are not white, Christian, and middle class. The notion of 'individual rights', for instance, is such a fundamental part of white Anglo-American rhetoric (and indeed is assumed to have universal relevance) that this abstract, complex, and highly ethnocentric concept forms the basis of many of the programs. However, as one team of educators discovered, the 'individual's right to be safe' makes little sense to some Latin or Asian children (cited in Finkelhor, 1986: 228).

Starting from the dominant race/class perspective most of the prevention programs have only belatedly (if at all) addressed issues relevant to children with less positive relationships with the state and multiple oppressions. As one North American activist asks: 'What about the children whose lives are not reflected in the skits, the images, the plays or the books? What of the Black child whose older brother was beaten by a policeman? Or the Chinese child who lives with her grand-mother, an undocumented worker whose presence at home must be kept from the white authorities?' (Butler, 1986: 10). What, also, of the child being raised by lesbians who must keep her 'life-style' secret or risk being taken into 'custody' by her father or the state? Children do not necessarily experience teachers, social workers and police-officers as potential allies. One attempt to encourage children to seek help from trustworthy adults, such as policemen, for instance, received a decidedly sceptical response from at least one group of children — in a Welsh pit village soon after a year-long miners' strike (during which the police were seen to be violent agents of the state). Although claiming to speak to all children, many of these programs thus fail to address the concerns of 'minority' children and rely on racist, classist and heterosexist assumptions about the 'nature' of childhood.

Empowering the Powerless

The central tenet of these child safety programs is not, however, only to assist children to identify abuse and seek help but to 'empower' children to help themselves. Rejecting assumptions of childhood pas-sivity and defencelessness they build on children's existing sense of self-protection and their ability to kick, yell and run. Rather than seeing all children as inherently vulnerable, these activists pay attention to extra 'risk factors' such as an individual child's low self-esteem and target them for 'ego-enhancing' action. Instead of presenting children as 'natural victims' this approach celebrates their spirited and deter-mined resistance (Caignon and Groves, 1989: 6). Rejecting the imposi-tion of restriction on children, restrictions which can undermine 'the sense of personal independence that is as important as caution' (Brown, 1986), these programmes try to help children to be 'streetwise' and confident. Books and videos with titles like 'Strong Kids — Safe Kids'; 'Speak Up, Say No'; 'You're in Charge' and 'Feeling Yes, Feeling No' urge children to be assertive, to express their own feelings and to develop a sense of control over their own bodies (Brassard, *et al.*, 1983).

This is the positive side of the action taken in response to the concept of vulnerability. Vulnerability, here, is seen not just in terms of the need for adult protection but as something that children themselves can change by modifying their behaviour. Role play, games, stories and songs are designed to help children resist abuse; the message is, as one catchy song boldly declares:

My body's nobody's body but mine
You run your own body
Let me run mine   [From 'Kids can Say No' video]

Such programs represent a challenging departure from the traditional approach to children and child protection. Indeed, they provoke considerable unease among those concerned with maintaining the status quo. These programs are accused of undermining parental rights, encouraging self-centeredness and failing to distinguish between the 'normal' and 'abnormal' exercise of parental authority. Gilbert (1988), for instance, bemoans the fact that only one of the programs he reviewed instructed teachers 'to point out that a bad touch is different from a spanking and to suggest that children may deserve to be spanked by parents if they do something naughty or dangerous' (Gilbert, 1988: 8). Another writer also concerned about 'strident' prevention compaigns concludes: 'Children who have been systematically taught to fight dirty, lie and be rude and unhelpful to strangers, may well be tougher propositions when it comes to resisting sexual abuse — but at what cost for the rest of their dealings with society?' (Tucker, 1985: 98).

Faced with such hostility, many people are understandably eager to protest that these programs are 'not subversive' (Frost quoted in Aziz, 1987). However, what change can be made to children's position within society *without* subverting existing hierarchies, *without* challenging 'society as we know it'? If these preventive programs are not subversive then what are they? Where do the activists in this area 'draw the line' and what contradictions and dilemmas do they face?

The Limits of Empowering

One of the dilemmas for activists seeking to 'empower' children is how to make them feel they *can* resist abuse without making them feel guilty if they don't or can't. Placing the primary emphasis on teaching children to 'say no' risks making them feel responsible for their own victimization. Indeed, after one prevention program, the children were found to have a *greater* tendency to believe that, if they were abused, it would be their own fault (cited in Hamilton, 1989). Some adult survivors too find that these programs reflect negatively on their own experiences: 'I thought I had said no. Maybe I didn't say no as though I *really* meant it.' Many survivors (including those whose ingenious strategies are described above), are made to feel that their victimization is evidence either of their collusion or their weakness. 'I let him do it to me' said Vida; 'Was it because I was a weakling?' asked Sadie, while another woman, reflecting on the abuse inflicted on her at a child-care centre, stated: 'Now I can see that I gave my power away' (Asherah, 1983: 179).

Seeing power in individualistic terms as something that can be 'claimed' or 'given away' by an 8-year-old is, for many people, reassuring. Even some survivors talk of 'wanting' to believe that they had some influence over events, if only to cling to some illusion of control. Louise Wisechild, for instance, describes her childhood powerlessness but also identifies a function in believing that her own badness caused the abuse: 'If it is my fault and I'm bad, then trying to be good offers hope. If we're not bad [. . .] then maybe we can't make anything happen, not even bad things.' (Wisechild, 1988: 132). To have had *some* power (even if it was the power to provoke maltreatment) is less humiliating and terrifying than to have been a total victim with no power at all.

The idea that children have the ability to stop abuse, or that 'vulnerable' children can have this vulnerability erased by judicially applied 'ego-enhancing' education, is also a way of 'selling' sexual abuse prevention programs. Commercially produced prevention packages are now a multi-million dollar industry in North America and it makes sense for anyone seeking permission for children to attend such programs to promote the idea that, as stated in one letter sent out to parents: 'When interviewing people who have sexually assaulted children, it has been determined that in 80 per cent of the cases, the abuser would have stopped if the child had said "No"' (quoted in Trudell, *et al.*, 1988: 105). Such a suggestion is an insult to the many women and children who try to resist but are still abused and who, when they confide in family or friends, face the question 'But why didn't you say no?' The emphasis on 'personal power' and 'the right to say no', by locating change within the individual, distracts attention from social structural issues[9]. It fragments common experiences of oppression and thus undermines our perception of the necessity for collective, political action.

When children are cowed and unresisting such behaviour should not be seen simply as a 'bad habit' that can be 'corrected' by a few hours 'intervention'. It is a reflection of their experience of powerlessness. One of the ironies of the prevention campaigns is that children who start off with lowest self-esteem in the first place appear to benefit *least* from such interventions (Gough, 1989: 14). In other words it is precisely the children who are most vulnerable, eager to please and easily-led who obstinately reject any idea that they have 'rights' and refuse to develop a 'sense' of their own power. Such unexpected conviction from the most vulnerable children is understandable if we accept that a 'sense' of powerlessness may in fact reflect their external 'reality'. Children are sometimes hopeless because there is no hope, helpless because there is no help and compliant because there is no alternative. Powerlessness is in the food they eat, the air they breathe and the beds they sleep in. As one 9-year-old, explaining her own abuse, said simply: 'He was big and I was little. I had to do what he said' (Gilgun and Gordon, 1985: 47). Abusers rarely have to display any great brutality to get their own way: the father-abuser's power runs like an undercurrent through the whole family. In sensationalizing perpetrators' grosser *abuses* of power we forget the routine use of power over children, 'That's what makes me angry now,' explains one survivor, 'when the media says that all kids are told to shut up and threatened — that is often the case, but you can threaten without any words at all'.

Changing children's sense of power or adults' use of such power cannot be achieved without reference to their actual state of powerlessness or control. Telling children that they 'have' certain rights is not enough — they need either some practical experience of those rights and/or some idea of the forces which deny them those rights and ways of fighting for them. As 'Liz' writes: 'A child's right to her own body, autonomy and privacy is still a radical concept *which would require the transformation of family power relations.* (Liz, 1982: 217, my emphasis.) The limits and contradictions of the campaigns to 'empower' children are, perhaps, most clearly illustrated by cases where children have 'over-generalized' or 'gone too far' in their understanding of their 'rights'. One child, for instance, generalized her right to say no to any request that she did not like or made her feel uncomfortable. Her parents were apparently 'forced' to endure 'much anguish and frustration' and 'had to punish her in order to convince her that she did not have the right to disobey them whenever she wanted to' (Conte cited in Haugard and Repucci, 1988). Clearly then adult intentions to permit, and children's ability to claim that, 'My body's no body's body but mine' is severely limited, intertwined as it is with notions of 'obedience' and parental obligations.

Helping children resist abuse depends on paying close attention to their existing strategies and exploring why these are often insufficient protection: insufficient because of a lack of alternatives, resources and power. Children's resistance strategies fail *in spite of* the child not simply because of her lack of confidence. We need to examine children's material reality and recognize that children are vulnerable because they *are* children — childhood is a state of oppression (an oppression compounded by discrimination based upon sex, race, class and disability). Powerlessness is not 'all in the mind.' (For a discussion of the ways in which the social construction of 'deafness' and 'mental impairment' accentuate these children's 'vulnerability' see Sullivan *et al.*, 1987, and Senn, undated.)

Many of the activists concerned with empowering children would probably agree with this analysis of structural power. There is even a tradition of ending reviews or evaluations of prevention programs with a caveat that goes something like: 'Of course, education is not enough — we need to look at wider power imbalances within society as a whole'. However, this understanding of structural power is not applied to the design, evaluation or review of prevention programs themselves. While writers pay great attention to the difficulties concerning, for instance, talking to children about sex, the dilemmas faced in talking with children about power are not even part of the debate. The implicit assumption is *either* that it is dealt with during discussion of such topics as 'bullying' *or* that it is not appropriate to talk directly to children about power at all. (Dealing with power is a big, grown up thing that the adults should just get on and tackle by themselves). Indeed, there seems to be a tacit agreement that talking to children about structural power is a dubious activity because it may erode their sense of 'personal power'. Identifying the odds stacked against children might be 'disempowering', making them feel helpless and vulnerable: to name power is to create it; to identify power is to activate it; once acknowledged its force increases. In fact, children are systematically denied a language of power and their experiences of powerlessness are obscured. Faced with children who are the victims of institutionalized bullying or sexist, racist or heterosexist abuse we often feel unable to explain the issue in terms of politics and oppression. We may not have a language of power with which we are comfortable ourselves, we may feel that children cannot grasp such abstract concepts or we may simply wish to protect them from confronting injustice and discrimination. Thus, a black child is told that the white children call her names because 'they are jealous', the bullies are 'just silly', the spanking was 'deserved' — 'because you were naughty' and the unjust teacher 'probably had a bad day' (Kitzinger and Kitzinger, 1989).

However, it is only by discussing power with children that we can explain why some children 'passively' comply with abusers and why some 'actively' resist but are still abused. It is only by discussing power that we can place responsibility with abusers rather than their victims.

When adults do find ways of talking about power then even quite young children are capable of understanding and working with the concept — power is, after all, part of their everyday experience and is a useful tool to make sense of their world (Kitzinger and Kitzinger, 1989). (The agility with which these programs are able to discuss sexual abuse *without* directly addressing either sex or power is testimony to the years of expertise built up around avoiding these two taboo subjects!) Preventive programs aimed at children need to explore ways of talking about power in accessible and directly relevant ways and must address issues such as: how are prevention programs affected by the context within which they are introduced (e.g., with the hierarchical and compulsory institution of school)? How do we usually *explain away* injustice and oppression? If power is 'given' can it also be taken away? What are the implications for adult 'caretakers' if children start questioning power?

A radical, deconstructionist approach to preventive work with children would focus *not* on 'giving' children a 'sense' of power and telling them their 'rights' but, instead, on supporting them to recognize and name their own oppression. Rather than encouraging adults to be nicer to children by simply negotiating with them or 'involving' them in decision making, a radical approach would explore ways of openly discussing power with children and would encourage us to consider how we, as adults, manipulate children in order to obfuscate our own power. As a feminist teacher writes: 'I am very aware of the problem of my control over them [my students]. I view it as part of my work to enable them to make a critical examination of their own position and mine. I don't want them to see me as one of their pals, because that could blur their awareness of all the structures in school which reproduce power relationships, dominating them here, at home and in their future work' (Elliott, K., 1982).

In recognizing the political oppression of children (on the basis of age and of gender, race, class and disability), a radical approach would also recognize children as resisters to those oppressions. This means refusing to collaborate in the censorship of children's contemporary and historical struggles against injustice throughout the world. It also means countering adult-centric and ethno-centric western perceptions of child activists as victims of the machinations of adults (e.g., children involved in anti-nuclear actions at Greeham Common were frequently portrayed as 'victims' of their uncaring, unmotherly mothers who were 'using' them as political footballs) (Kitzinger, J., 1985). Once we stop denying children a language of power and of resistance then we remove one of the barriers to the transformation of childhood from within.

We also open up the possibility for a different relationship between adults and their own childhoods, as well as between adults and other people's childhoods. While any 'education' bestowed upon children by adults is problematic, (and should certainly not be seen as the only or primary 'site of intervention') at least a 'consciousness raising' approach such as that suggested above does not gloss over inequalities or actually *undermine* the struggle against structural change.

Conclusion

Debates about the sexual abuse of children are deeply embedded in discourses about childhood — what it is and what it should be. However, much of the 'pro-child' discussion, even many of the most radical 'child-centered' or 'empowerment' approaches, have succeeded in problematizing child sexual abuse without problematizing childhood as a structural position within society. Indeed, the very term 'child abuse' allows an evasion of the issue of power because it takes the nature of 'the child' for granted: 'child abuse' is premised on the notion of the child, rather than say young(er), small(er), or weak(er) persons. Child abuse may be posed as a problem, yet in doing so the ageism of dominant social constructions of the child/ren may remain, even be perpetuated (Hearn, 1988: 534).[10]

Rather than relying on notions of 'protection' or even 'empowerment', activists engaged in the struggle against child abuse need to consciously grapple with the deconstruction and reconstruction of childhood. This means acknowledging and reinforcing children's strategies and identifying and challenging their powerlessness. It means dealing openly with children about power and thinking in terms of 'oppression' rather than 'vulnerability', 'liberation' rather than 'protection'. The deconstruction and reconstruction of childhood is also not something that just goes on in our own heads — it involves struggling to increase children's practical options and to transform the social and political context within which children exist. Children's need for protection (by adults, from adults) or their need for assertive self-defence strategies would be substantially reduced if they had more access to social, economic and political resources.

Ultimately, it is childhood as an institution that makes children 'vulnerable'. Millions of children endure different types of abuse every day. Abuse cannot be blamed on either 'the decay' of childhood or the inherent 'nature' of childhood; it is not a question of mothers going out to work, nor of 'incompetent' social workers; nor is it a question of the individual psyches of the abused or the abuser; rather, the risk of abuse is built into childhood as an institution itself. 'There is so much abuse of young people, as violence, as threatened and potential violence, and routine ageism, that it is not a "something" that can be solved by professional interventions and professional intervenors. It is a problem of this, patriarchal, society' (Hearn, 1989: 79).

Child abuse is not an anomaly but part of the structural oppression of children. Assault and exploitation are risks inherent to 'childhood' as it is currently lived. It is not just the *abuse* of power over children that is the problem but the existence and maintenance of that power itself.

Notes

Part of this chapter first appeared in the special issue of *Feminist Review* on child sex abuse, 28, Spring 1988.

1 The few images I found of clearly non-white children subject to sexual exploita-tion were in stories about wholesale child sexual slavery — exotic peeks into other cultures, at best, linked to a market created by white tourists but often, by implica-tion, a reflection of something rotten within the culture. This kind of cultural analysis is not, of course, applied to the widespread abuse of children within white mainstream culture. Although 'sub-cultural' explanations have been applied to incest among white people in isolated rural areas, among the over-crowded work-ing classes or within the individual 'dysfunctional family', it has certainly not been brought to bear on the large child prostitution and pornography rings organized by middle class white, professional men in Britain.

2 These themes appear in different guises and combinations — I am not claiming to describe a watertight and coherent body of beliefs propounded by one particular group of people.

3 Glib statements about 'the nature' of childhood obscure the fact that most children do not live in 'safe havens' but face disease, starvation, homelessness and war (Allsebrook and Swift, 1989). As Goode points out: 'For the eight year old guerilla in Nicaragua "doing the world" as a child is at best an occasional affair if not an impossibility' (Goode, 1986).

4 'Childhood innocence' is not just used against children; it is used to sell everything from soap to anti-homosexual repression (e.g., the North American 'Save Our Children' campaign and the UK Section 28). The 'cute effect' of the little innocent child (the meek who shall inherit the earth) is also now being cynically exploited in a rash of consumerist 'ecology' adverts selling cars, bank accounts and electric-ity (Stacey, 1989).

5 Unless otherwise specified, quotations come from my own research involving interviews with 39 women survivors of childhood sexual abuse. Psuedonyms have been used throughout. In using personal accounts I am not suggesting that these give the one and only 'true' and static understanding of events. We all experience and talk about out lives within particular frameworks, we construct and recon-struct accounts drawing, for instance, on notions of what it means to be a victim or a survivor and the meaning of sexual abuse in childhood.

6 Adult-centrism is evident in the calls to help children because they are 'the parents of tomorrow' and 'our most valuable human resource'. Children are valued because of the adults they will become and their pain is evaluated in terms of its effect on adult functioning. It is almost as if, on one level, childhood suffering is discounted because it is only 'a passing phase', an oppression that you, literally, 'out grow'. As Finkelhor points out: '. . . researchers and theoreticians persistently focus on the question of long term effect [. . .] The bottom line is always how does this event affect adult adjustment, adult feelings, adult capacities and adult attitudes?' (Finkelhor, 1984: 198).

7 One influential essay that *does* look at children's survival strategies is Summit's classic 'The Child Sexual Abuse Accommodation Syndrome'. However, the discussion is, ironically, packaged in medical terminology which, as feminists (among others) have pointed out, serves to depoliticize experience and reinforce the control of 'the experts' (Kelly, 1989).

8 These programs do, however, have to negotiate acceptance by parents and schools and are thus constrained by demands to preserve childhood innocence, obedience, and trust in parental and school authority. Thus, for instance, few programs even identify sexual anatomy let alone include any discussion of sexuality (Miller-Perrin and Wurtele, 1988: 316). Keeping children in ignorance about sex perpetuates their vulnerability and may be actively exploited by abusers. Gillian's father, for instance, obliged her to submit to his sexual demands as legitimate punishment after he discovered her masturbating, while Barbara, who was sexually involved with a female friend, submitted to her uncle because she thought he had a right to teach her about 'normal sex'. Similarly, another girl was made to feel responsible for the abuse by her father who deliberately set out to stimulate her sexually (Touch, 1987, 147). All three girls were made vulnerable by the stigma surrounding children's sexuality and felt implicated in their own violation.

9 In fact, the notion of 'empowering' children is explicitly part of some 'paedophilic' arguments. In *Paedophilia: The Radical Case*, for instance, O'Carroll (1979) argues that '. . . if we are going to make more than a pretence of taking children seriously, they must be enabled to say *yes* as well as *no*. Children have to have a *choice* and should not be bound to either an anti-sex approach (as usually taken by parents, religious leaders, etc.) or a pro-sex approach (usually confined to peers and paedophiles).' Dichotomizing attitudes into the 'anti-sex' and 'pro-sex' type ignores issues around the social construction of 'consent', 'desire' and 'compulsory hetero sexuality' (c.f. Jeffreys (1985), Dworkin (1987) and Leeds Revolutionary Feminist Group (1981)).

10 The category 'child sexual abuse' also separates out the abuse of women under 16 or 18 years old from the abuse of women over that age. This allows for the diminution of children's experiences — where adult women can now talk of being 'sexually harassed', deceptively cosy words are applied to children — 'being interfered with', 'fondled' or 'petted'. It also creates a false division between the abuse women suffer at different periods of our lives and obscures the fact that many fathers continue to assault their daughters well into adulthood.

References

ADAMS, C. and FAY, J. (1981) *No More Secrets*, California, Impact.
ALLEN, C. (1980) *Daddy's Girl*, London, New English Library.

ALLSEBROOK, A. and SWIFT, A. (1989) *Broken Promise*, Seven Oaks, Hodder and Stoughton.

ARMSTRONG, L. (1987) *Kiss Daddy Goodnight*, New York, Pocket Books.

ASHERAH, K. (1983) 'Daddy Kanagy', in BASS, E. and THORNTON, L. (Eds) *I Never Told Anyone: Writings by Women Survivors of Child Sexual Abuse*, London, Harper and Row, pp. 179–81.

AZIZ, C. (1987) 'Teaching children to say no', in *The Guardian*, 6 January, p. 10.

BACON, H. and RICHARDSON, S. (1989) 'Reflections on the psychology of the abused child', talk given at *Child Sexual Abuse: The Way Forward*, Teesside Polytechnic, 18–19 July.

BARR, A. (1986) 'Child sex abuse: We need money not sentiment' in *The Observer*, 9 November.

BARRETT, M. and COWARD, R. (1985) 'Don't talk to strangers', *New Socialist*, November, pp. 21–3.

BASS, E. and THORNTON, L. (Eds) (1983) *I Never Told Anyone: Writings by Women Survivors of Child Sexual Abuse*, London, Harper and Row.

BENDER, L. and BLAU, A. (1937) 'The reaction of children to sexual relations with adults', *American Journal of Orthopsychiatry*, **7**, 4, pp. 500–18.

BRADBURY, A. (1986) 'A model of treatment', *Community Care*, **4**, September, pp. 24–5.

BRASSARD, M., TYLER, A. and KEHLE, T. (1983) 'School programs to prevent intrafamilial child sexual abuse', *Child Abuse and Neglect*, 7, pp. 241–5.

BROWN, M. (1986) 'A parent's dilemma', in *The Sunday Times*, 19 October.

BUTLER, S. (1986) 'Thinking about prevention: A critical look' in NELSON, M. and CLARK, K. (Eds) (1986) *The Educator's Guide to Preventing Child Sexual Abuse*, Santa Cruz, Network Publications.

CAIGNON, D. and GROVES, G. (Eds) (1989) *Her Wits About Her: Self-Defense Success Stories by Women*, London, Women's Press.

CAMPBELL, B. (1988) *Unofficial Secrets: Child Sexual Abuse: The Cleveland Case*, London, Virago.

COOK, R. (1987) *The Cook Report*, ITV, 8.30pm, 29 July.

COOPER, S. (1986) 'Confronting a near and present danger: How to teach children to resist assault' in HADEN, D. (Ed) *Out of Harm's Way: Readings on Child Sexual Abuse, Its Prevention and Treatment*, Phoenix, Oryx Press, pp. 36–40.

DINGWALL, R. (1987) 'A parental prerogative?', *Nursing Times-Nursing Mirror*, **83**, 17, pp. 47–50.

DWORKIN, A. (1987) *Intercourse*, London, Secker and Warburg.

ELLIOTT, K. (1982) 'Diary of a feminist teacher', in ROWE, M. (Ed) *Spare Rib Reader*, Harmondsworth, Penguin, pp. 250–5.

ELLIOTT, M. (1988) 'Caring about safety', *Social Work Today*, **19**, 31, pp. 25–6, 32.

FINKELHOR, D. (1984) *Child Sexual Abuse: New Theory and Research*, London, Collier-McMillan.

FINKELHOR, D. (1986) 'Prevention: A review of programs and research', in FINKELHOR, D. and ASSOCIATES (Eds) *A Source Book on Child Sexual Abuse*, London, Sage, pp. 224–57.

FORWARD, S. and BUCK, C. (1981) *Betrayal of Innocence: Incest and Its Devastation*, London, Penguin.

GILBERT, N. (1988) 'Teaching children to prevent sexual abuse', *The Public Interest*, **93**, pp. 3–15.

GILGUN, J. (1986) 'Sexually abused girls' knowledge about sexual abuse and sexuality', *Journal of Interpersonal Violence*, **1**, Sept, 3, pp. 309–25.

GILGUN, J. and GORDON, S. (1985) 'Sex education and the prevention of child sexual abuse', *Journal of Sex Education and Therapy*, **11**, 1, Spring/Summer, pp. 46–52.

GOODE, D. (1986) 'Kids, culture and innocents', *Human Studies*, **9**, 1, pp. 83–106.

GORDON, L. (1988) *Heroes of Their Own Lives: The Politics and History of* Family Violence — 1880–1960, New York, Viking.

GOUGH, D. (1989) *Child Abuse Intervention: A Review of the Research Literature*, Research Report to DHSS. (Available from SPORU, 1 Lilybank Gardens, Glasgow University).

HAMILTON, S. (1989) 'Prevention of Child Sexual Abuse: An Evaluation of a Programme', MSc in advanced social work, Edinburgh University.

HANCOCK, M. and MAINS, K. (1987) *Child Sexual Abuse: A Hope for Healing*, Illinois, Harold Shaw Publishers.

HAUGARD, J. and REPPUCCI, N. (1988) *The Sexual Abuse of Children: A Comprehensive Guide to Current Knowledge and Intervention Strategies*, San Francisco, Jossey-Bass.

HEARN, J. (1988) 'Child abuse: Violences and sexualities towards young people', *Sociology*, **22**, 4, pp. 531–44.

HEARN, J. (1989) 'Child abuse and men's violence', in THE VIOLENCE AGAINST CHILDREN STUDY GROUP, *Taking Child Abuse Seriously: Contemporary Issues in Child Protection Theory and Practice*, London, Unwin Hyman. pp. 63–85.

HOLT, J. (1975) *Escape from Childhood: The Needs and Rights of Children*, London, Penguin.

HUBBARD, K. and BERLIN, E. (1985) *Help Yourself to Safety*, Chas, Franklin Press.

JANUS, S. (1981) *The Death of Innocence*, New York, Morrow.

JACKSON, S. (1982) *Childhood and Sensuality*, Oxford, Basil Blackwell.

JEFFREYS, S. (1985) *The Spinster and her Enemies*, London, Pandora.

KELLY, L. (1989) 'Bitter ironies', *Trouble and Strife*, 16, Summer pp. 14–21.

KELLY, R. (1988) 'Protect your child from sexual abuse!', *The Plain Truth*, September, pp. 10–11.

Kids Can Say No, Video, Exeter, Pergamon Educational Productions.

KITZINGER, J. (1985) '"Take the toys from the boys": The social construction of gender and the women's peace movement', in *Bulletin of the British Psychological Society*, **38**, May, p. 68.

KITZINGER, S. and KITZINGER, C. (1989) *Talking to Children About Things that Really Matter*, London, Pandora.

KOHN, A. (1987) 'Shattered innocence', *Psychology Today*, **21**, February, pp. 54–8.

LEEDS REVOLUTIONARY FEMINIST GROUP (1981) *Love Your Enemy: The Debate Between Heterosexual Feminism and Political Lesbianism*, London, Onlywomen Press.

LIZ (1982) 'Too afraid to speak', *The Leveller*, 2–15th April, pp. 18–21.

MACFARLANE, K. (1988) 'Current issues in child sexual abuse', Talk given at *Intervening in Child Sexual Abuse*, Glasgow, 1988.

MILLER-PERRIN, C. and WURTELE, S. (1988) 'The child sexual abuse prevention movement — A critical analysis of primary and secondary approaches', *Clinical Psychology Review*, **8**, 3, pp. 313–29.

NELSON, S. (1987) *Incest: Fact and Myth*, Edinburgh, Stramullion.

PARTON, C. and PARTON, N. (1988) 'Women, the family and child protection', *Critical Social Policy*, Winter 88/89, pp. 38–49.

RANTZEN, E. (1986) 'Dear Esther', in *The Sunday Times*, 9, November, p. 25.

RUSH, F. (1980) *The Best Kept Secret: Sexual Abuse of Children*, New York, McGraw-Hill.

Russell, D. (1986) *The Secret Trauma: Incest in the Lives of Girls and Women*, New York, Basic Books.

Sarnacki Porter, F., Canfield Blick, L. and Sgroi, S. (1982) 'Treatment of the sexually abused child', in Sgroi, S. (Ed) *Handbook of Clinical Intervention in Child Sexual Abuse*, Massachusetts, Lexington Books.

Seabrook, J. (1987) 'The decay of childhood', *New Statesman*, 10 July, pp. 14–15.

Senn, C. (undated) *Vulnerable: Sexual Abuse and People with an Intellectual Handicap*, Canada, G. Allan Roeher Institute.

Sgroi, S. (Ed) (1982) *Handbook of Clinical Intervention in Child Sexual Abuse*, Massachusetts, Lexington Books.

Shelter (1989) *One Day I'll Have My Own Place to Stay*, London, Shelter, Publications.

Stacey, C. (1989) 'How to get ahead', *Options*, November, pp. 26–7.

Stainton-Rogers, R. (1989) 'The social construction of childhood', in Stainton-Rogers, W., Hevey, D. and Ash, E. (1989) *Child Abuse and Neglect: Facing the Challenge*, London, Open University Press, pp. 23–9.

Sullivan, P., Vernon, M. and Scanlan, J. (1987) 'Sexual abuse of deaf youth', *American Annals of the Deaf*, **132**, 4, pp. 256–62.

Summit, R. (1983) 'The child sexual abuse accommodation syndrome', *Child Abuse and Neglect*, **7**, pp. 177–93.

Summit, R. (1986) 'Foreword', in MacFarlane, K. and Waterman, J. (1986) *Sexual Abuse of Young Children*, London, Holt, Rinehart and Winston, pp. xi–xv.

Summit, R. and Kryso, J. (1978) 'Sexual abuse of children: A clinical spectrum', *American Journal of Orthopsychiatry*, **48**, pp. 237–51.

Takanishi, R. (1978) 'Childhood as a social issue: Historical roots of contemporary child advocacy movements', *Journal of Social Issues*, **34**, 2, pp. 8–28.

Testimony of a Child Debate (1989) BBC2, 5 July, 11.15pm.

Tharinger, D., Krivacsk, J., Layemcdo, M., Jamison, L., Vincent, G. and Hedlund, A. (1988) 'Prevention of child sexual abuse — An analysis of issues, educational programs and research findings', *School Psychological Review*, **17**, 14, pp. 614–34.

Touch, P. (1987) 'Stories my body tells', in Portwood, P., Gorcey, M. and Sanders, P. (Eds) (1987) *Rebirth of Power*, Racine, Illinois, Mother Courage Press.

Trudell, B. and Whatley, M. (1988) 'School sexual abuse prevention — Unintended consequences and dilemmas', *Child Abuse*, **12**, 1, pp. 103–13.

Tucker, N. (1985) 'A panic over child abuse', *New Society*, 18 Oct, pp. 96–8.

Waksler, F. (1986) 'Studying children: Phenomological insights', *Human Studies*, **9**, 1, pp. 71–82.

Ward, E. (1984) *Father Daughter Rape*, London, Women's Press.

Wisechild, L. (1988) *Obsidian Mirror: An Adult Healing from Incest*, Seattle, Seal Press.

Chapter 9

Childhood and the Policy Makers: A Comparative Perspective on the Globalization of Childhood

Jo Boyden

Introduction

My interest in child welfare and children's rights is as a practitioner involved in the development of policy and operational programmes for especially disadvantaged children in the poor countries of the South (Note 1). Among other things, the work entails the assessment of both governmental and non-governmental responses to issues of childhood such as labour, homelessness and maltreatment.

The extension of welfare services to the most needy sectors of the population is seen as the benchmark of the successful nation state in the modern world. And, to an extent, the function of people like myself has been to encourage this process wherever possible by informing and collaborating with governments. However, my involvement in research and programme evaluation in a number of countries has caused me to have growing misgivings about the conception of childhood and children's rights used in much social planning. My unease is focused in particular on the solutions to the special problems of childhood that are widely adopted.

Despite extreme social and cultural diversity, there exists a core ideology in the South, around which official versions of childhood pivot. This ideology dictates that children are demarcated from adults by a series of biological and psychological, as opposed to social, characteristics that are universally valid. It also dictates that childhood is accompanied by a set of rights that can be enshrined in international law. It is the concern of this paper to explore the historical origins of this ideal of childhood, to trace its global export and examine its impact, especially on the children of the poor.

Constructing Childhood in Adult Eyes

Childhood in the twentieth century is regarded as being separate from adulthood. Partly because of this, children have been attributed with certain special qualities or disabilities and as the interest in children grows, so the images of childhood conveyed by the adult world become ever more poignant. Adult nostalgia for youthful innocence is symbolized by the whimsy of London's Museum of Childhood, with its display cabinets full of mechanical toys, china dolls, hand-painted doll's houses, tin soldiers, electric train sets and Dinky cars. There is no place in this kind of childhood for labour in the factory or mine.

Yet there is growing evidence globally that childhood is for many a very unhappy time. International media coverage of the young paints an especially stark picture, of innocent and vulnerable child victims of adult violence and maltreatment; of 'stolen' childhoods in refugee camps and war zones[1]. The widespread trafficking and sexual exploitation of minors in Thailand and the Philippines, the physical and emotional abuse of children in Europe and the United States and the bondage of young labourers in India are now all clearly documented. But children have also endured serious crimes committed by their governments, as in Argentina under the military regime when an unknown number were abducted by the security forces and subsequently disappeared. In South Africa and Namibia black school pupils have experienced repression and detention and in Iraq, Kurdish children have been victims of genocide.

Rights and welfare activists have sought the introduction of measures to protect children from intolerable conditions such as these, on the grounds that the child comes into the world 'defenceless in the face of an aggressive and violent society and that he is the first to suffer the terrible consequences of famine, war and socioeconomic crisis' (Vega Fuente, 1983: 23). Agencies such as The International Union for Child Welfare and, more recently, Defence for Children International, have been created specifically to monitor the exploitation and abuse of children worldwide. The anxiety about young people in the present day is such that the political and social condition of whole societies is now gauged by the status of their children.

The major tenet of contemporary rights and welfare thinking is that regulation of child life should give priority to making childhood a carefree, safe, secure and happy phase of human existence (Sommerville, 1982). Most modern strategies of child protection are, as I shall show, underpinned by theories of pollution; adult society undermines childhood innocence, thus children must be segregated from the harsh realities of the adult world and protected from social danger (Aries, 1962).

To this end, child life has been characterized by a range of appropriate contexts, experiences, relationships and behaviors: 'properly loved children, regardless of social class, belonged in a domesticated, non-productive world of lessons, games, and token money' (Zelizer, 1985). Thus, the contemporary, essentially sentimental, approach to childhood is at the same time both nurturing and constraining, so that in the modern industrial world:

> the instrumental value of children has been largely replaced by their expressive value. Children have become relatively worthless (economically) to their parents, but priceless in terms of their psychological worth (Scheper-Hughes, 1989: 12).

Significantly, the norms and values upon which this ideal of a safe, happy and protected childhood are built are culturally and historically bound to the social preoccupations and priorities of the capitalist countries of Europe and the United States. It is a model of childhood — along with the legislative frameworks, policies and codes of welfare practice applied in its pursuit — which has resulted from the historical interplay of the Judeo-Christian belief system and changes in the productive and demographic base of society corresponding with capitalist development. Childhood had not been a matter of much concern until the time of the religious reformations, when moralists and theologians began to apply the discipline of doctrine and training to children in the hope of securing converts. It was during the eighteenth and nineteenth centuries that qualities of innocence and nobility were first associated with children and the desire to foster these qualities through conscious parenting emerged (see Hendrick, this volume).

The expansion of capitalism, however, has given the greatest impetus to contemporary images of the ideal childhood. Industrial production and urbanization had a dramatic impact on the lives of children in Europe, with mechanization in its early stages resulting in a marked increase in the exploitation of child labour. But mechanization also highlighted the need to foster socially responsible and economically useful individuals to supply a skilled and differentiated labourforce. It was eventually realized that such individuals would not flourish by labouring while young in mines and factories. Besides which, with economic specialization and the advance in complex technologies, children were becoming less useful materially. Schools then became a training ground for industrial workers and a place for containing and shaping childhood.

As Qvortrup (1985) has shown, under capitalism the foundation for productive work in the family was eroded. In urban areas particularly the extended family fell into decline and the smaller nuclear family emerged as the predominant household form within which child-rearing took place. It is, therefore, not surprising to find that today much state effort to secure child welfare is expended on developing ways of improving the home environment and scrutinizing parenting practices. Governments blame problems of child development and the neglect or abuse of children on the collapse of family, abnormal or deteriorating inter-personal relationships, a lack of marital or parental responsibility or alcoholism. As the definition of acceptable conduct within the home has become more precise, so judgments about abnormal childhoods and family forms and lifestyles that do not conform have become harsher. Conformity in child rearing has now reached the point in the industrialized world that parents are condemned for allowing their offspring to miss school, watch violent or sexually explicit programmes on television, or remain unattended or even in the care of a child minder either in public places or in the home (Winn, 1984; Morgan, 1987; Barlow and Hill, 1985). And parents whose children work are accused of exploiting them as a commodity.

In this respect, current welfare philosophy and practice in fact reflects the historical attitudes among reformers towards social pathology that were both punitive and judgmental. Nineteenth century welfare concerns, for example, focused especially on homeless, vagrant or indigent families rather than directly on child labour (Zeitz, 1969). In Britain, therefore, the fierce ideology of the workhouse was developed largely to counteract idleness, which was seen as tantamount to crime.

But the moralizing ideologies of social reform were not restricted to adults; there was growing concern about the darker side of children's nature. In Britain children between the ages of 5 and 14 years old who were found to be living in idleness or begging were bound into craft or agricultural services. The abnormal development of children and juvenile delinquency in cities became one of the main public concerns of the late Victorian and Edwardian period and underlay the priority given to the reclamation and reform of children and young people in social planning (Pearson, 1985; Alcock and Harris, 1982 and Hendrick, this volume). The fear was that childhood innocence if not properly directed and trained at home and in school could give way to riotous and immoral behaviour.

Many of these negative images of childhood still prevail and many have gained currency throughout the world in countries with very varied and contrasting social and economic conditions. They are in common usage in urban areas especially. Thus, while disquiet about the suffering of innocent child victims grows in the twentieth century, there exists another, very different, perception, of the unsocialized or anti-social child, the deviant, or trouble-maker. In this image, children and young people are characterized as being 'deficient' through immaturity (Alcock and Harris, 1982). Adults seem occupied by the idea that young football hooligans, school terror gangs, vandals, muggers and the like might represent human nature in its untamed state. Hence the intense curiosity about feral children and the portrayal in fiction such as Golding's *Lord of the Flies* of wilful and depraved children.[2] Adult protectiveness towards children, then, is tempered by the perceived need for control.

Crime statistics are frequently used to confirm adult fears about young people out of control, roaming the streets and indulging in acts of vandalism and violence. For example, official sources indicate that juveniles between the ages of 10 and 17 years old account for one-third of all the more serious offences dealt with by the police in England, Ireland and Wales (Hoghughi, 1983). Juvenile crime thus represents for many adults the most worrying symptom of urban chaos and decay in the modern world, the largest cities with the highest growth rates globally reporting the highest rates of youthful crime per capita (Clinard and Abbot, 1973). In cities as disparate as Abidjan, Bogota, Cairo, Manila and Seoul, children playing in the streets and other public spaces and young teenagers congregating on street corners, outside cinemas or bars, have become synonymous in the mind of the general public with delinquent gangs.[3]

Historically, it can be shown that among the young people most disparaged during the first decades of industrialization in Europe were those who worked on the street — street traders, newspaper vendors, match and flower sellers, messengers and van boys. However, the problem was not so much that these children were working rather than attending school, but more that the street itself was thought to be physically and morally damaging to minors. Whitehouse, writing about the problems of 'boy life' in 1912, says:

> The evidence is . . . clear and widespread as to the evils resulting to children and young people through trading in the streets. . . . The chief of these are the physical injury sustained by children through standing about the streets in all weathers, often insufficiently clothed; the moral injury following upon a life on the streets, which in the case of girls generally means their ruin, and in the case of boys rapidly leads to gambling and crime. At the best it unfits those who engage in it for any regular work in life. Fresh from school, and in many cases before they have left school, they enter upon a wild, undisciplined life, and suffer both mental and moral degeneration (Whitehouse, 1912: 167).

But the idea that the street is morally dangerous for children was a peculiarly northern European conception. Bedarida and Sutcliffe (1981), for example, suggest that while in nineteenth century Paris, one might have strolled down a street, in London this would have been seen as loitering. Whereas in northern Europe street life — especially in the poorest districts — was equated with a criminal sub-culture, in the Mediterranean countries the street was crucial to a variety of social and commercial activities (INGO, 1983). The sharp distinction between the street and the home took place alongside changes on the domestic front and in patterns of property ownership and lifestyle initiated by the urban rich. Among the middle classes of Northern Europe, whose women and children were in retreat from industrial life, the home provided the focal point for all things private (Meyer, 1983). As the fear of crime in public spaces in cities grew, the wealthy built more barriers against the encroachment into their domestic lives of immoral and illegal influences.

The concept of private property and privacy within the home is now closely protected by the rich in all continents. They live in culde-sacs, mews, or closes with obstructions of various kinds to stop through traffic. Fear of burglary causes them to put bars on their windows and build high walls around their gardens, and to set spyholes and double locks in their doors. In Latin America particularly, many families keep guard dogs on the roof, or hire guards — often armed — to keep watch at the front gate. Others live in closed, radio-controlled, complexes containing luxury housing, leisure facilities, shops, restaurants and banks.

Shielding middle class children from public life entails certain costs. It means that they must become accustomed to a world without freedom of movement. They may never play on the streets. Instead, they are confined to designated play areas in schools and parks and to designated play time — play in other spaces and at other times being disapproved (Munday, 1979). In many countries, rather than walking or travelling to school on public transport, children are taken by car, sometimes in the company of a bodyguard. In compensation for restricting the child's movement, the wealthy home contains a variety of recreational tools, such as a swimming pool, squash or tennis courts or a gymnasium, and recreation outside the home takes the form of family outings in the car or attendance at private functions, clubs or beaches rather than public facilities.

The notion that children should be kept off the streets coexists happily with the view that the family and the school are the chief legitimate agents for the socialization of children. In nineteenth century Europe, children were the leading colonists of the street and their streetlife was to be curtailed drastically by schools (Bedarida and Sutcliffe,

1981). Nowadays children present on the streets of Northern Europe during school hours run a high risk of being apprehended by the police for commiting a status offence.[4] School is therefore not simply an alternative to work, but also to life on the streets. Phillips, for example, remarked in 1912 that in England 'the whole system of national education has been reared on the foundation of the Ragged Schools, whose avowed object it was to draw children away from the fascinating misery of the streets' (1912: 206).

It is now generally accepted well beyond the frontiers of Europe that street life is morally polluting for the young. And in most countries convention holds that street children are both the most deprived and the most depraved members of society, living by theft, prostitution and drug running. The overriding concern, though, is not with the dangers for children associated with street life, but more the damage street children may do to the community (see Glauser, this volume). Take, for example, the views expressed in an article published in Dakar in 'The Politician':

> The invasion of aggressive and rather shady-looking beggars who rage all the thoroughfares of our capital constitutes the open and stinking wound which degrades and infects our daily lives. Traffic lights, bank entrances, department stores, post offices . . . hotels, are all stormed by an unqualifiably dubious crowd. . . . Even if they are physically handicapped, it goes without saying that as soon as darkness settles in, they change to clandestine prostitutes. The . . . children transform into dangerous burglars and wrongdoers. . . . For goodness sake, clear these beggars . . . out of the way (Abdoulaye Tall, no date: 6).

For many people the street child is the embodiment of the untamed, feral child; an outcast whose very existence threatens social chaos and decline. Because of their unkempt appearance, their involvement in illegal activities, their frequent substance addiction and their generally poor state of health, street children are frequently judged by officialdom to be lacking in moral or social values or somehow impaired mentally.

Yet the evidence from many countries is quite the contrary (Espinola, Glauser, Ortiz and Ortiz de Carrizosa, 1987; Swart, 1989; Fernandez, Godoy, Morales, *et al.*, 1985; Boyden, 1985). Street children generally organize into groups, often with clear internal hierarchies and strong attachments to a territory. Group solidarity extends to the sharing of food and other goods and provision of protection and support in crises. The street child is very often more intelligent, more creative, more aware and more independent than the child at home. Activities such as shoplifting or picking pockets which the community designates criminal are essential survival strategies on the street. Research shows that street children may well live with insecurity, danger and crime, but they are usually runaways and street life is an option they choose over the frequent subjugation and violence within the home. There is particularly strong evidence, for example, that a large proportion of runaways have experienced incest or sexual or physical abuse prior to leaving home (Reppond, 1983).

Setting the Agenda for Happy Childhoods

As the twentieth century has progressed, then, highly selective, stereotyped perceptions of childhood — of the innocent child victim on the one hand and the young deviant on the other — have been exported from the industrial world to the South. They have provided a focal point for the development of both human rights legislation at the international level and social policy at the national level in a wide range of countries. It has been the explicit goal of children's rights specialists to crystalize in international law a universal system of rights for the child based on these norms of childhood. The present United Nations Convention on the Rights of the Child comes closer to this goal than any previous international instrument. At the national level, child welfare has been a major pretext for state manipulation of the affairs of family and community.

One of the main links between international rights legislation and traditional child welfare thinking is that both have been deeply influenced by the ideologies of the social work and legal professions. This influence is extremely significant for the development of a global standard of childhood because both tend to play down the impact of wider social, economic, political and cultural conditions in the shaping of social phenomena and therefore to advocate individual, remedial solutions to social problems. Priority is given to individual causation, highlighting individual dysfunctioning or pathology, and rehabilitative strategies based on individual case history are used in the 'cure' of social problems.[5]

For example, social work has been dominated traditionally by medical psychology; pioneers in the field were drawn to moralistic rather than sociological interpretations of social phenomena. For them, problems such as juvenile delinquency, poverty or homelessness were the result of individual psycho-pathology — immorality or a lack of thrift, for example — rather than the 'iron constraints' of social conditions (Younghusband, 1981). Welfare practice consisted of moral rearmament and the strengthening of character. Whilst contemporary approaches in social work in many industrialized countries may have moved a long way from these beginnings — setting social problems more firmly in the context of social structure and organization — their influence can still be seen in welfare practice in a large number of countries, in the South especially, and is gradually having the effect of creating a universal standard of childhood.

This global standard of child rearing and child welfare sought by welfare practitioners is increasingly upheld as a basic human right. In fact, it is argued that the right to welfare — to adequate nutrition, medical care and so on — is perhaps the most fundamental of all human rights (Freeman, 1983). By setting this standard of welfare in the rights framework, it is implied that there exists a contractual obligation to guarantee child welfare, since embodied in the concept of right is a direct claim upon someone else (Alston, 1987; Smyke, 1979). In this sense 'right' is a far more powerful concept than 'need', the term that dominated early welfare thinking, because the latter amounts to little more than a general statement about moral entitlements (but see Woodhead, this volume). Thus, it is now,

> widely accepted that the characterization of a specific goal as a human right elevates it above the rank and file of competing societal goals, gives it a degree of immunity from challenge, and generally endows it with an aura of timelessness, absoluteness, and universal validity' (Alston, 1987: 2).

In the case of international humanitarian law, the contractual obligation to uphold children's rights lies with the state as signator to international treaties. The rights of the child in the modern nation are encapsulated in the doctrine *parens patriae* which grants the child the right to care and protection before the law and defines the duty of the state to act as the guardian and ultimate guarantor of child welfare through social planning.

Whilst international law has traditionally embodied the image of the dependent child, the potential victim, many national welfare programmes, in addition to protective measures, contain a large element of control or constraint. Indeed, moves at the international level to secure happy childhoods have been largely motivated by the gradual growth in awareness over the twentieth century that many governments are failing in their protective duty towards children.[6]

The foundations for a global standard of childhood were laid down by witnesses to the suffering of children in the First World War who wrote the Declaration of the Rights of the Child. The Declaration provided the blueprint for a universal ideal, specifying a series of rights for children that were separate from and additional to those of adults. In effect, these rights were little more than a collection of general moral entitlements and few — the right to love and understanding, for example — could be guaranteed. The prime aim of the treaty was to protect and nuture childhood rather than to encourage equality for children with adults, in that while it purported to work in the best interests of the child, these interests were identified entirely by adults. Also, child welfare was identified with that of the family and no allowance was made for the possibility of conflict within the family.

As this century has advanced, successive international instruments and human rights events have progressively refined their understanding of the special attributes and needs of childhood. Measures like the United Nations International Year of the Child and the UN Convention on the Rights of the Child, have given greater scope for self-representation and self advocacy than the Declaration. Also, they are more clearly focused on especially disadvantaged groups — addressing the rights not only of children living in 'average' situations within the family, but also of those experiencing exceptional circumstances such as war, abandoment or abuse. The Convention is seen as an important advance on the Declaration because it is not just a general statement of good intent, but an instrument legally binding those states that ratify it. More than previous treaties, the Convention recognizes the child's capacity to act independently, bestowing not just protective, but also enabling rights, such as the right to freedom of expression and association (Cantwell, 1989).

The United Nations, through its constituent agencies, has played a prominent role in the effort to promote enlightened and benign government on behalf of children, encouraging the establishment of social welfare, compulsory education, child labour legislation and health services throughout the world. The organization's concern with matters of social welfare began with the creation of the Social Commission in 1946 and eventually the United Nations became the main international body promoting social planning (Hardiman and Midgley, 1982). Membership of the United Nations increased from fifty-five to 154 countries between 1946 and 1980 and, as the supreme mediator of the principle of liberal democratic rule globally, it has a strong interest in spreading to the poor countries of the South the values and codes of practice devised in the public sector in the industrialized North. The organization has encouraged the development of social services and creation of schools of social work in the South as training centres for employment in Ministries of Social Welfare (*ibid*).

The earliest attempts at state regulation of childhood at the national level took place in Western Europe and the United States; in the South it was, therefore, through colonial rule that formal welfare provision first arose. The welfare priorities devised at that time continue to shape the structures and forms of provision in the present. For example, the countries previously controlled by the British tend to emphasize personal social services and rely heavily on voluntary agencies in implementation (Midgley, 1986; Kadushin, 1974). The former French colonies link social services with health and nursing activity and stress family allowances, whilst in Latin American countries, it is the Catholic church which is prominent in the provision of social services. The Silesian order, for example, has become closely associated with the education and vocational training of children and custodial care for the orphaned and destitute.

Nowadays the means by which childhood is regulated are becoming ever more sophisticated, stretching far beyond simple population issues and giving priority to the quality of child life. In the modern nation, provision for average or normal childhoods for the mass of children, has four main components; survival (health care and nutrition), regulation of population, schooling, and anti-labour legislation. The wealthier industrialized countries also cater for the majority of children through explicit policies on family and childhood, with a network of social benefits and social services designed to prevent or counteract dysfunctioning. The most comprehensive programmes have been developed in the Socialist Bloc and the Scandinavian countries, where measures such as family counselling, family planning, income maintenance, day-care and public housing for all coexist with specialist interventions for families in trouble.

The prime aim of health care in the South has been to reduce infant and child morbidity and mortality; In this task the World Health Organiation and UNICEF, in close collaboration with international non-governmental bodies like OXFAM and Save the Children Fund, have played a major role. In recent decades, the most important strategy promoted by these agencies has been primary health care at the community level, which relies on preventive measures, as opposed to curative medicine. UNICEF'S fortieth anniversary issue of 'The State of the World's Children' (1987) stressed that the major achievement of the period since the agency was founded was the halving of infant and child mortality globally. Low cost techniques for improving child health include oral rehydration therapy, immunization, breast — as opposed to bottle — feeding, birth spacing and appropriate weaning practices. Key national figures such as sports personalities and politicians have collaborated closely with national media in many countries in support of mass immunization campaigns and the dissemination of the general principles of preventive health care.

Whilst preventive health care has had a direct impact on child morbidity and mortality, schooling has been conceived as the panacea for underdevelopment and undemocratic processes (Hall, 1986). In the 1950s and 1960s, when many countries in the South became independent, education was a major growth industry, with school enrolments increasing at twice the rate of population (Coombs, 1985). In the early 1960s UNESCO organized a series of regional conferences at which education ministers from Asia, Africa and Latin America set their timetables for achieving universal primary education.

In the modern era, mass education is believed to be a fundamental human right, a goal all societies should seek to achieve.[7] Universal literacy and numeracy are seen as vital to the economic development and general welfare of society. These skills facilitate the acquisition of knowledge necessary for improving the quality of human life in areas such as birth spacing, health care, nutrition and hygiene. They also prepare the labour force for technically advanced productive processes. Furthermore, in democratic societies, universal education is seen as crucial to the proper functioning of the political process. As in the industrialized world in the past, compulsory full-time schooling is now also thought to be the best way of keeping unoccupied and potentially delinquent young people out of trouble in the South.

But despite the spread of schooling, children still play a major part in the labourforce in many countries. In some areas, more than a quarter of school age children work. Whereas at one time the International Labour Office advocated total abolition of child labour, the overwhelming impact of poverty in the South has forced it to adopt a compromise in recent years. The present aim, therefore, is to encourage policies that prohibit child labour in occupations damaging to health and development and to regulate child labour in non-hazardous occupations (Bequele and Boyden, 1988). A further distinction is made by the International Labour Office between child work and formal labour or employment, on the grounds that while the latter is often highly exploitative, the former may not be harmful to children and may even be beneficial. The only real concern of labour policy is to regulate the waged or semi-waged occupations of children; non-remunerated labour, self-employment and so called 'informal' activities are considered to fall within the confines of social welfare intervention. Family labour and labour on the farm or in domestic chores is also excluded, because exploitation or danger resulting from hazardous processes in agriculture or in the home is believed to be far less likely than in situations where children are employed by non-related adults in industry, commerce or services.

All countries now have specialist interventions that target children with social problems. Indeed, in many countries in the South formal welfare is restricted to dealing with problem childhoods, as both the resources and the will to implement preventive welfare measures to secure the wellbeing of the wider population of children are in short supply. The majority of governments now have a fairly clear definition of what for them is an abnormal childhood and which are the appropriate procedures for dealing with such abnormality.

For example, children who are thought to require state intervention generally include, on the one hand, those in need of supervision and the delinquent and, on the other, the dependent or neglected (Stein, 1981). The delinquent and the child in need of supervision is the deviant child of modern society; those children who have engaged in theft or vandalism, and runaways and school truants, who have broken the special rules of childhood. Dependent or neglected children fall into a very different category; they are perceived as society's victims rather than its scapegoats. Among these children are included the morally and materially neglected, whose parents are either unable or unwilling to shelter and care for them or consciously expose them to moral danger by influencing them to commit or witness illicit acts. The school, the juvenile court, welfare agencies, children's sections in the police force and correctional establishments all exist as mechanisms through which compliance with the standards of child care set forth in law can be enforced.

But because of budgetary constraints, formal welfare provision in the South usually responds only to the most public and extreme of cases, such as the infant abandoned on a rubbish heap, alongside the road or in a doorway, or the child living on the streets; problems within the home are largely ignored. Most countries also focus mainly on urban rather than rural populations, assuming that the latter have long since developed customary measures to provide for children in trouble (Macpherson, 1982).

Obstacles in the Export of Ideal Childhoods

As shown in the previous section, under colonial rule and the more recent influence of the United Nations and international legislation on children's rights, the images of childhood favoured in the industrial

North have been exported to the South. The view that childhood is a fixed notion, 'determined by biological and psychological facts' rather than culture or society is explicit in international children's rights legislation (Freeman, 1983). The rights lobby is in the forefront of the global spread of norms of childhood which are integral to the history and culture of Europe and North America. For example, as Alston has commented, lawyers tend to speak of the 'international human rights system' as though there were indeed a single system 'based upon sound and essentially unchallenged foundations, applying a reasonably clear, coherent and internally consistent set of norms' (1987: 7).

International children's rights lawyers largely ignore the evidence that the conception of rights is intimately tied up with cultural values and the outlook of any given society. Lejeune (1984) takes up the argument specifically in relation to the UN Convention on the Rights of the Child which, since it does not make general statements, but sets out rights in detail, he says, can only apply to a geo-political area in which the same attitudes to law, the same political system and compatible cultural traditions are firmly rooted.

The view that equality of opportunity should exist for all children is very attractive and is certainly extremely just and humane — especially in light of the widespread exploitation and maltreatment experienced by so many young people in the world today. However, research in sociology and social anthropology suggests that childhood, within certain biological constraints, is a social construct which appears in a variety of forms (see Prout and James, this volume). The different competencies and incapacities perceived to be associated with childhood in different societies are numerous and often imply contradictory conceptions of the child. For example, while in many countries children are seen as dependent until well into their teens, in many others they are expected to be fully independent from an early age. The contrast between Britain and Peru, for example, is instructive. In the former it is illegal to leave infants and small children in charge of juveniles under the age of 14. In the latter, on the other hand, the national census records a significant group of 6 to 14 year olds who are heads of households and as such are the principal breadwinners in the family, sometimes even the sole person in charge of the care of younger siblings (Boyden, 1985). Similar findings are reported in a survey of 600 children in Bangalore, India, in that over 6 per cent of these children were the sole working and earning member of the family (Patil, 1986).

The manner in which the transition to adulthood is achieved may also differ radically from one country to the next. Thus, whereas age grade system normally represent a progression by stages of ever increasing responsibility, in many countries the age of majority signifies a watershed, in which adult rights and obligations are assumed all at once. In some countries there are even considerable internal inconsistencies, with different capacities being bestowed at different ages. This situation may also be further compounded by gender distinctions.

The discomfort among certain welfare practitioners from the South about the global export of perceptions of childhood and family is most explicit in recent consultations on the content of the draft Convention on the Rights of the Child. During discussion, several of the delegates from the South expressed dissatisfaction that the drafting group was 'predominantly Western in its orientation', and argued that greater account should have been taken 'of the cultural diversity and economic realities of developing countries' (Newman-Black, 1989: 36). Indeed, as Fyfe (1989) has pointed out, the majority of countries in the South showed little interest in the drafting process, precisely because it embodies values of 'normal' childhood and child development that are foreign to them. It was suggested by some delegates that each country should be able to interpret the instrument as it wishes and proposals were made for an African charter of children's rights, to address the specific cultural and social circumstances of that region (Newman-Black, 1989).

Other criticisms focused on the definition of family and family responsibility. For example, the draft text referred throughout to 'parents', meaning those people who have special rights and obligations with regard to children. However, in many societies customary law dictates that children are the responsibility of the extended rather than the nuclear family and the role of relatives other than parents in child care is vital. Use of the term 'parents', it was suggested, implies that the nuclear family is more 'natural' than the extended family (*ibid*).

Formal interventions by the state can be seen to threaten the rightful fuctions of the family. This is especially true in the Middle East and other areas where shared parenthood within the clan or extended family system remains deeply embedded in the social structure. Adoption, as a state intervention, also presented a particular problem since it runs counter to the culture and traditions of a large number of societies in the South. In many Islamic countries, for example, adoption is prohibited altogether, whereas, according to Hindu custom, it is confined almost exclusively to males within the descent group (Goody, 1976).

National welfare programmes in the South are generally less explicit about their use of norms of childhood borrowed from the North than are international treaties. Nevertheless, these norms are employed widely in social policy in the South, often as an inheritance from colonial times. For instance, one of the earliest examples of statutory child care comes from the Philippines, where the Bureau of Dependent Children was established in 1918 along the lines of the Children's Bureau in the United States (Midgley, 1986). But many of these models have proved inappropriate. As Edobor Igbinovia (1985) notes, the use of imported procedures, such as juvenile courts, probation services, approved schools and reformatories, guided by non-African philosophy and law has proved ineffective in the control and treatment of juvenile offenders in Nigeria.

The types of welfare services provided in the South during the colonial period reflected the concerns of the rulers rather than the needs of the ruled. One of the explicit priorities of colonial govern-ments was to provide protection for the expatriate community against a hostile physical environment. The Nigerian health service, for example, was established in areas where expatriates lived primarily as a result of the great fire that consumed Lagos in 1877 and the outbreak of bubonic plague in 1924 (Sanda, 1987). The expatriate settlers and colo-nial administrators were also worried about the threat to themselves from youth crime, and made begging and vagrancy and public order concerns predominant.

The ideologies and structures of state provision developed in the colonial period generally reflected a very narrow interpretation of so-cial welfare and the priority awarded to public order was to remain intact under the subsequent influence of the United Nations. Even as late as the 1950s, United Nations interest in social issues was confined largely to destitution and social pathologies in urban areas (Hardiman and Midgley, 1982). Although this policy eventually attracted criticism and the Economic and Social Council undertook a major reappraisal of the organization's social welfare activities, the welfare bureaucracies and their modes of practice were by this time firmly established in the South and few were eager to adopt a new approach. Moreover, despite the information collected globally by the United Nations on social and economic indicators, there is still a serious lack of reliable data to aid the development of new, effective policies in welfare (Livingstone, 1969). As a result, many of the principles of existing policies are based on assumption, or even guesswork.

It could perhaps be argued that global uniformity in policies to-ward children is justified because the patterns of socio-economic change in the South in the present day seem to resemble closely those which took place in the North in the past. For example, recent research indic-ates that in urban areas in the South the extended family has largely been replaced by nuclear family units (CEPAL, 1983; Centre for Social Development and Humanitarian Affairs, 1984; De Souza, 1983; Michel

Zinzou, 1985). And, crucially, problems such as alcoholism and crime have apparently increased in cities in the South at precisely the moment that traditional solutions are becoming progressively less viable (Kayango-Male and Onyango, 1986). Welfare professionals point to the decline of traditional values of social control and the loss of critical support mechanisms with the dispersal of joint or extended families, detribalization and the weakening of clan structures as justification of state intervention (Sanda, 1987; Hasen, 1969; Macpherson, 1982; CEPAL, 1983).

The weakening of affective ties and resultant family disorganization in urban areas in the South is believed to have had a particularly devastating effect on the young. Changes in the roles within the family, with the husband and father no longer playing the central part in income generation, have apparently led to the widespread abandonment of women and children (Tacon, 1981). Marital discord, female headed households and working mothers have all been cited as causal in abuse and neglect, homelessness and other problems of children; control over and care of the young has become a major preoccupation in urban areas. 'Under such situations where parental care is lacking or deficient, there is a tendency for the children to show deviant patterns of behavior. They may become undisciplined, delinquent and sexually promiscuous' (Oyemade, 1986: 195). As the network of mutual aid and support is seen to weaken, a growing number of institutionalized child welfare services such as day and custodial care are needed to reinforce, supplement or substitute parental care (Midgley, 1986; Macpherson, 1987).

Yet, recent evidence suggests that far more caution needs to be exercised in the use of social data such as these to determine policy. Lobo, for example, has argued that there is a tendency to underestimate the role of kinship ideologies, and of networks and alliances in Third World cities (1982). Planners may wrongly assume that social chaos corresponds with the visual disorder of self-help housing, makeshift services, high population densities and poor infrastructures. Also, they may fail to appreciate that a decline in traditional values and networks is often matched by the appearance of new alliances and innovative survival strategies:

> The development process, in particular, seems to produce changes in family roles and functions that may, on the one hand, be associated with the breakdown of the family and may, on the other, promote resilience and flexibility in adapting to new circumstances and may even foster the change process itself (Centre for Social Development and Humanitarian Affairs, 1984: 2).

For example, where the incidence of female headed households is high or where extended family ties are weak, neighbours frequently collaborate closely in matters such as child care or income generation.[9]

Caution is also necessary when transplanting the concept of individual rights. While the industrialized world places a premium upon the development of individuality and the guarantee of individual rights, in many peasant-based societies the desire to sustain group solidarity prevails over individual needs and interests (Poffenberger, 1983). Therefore, what might be considered an abuse of individual rights in the Northern context, may in many countries be perceived as a vital mechanism for maintaining group cohesion and solidarity. Thus, African nationalism has tended to identify national repression with the erosion of pre-capitalist societies and to insist on the sanctity of the pre-capitalist family, embodying though it did the subordinate position of women (Burman, 1984).

Ascriptive systems such as that of the Hindu caste structure, for example, can be especially tyrannical towards the individual. Caste affiliation determines not only children's social status, place of residence, educational attainment and future position in the division of labour, but also their health and survival rates. For example, while overall child mortality in New Delhi in the 0 to 5 year age group is 221 per 1,000 births, it is twice as high amongst certain Scheduled castes (Earthscan, 1986). There is growing concern among women's groups that Hindu practices once considered normal or even beneficial to child welfare and development may in fact be abusive in the context of modern Indian society. The dowry system, for example, has led to the widespread abortion of female foetuses and female infanticide (Sen, 1986; Miller, 1981).

Because they are associated with modern with 'progressive' lifestyles, the ideologies and solutions of formal welfare have therefore in many areas become more highly valued than traditional ones. As the globalization of childhood progresses, they present an increasing challenge to customary law and practice in the conduct of family and community affairs.

Penalizing the Children of the Poor

Social policy can be an extremely blunt instrument and its application in the consolidation of a universal standard for children can have the effect of penalizing, or even criminalizing, the childhoods of the poor, often for the simple reason that poor families are unable to reach this standard. The unequal distribution of resources and the overwhelming impact of poverty, unemployment and ill health in many communities makes it impossible for children and families to meet the goals of social planning, especially when these goals run contrary to traditional values and customary law.

In many countries juvenile justice and child welfare have evolved as a means by which one group in society imposes its values on others. Statutory welfare bodies are run mainly by the urban wealthy and it is they who are charged with interpreting legislation. But it is the poor who are normally the targets of welfare intervention and also, there-fore, the objects of moral judgment. We have seen that since the outset, services aimed at meeting the needs of children have also existed to reduce the threat of social disequilibrium, humanitarian and ethical considerations often being secondary to the need to provide the neces-sary social arrangements to deal with dysfunctioning (Kadushin, 1974). It has been argued that nowhere is the oppression of the poor more evident than in the advance of the ideology of the nuclear family through welfare philosophy (Martinez de Duran, 1983; CEPAL, 1983; Scheper-Hughes, 1989; Donzelot, 1980; Meyer, 1983).

For example, maternal bonding, a concept which underlies many modern theories of mother-infant interaction, is believed to be funda-mental to the successful nuclear family. Failure of bonding is thought to lead to abuse and neglect and in the North is used as a pretext for monitoring family life. Scheper-Hughes in her attack on such psychobio-logical theories of human behavior suggests that they 'have been uncritic-ally derived from assumptions and values implicit in the structure of the modern, western, bourgeois family' (1989: 201–2). In her study of women in a Brazilian shanty, she found that material detachment or indiffer-ence, far from signalling the collapse of affective ties within the nuclear family, was a highly selective pattern of behavior developed in response to the conditions of shanty town life. Maternal neglect was focused on passive, docile or inactive babies who were judged too weak or too vulnerable to survive. The women expressed anxiety about the possibil-ity of having to care for a permanently disabled, frail or dependent child and many babies remained not only unchristened, but also unnamed until they began to walk or talk and the risk of death had passed. Thus, what is believed by some people to signify family disorganization or breakdown and social chaos may in fact simply indicate a different way of organizing the family (*ibid*; CEPAL, 1983).

In fact many attempts by government to avert social crises hinge on the fear that it may lead ultimately to uprising. It is believed that this is most likely to occur among the urban poor, especially the disenfranchized ethnic minorities. The worry is that impoverished urban communities such as Shek Kip Mei in Hong Kong, Mathare valley in Nairobi, La Parada in Lima and the Bronx in New York may flourish — with a life and outlook entirely of their own — beyond the reach of city planners, policy makers and the state generally. Run-down, inner city tenements or suburban squatter settlements and informal, poorly paid jobs are thought to correspond with unauthorized and subversive lifestyles. High population density, crowding and self-help housing have been cited as presenting criminal, moral and political hazards (Palen, 1981; Goldfield and Brownell, 1979; Habitat, 1987) as well as the more obvious ones of health and fire risk. Such criminalization of working class life is evident in many aspects and penalizes the children of the poor.[10]

Paradoxically, measures intended to resolve children's problems can in themselves be harmful. This is especially true of interventions such as child sponsorship and institutionalization which, whilst being common in the South and imported originally from the North, and indeed still largely sustained by Northern charities and aid agencies, have now been largely discredited in most Northern countries.[11] Children's dealings with the state often expose them to a myriad of formal rules and procedures that may make them more marginal socially and economically, without giving access to services or benefits (Alcock and Harris, 1982). Moral or material abandonment, vagrancy or delinquency are grounds frequently cited in interactions between children and the state. Among the children who might be defined as abandoned are those that participate in school infrequently, those that work and those who are left unattended whilst their parents work.

As in the industrialized world in the past, the children who work or live on the streets are the ones of greatest concern to the state. Welfare policy dictates that a child's presence on the street and absence from school proves a failing on part of parents or guardians to provide adequate care and protection. Young street workers engaged in retailing or services are not recognized as workers but are instead brought before the magistrate as vagrants, abandoned or perpetrators of antisocial acts. In fact, it has been suggested that protective bans on the employment of minors increases the vulnerability of street children to becoming involved in prostitution or criminal activity (Allsebrook and Swift, 1989). 'Begging or busking increase the risk of a child being picked up by the authorities. Unable to sell their labour, children have only their bodies to sell' (*ibid*: 138). Also, defining street workers as abandoned can result in their removal from a perfectly secure and stable home. Many of those brought before the juvenile magistrate face a custodial sentence of one sort or another, ranging from imprisonment in a correctional institution to forced enlistment into a military establishment or placement in an orphanage. Children used to the freedom of the streets do not normally adapt well to life in an institution and many eventually escape, setting up a cycle of further arrests, detainments and escapes.

Because of the limited resources allocated to welfare ministries, many of the functions of social work in the South are left to the police, the army and juvenile courts — the control or correctional element in welfare provision being better funded than the promotional or preventive. Welfare services tend to be concentrated in highly centralized, urban institutions. There may exist social workers and other welfare professionals in key institutions such as the courts, orphanages and hospitals, but outreach is very poor and there are none available for working within the community. Thus, state presence at the local level may be confined to the army post or the police station and to police patrols. Children's experience of statutory bodies may be both repressive and frightening, since of all sectors of the population children are the easiest to arrest. In countries as widely dispersed as Colombia, India, and Ethiopia, street children are constantly harassed by the police. In Puerto Plata, in the Dominican Republic, they are rounded up periodically to keep them from pestering the tourists who arrive by ship (Dorfman, 1984). They are usually held for some hours in penal establishments without food or drink. When the tourists have gone they are transported to distant beaches and left to make their own way back to town on foot. Similarly, a survey of street children in Manila showed that they regularly experience extortion and brutality at the hands of the police (UNICEF, 1985). And in Brazil, many street children have been killed by the police (Henriques, 1986).

It is usually the police patrols who pick up the children sleeping on the streets at night and those working on the streets during the day. And it is the police who find the babies and young children abandoned on waste land or in shop doorways and who detain child prostitutes and drug addicts. As a result, much social research into childhood problems in the South depends on the records of the police and legal system. This is the case of Oyemade's survey of child rape victims and street traders, children wandering the street and the abandoned in Nigeria, for example (Oyemade, 1986). In Peru, the few studies that have been made of issues such as child abandonment, drug abuse and maltreatment were all sponsored by the Ministry of Justice (Ministerio de Justicia 1983; 1984a; 1984b; 1984c; 1984d). Dependence on the agencies of law enforcement for primary data in social research perpetuates further the negative perceptions of childhood, since the recording of information by these bodies is usually conditioned by stereotypes that are subsequently published by social scientists as fact.

The low levels of investment in social welfare in the Third World have the effect of setting priorities that are in contrast with those of the industrialized world. We have seen that, whilst in the latter concern with private behaviours within the home such as violence against women and child abuse and neglect is paramount, in the former, only the most public or visible social problems are dealt with. But the poor experience far less privacy than the rich — much of family life, including work, eating, washing, children's play and even defecation and sleep, is conducted in public on the street. The distinction between the public and private sphere is not clear. For many families it is impossible to withdraw children from public life and for those playing or working in public places there is a constant risk of state intervention.

Yet, there is no evidence that work is in itself a damaging experience for children and nor is there any evidence that working children inevitably become involved in illicit activities. In many societies, in rural areas particularly, work is and has always been a traditional activity of childhood and it may be fundamental to the transmission of skills and knowledge between generations. 'Many children welcome the opportunity to work, seeing in it the rite of passage to adulthood' (Fyfe, 1989: 4). What is harmful is child involvement in work processes that impede normal development and health, and child labour that is exploitative. In many countries in the South children are the backbone of the informal sector. In Moslem societies where women live in purdah children replace female labour in public spaces (Schildkrout, 1981). In countries where female labour is concentrated in outwork, children are an essential, if unseen and often unpaid, component of the labourforce. Many occupations rely more on child labour than on adults and some are restricted exclusively to children. Even when children are not directly involved in generating income, they are responsible for domestic chores and the care of younger siblings.

Given the policy divide between formal employment or waged labour and more informal types of child work, the majority of working children in many countries fall under the confines of social welfare departments rather than labour ministries. They cannot therefore receive the services and benefits associated with the organized labour market. In fact many of the activities in which children are engaged are perceived by the authorities as hobbies rather than work, despite their crucial role in family survival.

As in the industrialized world, school in the South is increasingly being seen as an alternative to labour and the apparent part schooling plays in securing the withdrawal of children from the labour market is one of the motives behind calls for compulsory full time education. However, because of the cost entailed in the loss of the child's labour, large numbers of children in the South are forced to remain in the labour force and either attend school only sporadically or not at all, even where education is free. Moreover, policy-makers rarely notice the irony that school attendance consistently results in an increase in child labour because children must work to buy their uniforms and utensils. This is one explanation for the large percentage of children in many countries who attend school whilst also working in out-of-school hours.

The mistaken assumption that if parents had a choice they would always send their children to school and that it is poverty that forces children to work does not accord with ethnographic research. Many parents, for example, believe that rather than shield their children from adult life, their main duty is to prepare them for adulthood by teaching them a trade early. Research in Bangalore, for example, shows that economic compulsion is only one of the motives behind child work (Patil, 1986). Of 600 working children, 42 per cent indicated that they worked for reasons such as failure to advance at school or the desire of their parents for them to receive a training or enter what in adult-hood will amount to lucrative employment. Approximately 5 per cent of the children said that they worked simply because they wanted an income like their peers.

The poor quality of education and the lack of opportunities for skilled employment in many countries is a contributory factor to parents' often very negative attitudes to schooling. This is true especially in societies based on an ascriptive status hierarchy, where education makes no impact on social and economic circumstance. In India, for example, the Scheduled Castes and Scheduled Tribes and others are 'generously offered free, impoverished education in backward schools and colleges', while the children of the wealthy are placed in 'an elite education system . . . [that is in the] English medium . . . and American export-oriented, from nursery schools to high-class college and tech-nical institutions' (Iyer, 1984: 6). Thus, the literacy rate of Scheduled Castes is, at 15 per cent, half of the national figure (Hiro, 1982). Parents are wary of an education system that is of poor quality and, in addition, is no asset for the occupations such as street sweeping, scavenging, cleaning latrines, skinning carcasses and agricultural labour that are associated with untouchability.

Finally, the decision to send a child to school involves assessing the possible material and social benefits and weighing these against the costs. For example, teaching in many areas in the South takes place in the language of the former colonists. Use of the colonial language also doubly disadvantages the poor child. The rich may use this language at home habitually or even deliberately in order to facilitate their children's learning. Parents in poor homes, on the other hand, are frequently unable to speak the colonial language. This is the situation in Jamaica, for example, where teaching is in standard English, while children in most poor urban communities speak Creole (Jervier, 1977). Failure in school leading to repetition of years or dropping out is more likely among pupils whose parental language differs from that of school instruction. It is not unusual, for example, for children to be illiterate even after completing the primary cycle.

Thus, for many children, schooling acts neither as a channel of upward social mobility nor as an instrument of social change and personal development but as yet another medium of social control. Worse still, it can further disadvantage the poor child by acting as a drain on income and undermining the direct transmission of culture (Meyer, 1983).

Conclusion

The discontinuity between the protective ideologies of child welfare embodied in both international rights legislation and national policy and the socio-economic and cultural realities of countless children in the South is marked. The beliefs of welfare and rights practitioners about the activities and experiences suitable for child life may differ radically from those of parents and children. From the point of view of the former, children present in public spaces — regardless of the motive — and absent from the school or the home, and children at work or living on the streets all signify family or personal dysfunctioning. Under these circumstances the children and, consequently, their families, are considered legitimate targets for state intervention. But the perceptions of parents and children may be that these are not pathological behavior patterns; on the contrary, the development of precocious mechanisms for survival is seen by many as integral to normal socialization.

More important still, some of the measures for child welfare — advocated often on humanitarian grounds — have the effect of isolating children further from their family and community and increasing their social and economic disadvantage. Innovative responses to the problems of childhood that are sensitive to customary law and practice and meet the needs of children — that they themselves identify — are rare. On the other hand, judgmental or repressive responses, involving elements of containment and correction are all too common. In this respect, the move to set global standards for childhood and common policies for child welfare may be far from the enlightened step anticipated by its proponents.

Notes

'North' and 'South' have been used throughout Chapter 9 as the commonly accepted terminology for industrialized and developing countries. 'South' is taken to exclude countries like Australia and Japan.

1   'Stolen Childhood' is the title of a series of programmes made by North South Productions and directed by Richard Keefe which was shown on Britain's Channel 4 Television in the Autumn of 1989. It explored some of the major aspects of childhood in a range of countries from the perspective of the UN Convention on the Rights of the Child, stressing in particular disadvantaged childhoods and the many deprivations suffered by children globally.

2   The novel describes how a group of schoolboys left on an island after a plane crash, having attempted to organize themselves along adult lines, eventually revert to 'primitive' behaviour, leading to the ritual killing of one of their number. The story is a myth about people's essential inhumanity towards each other, but it also depicts adult fears with regard to the hidden powers and characteristics of children.

3   Despite the weighty evidence mustered to support many of the images of childhood in common usage globally, these images are highly selective and can be extremely distorted. Thus, for example, the widespread fear of juvenile delinquency is greatly disproportionate to the actual threat it represents to society (Hoghughi 1983; Muncie 1984; Sumner, 1982). Young people only figure so prominently in crime statistics because they are highly visible and relatively powerless and are therefore easy prey for alleged police persecution. Statistics on juvenile crime are likely to be inflated, especially in countries where career advancement and increases in departmental budgets in the police force are achieved by successful arrest and prosecution. As we shall see, juveniles are frequently detained on imprecise grounds such as 'loitering' or 'vagrancy'.

4   Status offences, such as running away from home and truancy from school, are indicated by a failure to obey the special rules of childhood and are therefore one of the more controversial features of juvenile justice. Described by Freeman as the 'wrongs only children can commit', they are highly discriminatory (1983: 79). Moreover, although in many countries certain status offences, such as truancy, may not be criminal, the measures for dealing with them can be highly punitive.

5   The stress on the individual, pathological behaviour of parents in cases of child abuse and neglect, for example, show how deeply explanatory theories are influenced by medicine. After all, it was the advance in medical technology — and especially the development of the x-ray — that first enabled detection of physical battery (Kempe and Kempe, 1983). The image of abusers as caregivers out of control is politically expedient for governments who wish to avoid taking major

measures to reduce social and economic distress and also paves the way for criminalization of the problem and legal intervention.

6 Despite the moves internationally to guarantee child protection, there exists no means of enforcing International Law and there is no agency even to monitor developments in children's rights at the national level. The recent creation of a special item for children on the agenda of the UN Sub-Commission for the Prevention of Discrimination and the Protection of Minorities was heralded by many as a step forward in this respect because it provided a forum for the exposure of specific instances of rights abuse. However, the item is awarded low priority and is often suspended altogether when the Sub-Commission falls behind schedule.

7 Smyke (1979) highlights the the way in which the evolution of the concept of a 'right to education' entails some ambiguity, if not a direct contradiction. There was a time when education was available only to a small elite. At this stage it would not have been considered a 'good' for everybody and the majority of the population had no *need* of it. But as times changed, formal education came to be seen as a good that was desirable for everyone and as it was extended to include a wider circle of people, it came to be thought of as a necessity. It was agreed that everyone had a need for some formal education. Finally, when agreement on this point was widespread enough, it began to be seen as a 'right' and was included in the Universal Declaration of Human Rights and the Declaration of the Rights of the Child. But the move to make primary schooling compulsory raises the question as to whether education under these circumstances is properly described as a right or whether it is better thought of as an obligation. As Smyke (1979) points out, it is not a case of mere semantics, because in some countries where education is compulsory, children are asserting the right not to go to school. The right to resist formal education takes on special meaning among ethnic or religious minorities faced with enforced assimilation into the nation state.

8 It has been said of the Convention that it is 'an unprecedented framework for presenting children's global needs — since it is in response to needs that rights are formulated' (Cantwell, 1989: 38), thereby refering overtly to the global model of childhood, defined by a fixed range of characteristics and attended by a set of predetermined needs and rights.

9 Scott (1987) and Lobo (1982) found that the residential clustering of kindred brought about by migration and inter-marriage was common and that such networks functioned to provide support in the form of loans, accommodation and employment, as well as being fundamental to the formation of squatter's rights. For similar findings for other countries, see also Singh and De Souza, 1980; Bohman, 1984; Nelson, 1978/9; Warnock Fernea, 1982.

10 Because squatters and inner-city tenants rarely possess property deeds, their dwellings are usually described as 'illegal' (Hardoy and Satterthwaite, 1985) and they are subject to continual violence and eviction and to persecution by protection racketeers. The poor also tend to be concentrated in unregistered enterprises with neither contractual labour arrangements nor benefits which are often defined as illegal (De Soto, 1987).

11 Whilst in the North there are moves to provide for children in trouble within their own communities and families, welfare bodies in the South still rely on measures such as institutionalization and child sponsorship, both are remedial rather than preventative and are liable to create a serious dependence in the client population, isolating it from the wider society. Children's towns and villages, large orphanages,

remand homes and similar institutions abound in many countries, despite their cost to maintain and use of models of child rearing that are often highly inappropriate in the local context. Moreover, the conditions in many institutions, which are often overcrowded, poorly resourced and badly designed, can cause major health and safety problems for the children.

Postscript: Implementing the Convention on the Rights of the Child — Who Decides about Children's Welfare?

In the six years since I first wrote about the global construction of childhood, events at the international level have moved at a remarkable pace. There has been an unprecedented rise in enthusiasm for children's issues throughout the world, the concepts and ideas having now become firmly embedded within the human rights discourse. The UN Convention on the Rights of the Child, which in record time has achieved almost universal ratification, has done much to kindle this fervour, providing a consensus on universally agreed norms and prerequisites for children's full development (Base and Larson, 1994: 6). What we have in 1996, then, and what was absent in 1990, is an instrument with very real institutional power which frames in international law the global childhood ideals which were the subject of my original article.

Certainly the Convention has fostered some very significant achievements in children's welfare in the last few years. For one thing, it makes states directly responsible for children in ways they have never before been responsible. Recalling the earlier resistance of many governments to the very notion of children's rights, some observers might be surprised by what has been termed the 'stampede towards ratification' (Black, 1994: 7). Indeed, given the intense activity generated by ratification and promotion of the treaty, 'the global standards it has set for children can now scarcely be ignored' (Ennew, forthcoming: 2).

The Convention has also brought non-governmental agencies into the children's rights field. In fact, most of the debate around children's rights has been spearheaded by non-governmental agencies, experts from this sector having led the treaty drafting process. Since 1990 organizations, coalitions and networks focusing on children's rights have mushroomed everywhere. Even the more established agencies like The Save the Children Fund (UK) and Radda Barnen, the Swedish Save the Children, that once confined themselves to development work have begun to shape their programmes and policies according to the Convention. Several UN agencies are also playing their part. UNICEF, for instance, initially reluctant to endorse children's rights, has now thrown its weight behind the instrument and was the prime mover in obtaining the commitment at the first World Summit for Children of 159 countries to a Plan of Action for Children, which includes specific targets and goals in line with key provisions of the Convention to be reached by the year 2000.

Raising children's rights on political and social agendas — local and national — media and community advocacy has proved the most powerful weapon in the activists' armoury. In the Philippines, for example, in the 1980s even before the treaty, a series of television programmes and newspaper articles drew attention to the problem of child prostitution and the activities of paedophile tourists in the resort town of Pagsanjan (Rialp, 1993). Law enforcement agencies were mobilized together with Interpol to trace, detain and deport known paedophiles. This campaign was the precursor to wider civil society action on the behalf of children who are homeless, engaged in hazardous labour or exploited sexually throughout the Philippines. Research on these issues in the capital and several other towns provided baseline data for further advocacy. Awareness was raised between families and communities of the hazards of street life and the sex industry and a campaign was mounted to secure the passage of legislation protecting Philippino children against exploitation and abuse. Police officers and other professionals working at the community level were trained in children's rights and an array of children's services was established.

Much of the energy expended on children's rights internationally has been directed at research and monitoring. States, parties to the Convention, are required to present an initial report to the Committee on the Rights of the Child two years after ratification and thereafter every five years, providing general information about their country and its children, and indicating measures and progress, as well as difficulties, in implementing the treaty. Monitoring has revealed some priority concerns in relation to children's welfare. In 1993, for example, at the behest of the Committee on the Rights of the Child, the body officially responsible for monitoring, the UN General Assembly passed a resolution calling for a comprehensive international study of children affected by armed conflict. And the sexual exploitation of children is to be addressed in a world congress to be held in Sweden this summer. The Committee has encouraged the involvement of non-governmental agencies in monitoring, in part to improve the quality of information but also to sustain the momentum of monitoring. UNICEF has developed its own strategy, publishing childhood statistics from all over the world as a means of rallying governments:

> The day will come when the progress of nations will be judged not by their military or economic strength, nor by the splendour of their capital cities and public buildings, but by the well-being of their peoples . . . and by the protection that is afforded to the growing minds and bodies of their children.
>
> The Progress of Nations, published annually by the United Nations Children's Fund, is a contribution towards that day. (UNICEF 1994, frontpiece)

Using a device termed 'the National Performance Gap' nations are ranked according to their achievements in areas like child survival and health, nutrition, education, family planning and progress for women. The Gap refers to the difference between the actual level of progress achieved and the expected level of progress for each country's per capita GNP. For each indicator used, the expected level of achievement has been calculated from the per capita GNPs and the relevant social indicators of all countries. The expected level therefore represents the level that the average-performing country could be expected to have reached for its level of GNP per capita.

Monitoring has also created a demand for better data and better research methods. Several initiatives serve this end. The recent Childhood as a Social Phenomenon project, for instance, examined social statistics from seventeen European countries and came up with a series of recommendations on how to make children more visible in research through more effective presentation and tabulation of data. Recognizing the need to improve qualitative information about especially disadvantaged children, Radda Barnen and other member agencies of the International Save the Children Fund Alliance are supporting training in participatory children-centred research in Africa, South and South East Asia and Latin America. And Childwatch International, a network serving institutions and individuals involved in research with children, is devising methods for collecting and measuring childhood indicators.

Developments in children's rights at the local, national, regional and international levels are both numerous and varied. As all these efforts to instill global standards would indicate, there surely exists an underlying core of universal biological and psychological processes in child development and welfare. Indeed, some commentators are very clear that cultural relativism cannot be allowed to undermine global standards, arguing that whatever the cultural or economic circumstances, when the 'best interests' of children are at stake, global norms should prevail. As Thomas Hammarburg, a prominent champion of children's rights internationally and a member of the Committee on the Rights of the Child, has stated: 'When there is a clash between cultural practices (like female circumcision in Sudan) and the rights of the child, we defend the latter' (Hammarburg, quoted in Singh, 1995: 17).

Nevertheless, children's rights advocates generally concede that entrenched cultural and economic diversity continues to be a serious challenge to implementation of the treaty. And Blanchet (1996: 223) reminds us that exposure to global thinking may actually reinforce relativism, giving rise to a fundamentalist reaction. Globalization certainly creates new awareness, but it also makes explicit the contrasting norms and values of local and global models, generating a sense that things local are morally superior and leading to the rejection of things global. Precisely how global, national and sub-national models of childhood and child-rearing will be reconciled in the application of the Convention remains to be seen.

This brings us to the central issue in the whole debate, which is: what kind of globalization is the Convention going to bring? The answer is largely dependent on what implementation strategies and what theoretical concepts and values it inspires. The outcome cannot yet be predicted, since several models and trends are beginning to crystallize internationally and these are potentially quite contradictory. As a theoretical and conceptual framework, there is the fact, often mentioned, that the global model of the Convention draws primarily on northern, and especially Christian, thinking. For some this means that it is a model imposed on the South: 'many southern governments are now struggling to report on and implement Articles that are at best barely comprehensible and at worst irrelevant in the local context' (Ennew, forthcoming: 2). And the possibility that the childhood ideal of the Convention may not always be better for children's welfare than the childhoods of other cultures and other times lingers on, even with the broad acceptance of the treaty (Stephens, 1995). Studies by Cho (1995) and Field (1995), for example, show how making the State the guarantor of global standards of children's rights gives little assurance that children's best interests will be served. They describe the modern compulsory education systems of Japan and South Korea as a tyranny of labour for many children, suggesting that the 'universalizing modernist discourses on children's rights . . . may actually be brought into service to legitimate situations that constitute new sorts of risks to children' (Stephens, 1995: 40). Compulsion is hardly the most effective way of accomplishing children's right to education and indeed, as Cunningham (1996) argues, it was conceived in the last century as a way of dragooning children into school primarily for their discipline.

That international thinking about children is now steered by a human rights discourse has other conceptual implications. Not only are some things that are just different seen as abnormal but also the spectacular problems of childhood, such as the traffic in children or their involvement in prostitution, are brought to the fore. In this paradigm children are cast both as dependent and as victims [see Woodhead this volume]. Thus, the bulk of the Articles in the Convention deal with the special protection rights of children in exceptionally difficult situations. Paradoxically, one of the main preoccupations generated by this thinking is the danger to children resulting from the globalization process itself. The encounter between agents of the world's rich and poor countries is believed to invite the exploitation of poor children and to threaten childhood innocence. People who traffic children and paedophile tourists, among others, are singled out as predators, as are multinational corporations who profit by flooding industrialized countries with goods made by cheap child labour in the South. Undoubtedly countless children in poor countries live extremely precarious lives and are deeply exploited; these children deserve all the support and assistance they can get. But the point is that the human rights discourse tends to detract from careful ethnography, as often as not calling forth simplistic explanations and solutions, many of which are inappropriate or ineffectual.

In one of the most potent models of globalization emerging at present, the Convention is used as a policing mechanism to bring governments and others to account. In these cases, so confident are the enforcers of international standards that they inhabit the higher moral ground, that they believe unilateral action to be fully justified. Of course, the treaty is 'weak law', as such largely unenforceable at the national level (Gautam, 1994). All the same, it can and has been applied to great effect to bring pressure to bear on violators, if only by making public information about the status of children's rights within different countries. In some cases penalties have been used to enforce children's rights, as in Guatemala, where official aid disbursements were made conditional upon the cessation of the arbitrary detention and extrajudicial executions of street children by members of the police and armed forces (anon, personal communication). In another more recent example — applied against private companies rather than governments — a diverse lobby for social responsibility in trade has been putting pressure on enterprises selling goods in industrialized countries to have children removed from the workforces of their business partners in the non-industrialized countries of the South. The grounds given are that employment below an internationally defined minimum age is an exploitation of children. Consumer boycotts and legal measures are called for to ensure compliance. Accordingly, in 1992 proposed legislation was introduced into the

United States banning importation of products from foreign industries in which children less than 15 years of age are employed.

The Bill was received with much interest by several European governments, who began discussing similar measures. But it caused serious disquiet in many countries in the South, where export production uses child labour to a varying degree, the more so because it was perceived as a breach of sovereignty in which one nation had appointed itself to police others without understanding the many complex cultural and economic issues involved. Some countries hold that children working is compatible with their welfare and that the Bill was therefore policing them to do the wrong things for children.

The crucial issue about some of these more strident efforts to enforce the Convention is that the focus is on whether countries are complying or meeting their obligations rather than whether or not children are better off as a result of intervention. It is even doubtful whether the State is the best agent for operationalizing children's rights in some of the more acute cases, not least because government forces may be the perpetrators. Besides, the instruments of government tend to be very blunt, failing to address the complex social forces that apply at the local level. Thus, senior government officials in Guatemala blamed local welfare workers for the donors' decision to make aid conditional, veiled threats were made and there was a very real risk of increased harassment of street children and programme staff.

When contemplating the role of the State as guarantor of children's rights, it is worth bearing in mind that many governments in today's world are not democratically accountable. If the spirit of the Convention is to prevail, the concern is surely not so much with obligations, enforcement and compliance as with what the application of global standards actually means for children.

The tabling of the US Bill provided a rare opportunity to research the effects on children of an attempt to enforce global childhood standards through a penalty. The ILO, with support from UNICEF, conducted a study of children involved in the production of garments for export in Bangladesh (Boyden and Myers, 1995). The industry was found to be an important income source for the families of child employees, many of whose fathers were either unemployed or not contributing financially to the household due to marital breakdown and remarriage. It provided employment for girls and women especially, this being very significant in a Muslim society where opportunities for females to obtain socially legitimate paid work outside the domestic domain are very few. The children would mainly undertake light finishing work.

The mere threat of the Bill led to many thousands of children being removed from the garment sector. The study showed a sample of former garment children to be worse off than children still in the industry in a number of ways. None were attending school and many were involved in activities such as brick chipping and rickshaw pulling which are more hazardous than garment work. Children outside the industry suffered both acute and chronic illnesses at rates four times those of the children inside and also ate less food, which was of poorer quality.

It is evident that the best interests of the garment children in Bangladesh were not served by an intervention which was ultimately based on a set of assumptions far removed from the children's reality. This highlights that there are no short cuts in achieving children's rights, and that applying solutions which have been developed elsewhere and in a different context can make a mockery of the underlying intentions of the Convention. For these children there was never really a choice between employment and schooling since they were obliged for economic reasons to work. Besides, there was no evidence that the work they were doing in the garment industry was harmful in any sense other than that, while at work, they were not at school; more evident were the perils of subsequent employment outside the industry in other sectors of the economy. Significantly, the children's views about their employment were not even considered by those who devised the Bill.

This brings us back to a point merely touched on in my original article that now seems of paramount importance, which is that the global construction of childhood is one in which children have played no part whatsoever: children definitely did not participate in the drafting of the Convention; nor have they been consulted as to the most effective manner of implementation. This is in spite of the fact that the treaty not only recognizes the vulnerabilities of children but also their capacities, endorsing in articles 12 to 15 the notion that children capable of forming their own views have a right to participate in decisions and all matters affecting them. Herein lies a major innovative feature of this most recent global construction of childhood, which is that children are not just to be protected from, but also empowered to.

For some, the idea that children might take an active part in decision-making is still be very novel; others may fear the consequences. But this is hardly logical, as Johnson (1966, p. 34) indicates: 'if children are old enough to collect fodder and fuel, look after siblings and work for waged labour, they are certainly old enough to consult about decisions which effect their development. It has been emphasized by several authors that in all social processes children are protagonists and not passive recipients: 'children . . . are social actors in their own social, economic and cultural contributions to society' (Theis, 1996: 70–1). Child-hood identity is not just attributed but actively negotiated and managed as a set of social relations within which the early years of human life are constituted (James, 1993; Prout and James, 1990). Undoubtedly adult society and the institutions created by adults for the care and nurture of children — the school, the family and the like — play the major part in this process. But children have a role too: childhood is a social space within which children also negotiate their own and each other's iden-tity (James, 1993).

It is incumbent upon social planners to listen to and learn from children directly. Obviously children are not always right and do not always make decisions that are in their own best interests. Nevertheless, parents and children have lots of reasons, both strategic and practical, for favouring children's work. Research by White and Tjandraningsih (1992) in Indonesia, Johnson, Hill and Ivan-smith (1995) in Nepal and Szanton Blanc *et al.* (1994) in Brazil shows that work can bring import-ant social rewards for children. Moreover, appropriate and safe work may well offer benefits to children of which we are as yet little aware and in any case, given the serious problems with much of the educa-tion on offer in different parts of the world today, it is hardly illogical that children sometimes prefer to work. When social planners ignore the reasons why parents and children make their particular choices, they risk undermining the welfare of both children and their families. At the very least, children's participation in decisions made on their behalf may provide some protection against exploitation and abuse since it implies that they should be provided with appropriate information and an opportunity to articulate their problems and needs.

Already children's participation in planning is being fostered mean-ingfully in different ways and at different levels in a variety of countries. In Brazil children were consulted in the development of the national Statute on Children and Adolescents, which gives children absolute priority in public services and regards them as full citizens in a special condition of physical and mental development with a claim to exclusive rights appropriate to their age. In Nepal (Johnson, Hill and Ivan-Smith 1995), Uganda (Guijt, I., Fuglesang, A. and Kisadha, 1994) and Sri Lanka (Stephens, M., 1996; Coomaraswamy, P., 1996) non-governmental agen-cies are using participatory research with children and their families as a basis for planning policies and programmes that respond to their concerns and give children priority.

These recent attempts to include and empower children to invoke an interpretation of globalization very distinct from that based on enforce-ment with a penalty or the transport across the world of ready-made solutions to age-old and culturally defined problems. They embody a more liberal vision, in which the Convention provides a flexible framework that brings cultures together around children's rights and children's welfare rather than an instrument of censure endorsing a single model of childhood. In this vision cultures are allowed some latitude to proceed towards the global goal in their own way and in their own time, solutions are negotiated and not imposed and children assume an active role in these negotiations. Implicit in this vision is the suggestion that, if globalization is to become an opportunity for children to grow and develop in security and respect and with access to all the benefits and services that are their right, the Convention needs to pay due regard to children's own views and to their culture and economic condition, for the chances are that strict enforcement of a universal set of values without proper contextualization may have unforseen adverse consequences for children.

Applying globalization as a vision of inclusion and empowerment carries many challenges. It confronts the need to develop appropriate methodologies, methods and tools for learning about and working with children. To capture and reflect children's concerns can be extremely difficult, especially given the power imbalance between children and adults, the situated character of children's meanings and the fact that children frequently apply concepts and interpretations which are unfamiliar to adults (Fine and Sandstrom, 1988: 35). Young children in particular inhabit a universe that is phenomenologically very distinct. There are also ethical concerns, for example that high levels of consultation with children may raise expectations which cannot be fulfilled, or that awarding priority to children may cause conflict with families or other social groups. And incorporating children's views within legislation, policy and programmes definitely involves major institutional changes. It is evident that there is still a long way to go and much still to learn. As a minimum requirement, someone somewhere should be monitoring the monitoring, as well as the implementation and enforcement of the Convention: analysis internationally of the potentially conflicting vision of globalization and their comparative impact on children is long overdue.

References

ABDOULAYE TALL, P. (nd) 'Do human rights mean anything to homeless children and youth' *ENDA*, Jeuda no 49/E Dakar, Senegal.

ALCOCK, P. and HARRIS, P. (1982) *Welfare Law and Order: A Critical Introduction to Law for Social Workers*, London, Macmillan.

ALLSEBROOK, A. and SWIFT, A. (1989) *Broken Promise: the World of Endangered Children*, London, Hodder and Stoughton.

ALSTON, P. (1987) 'The nature of international human rights discourse: The case of the "new" human rights', Paper presented to conference at Oxford University, *An Interdisciplinary Inquiry into the Content and Value of the So-Called New Human Rights*, 29–31 May.

ALSTON, P. (Ed) (1994) *The Best Interests of the Child: Reconciling Culture and Human Rights*, UNICEF-ICDC, Oxford UK, Clarendon Press.

ARIES, P. (1962) *Centuries of Childhood*, London, Jonathon Cape.

BARLOW, G. and HILL, A. (1985) *Video Violence and Children*, London, Hodder and Stoughton.

BASE, K. and LARSON, H. (1994) 'The Convention on the rights of the child: Implications for health and wellbeing of Pacific Children Pacific', Health Dialog, **1**, 2, pp. 6–13.

BEDARIDA, F. and SUTCLIFFE, A.R. (1981) 'The street in the structure and life of the city; Reflections on 19th century London and Paris', in STAVE, B.M. (Ed) *Cities, History, Policy and Survival*, California, Sage Publications.

BEQUELE, A. and BOYDEN, J. (Eds) (1988) *Combatting Child Labour*, Geneva, International Labour Office.

BLACK, M. (1994) *Monitoring the Rights of Children*, Summary Report of Innocenti Global Seminar 23 May–1 June 1994, Florence, UNICEF International Child Development Centre.

BLANCHET, T. (1996) *Lost Innocence, Stolen Childhoods*, Bangladesh, University Press Limited, Radda Barnen.

BOHMAN, K. (1984) *Women of the Barrio: Class and Gender in a Colombian City*, Sweden, Stockholm Studies in Social Anthropology.

BOYDEN, J. (1985) *Children in Development: Policy and Programming for Especially Disadvantaged Children in Lima, Peru*, Report for UNICEF and Oxfam, UK.

BOYDEN, J. and MYERS, W. (1995) *Exploring Alternative Approaches to Combating Child Labour: Case Studies from Developing Countries* Innocenti Ocasional Papers Child Rights Series, Number 8, Florence UNICEF International Child Development Centre.

BURMAN, S. (1984) 'Divorce and the disadvantaged: African women in urban South Africa', in HIRSCHON, R. (1984) *Women and Property, Women as Property*, London, Croom Helm, pp. 117–39.

CANTWELL, N. (1989) 'A tool for the implementation of the UN Convention', in RADDA BARNEN (Ed) *Making Reality of Children's Rights*, International conference on the rights of the child, pp. 36–41.

CENTER FOR SOCIAL DEVELOPMENT AND HUMANITARIAN AFFAIRS (1984) *The Family: Models for Providing Comprehensive Services for Family and Child Welfare*, New York, UN Department of International Economic and Social Affairs.

CEPAL (1982) *Five Studies on the Situation of Women in Latin America*, Santiago, Chile, UN publication.

CHO, H. (1995) 'Children in the examination war in South Korea: A cultural analysis', in STEPHENS, S. (Ed) (1995) *Children and the Politics of Culture*, Princeton, NJ, Princeton University Press.

CLINARD, M.B. and ABBOT, D.J. (1973) *Crime in Developing Countries: A Comparative Perspective*, New York, John Wiley and Sons.

COOMARASWAMY, P. (1996) 'Coping mechanisms of a village community in the border areas of Anuradhapura District affected by the conflict, Unpublished report for Save the Children Fund (UK), Colombo, Sri Lanka.

Coombs, P. (1985) *The World Crisis in Education: The View from the Eighties*, New York, Oxford University Press.

Cunningham, H. (1996) 'Combatting child labour: The British experience', in Cunningham, H. and Viazzo, P.P. (Eds) *Child Labour in Historical Perspective 1800–1985*, Florence, ICD-UNICEF.

De Soto, H. (1987) *El Otro Sendero*, Peru, Instituto Libertad y Democracia.

De Souza, A. (1983) *The Indian City, Poverty, Ecology and Urban Development*, India, Manohar.

Donzelot, J. (1980) *The Policing of Families*, London, Hutchinson.

Dorfman, A. (1984) 'Arroz quemada y pan; Cultura y supervivencia economica en America Latina', in Desarrollo de Base, *Journal of the Fundacion Interamericana*, **8**, 2, pp. 9–20.

Earthscan (1986) *On Mean Streets: the Challenge of Children in Cities*, Preliminary briefing document prepared for the Save the Children Alliance, Mexico City.

Edobor Igbinovia, P. (1985) 'Old wine in new bottles: Juvenile justice and care of juvenile offenders in Nigeria', *International Child Welfare Review*, **64/5**, pp. 14–24.

Ennew, J. (Forthcoming) 'The child business: Comments on the management of international policies for children', *Journal of International Development*.

Espinola, B., Glauser, B., Ortiz, R.M. and Ortiz de carrizosa, S. (1987) *En la Calle; Menores Trabajadores de la Calle en Asuncion Paraguay, Imprenta El Grafico*.

Fernandez, F., Godoy, O., Morales, A., *et al.* (1985) *El Menor Callejero: Una Investigacion Basica en la Ciudad de La Paz*, La Paz, Bolivia, Division de Publicaciones Junta Nacional de Solidaridad y Desarrollo Social.

Field, N. (1995) 'The child as labourer and consumer: The disappearance of childhood in contemporary Japan', in Stephens, S. (Ed) (1995) *Children and the Politics of Culture*, Princeton, NJ, Princeton University Press.

Fine, G. and Sandstrom, K. (1988) *Knowing Children: Participant Observation with Minors*, Qualitative Research Methods Series, 15, California, Sage.

Freeman, M.D.A. (1983) *The Rights and Wrongs of Children*, London, Francis Pinter Publishers.

Fyfe, A. (1989) *Child Labour*, Cambridge, Polity Press.

Gautam, K. (1994) Preface to Black, M. (1994) *Monitoring the Rights of Children*, Summary report of Innocenti Global Seminar 23 May–1 June 1994, Florence, Italy, UNICEF International Child Development Centre.

Goldfield, D.R. and Brownell, B.A. (1979) *Urban America: From Downtown to No Town*, Boston, Houghton, Mifflin Company.

Goody, J. (1976) *Production and Reproduction: A Comparative Study of the Domestic Domain*, Cambridge, Cambridge University Press.

Guijt, I., Fuglesang, A. and Kisadha, T. (Eds) (1994) *It is the Young Trees that Make a Forest Thick*, A report on Redd Barna learning experience with Participatory Rural Appraisal, Kampala, International Institute for Environment and Development (IIED) London and Redd Barna.

Habitat: UN Centre for Human Settlements (1987) *Global Report on Human Settlements 1986*, New York, Oxford University Press.

Hall, T. (1986) 'Education, schooling and participation', in Midgley, J. *et al.* (1986) *Community Participation, Social Development and the State*, USA, Methuen.

Hardiman, M. and Midgley, J. (1982) *The Social Dimensions of Development, Social Policy and Planning in the Third World*, New York, John Wiley and Sons.

HARDOY, J.E. and SATTERTHWAITE, D. (1985) *The World Cities and the Environment of Poverty*, London, IIED.

HASEN, S.Z. (1969) 'Social security in India: Limited resources — Unlimited need', in JENKINS, S. (Ed) (1969) *Social Security in International Perspective*, New York, Columbia University Press.

HENRIQUES, J. (1986) 'Where little children suffer', *Observer Colour Supplement Special Report*, 24 June.

HIRO, D. (1982) *The Untouchables of India*, Minority Rights Group Report no 26, London.

HOGHUGHI, M. (1983) *The Delinquent: Directions for Social Control*, London, Burnett Books Ltd.

INGO: INTER NGO PROGRAMME ON STREET CHILDREN AND STREET YOUTH (1983) *Summary of Proceedings of Sub-regional Seminar for the Mediterranean on Street Children*, Marseilles, 24–7 October, Geneva, International Catholic Child Bureau.

IYER, K. (1984) *Justice in Words and Injustice in Deeds*, Delhi, Indian Social Institute.

JAMES, A. (1993) *Childhood Identities, Self and Social Relationships in the Experience of the Child*, Edinburgh, Edinburgh University Press.

JERVIER, W.S. (1977) *Educational Change in Post Colonial Jamaica*, New York, Vantage Press.

JOHNSON, V. (1996) *Introduction: Starting a Dialogue on Children's Participation*, PLA Notes 25 February, London, IIED.

JOHNSON, V., HILL, J. and IVAN-SMITH, E. (1995) *Listening to Smaller Voices: Children in an Environment of Change*, London, Action Aid.

KADUSHIN, A. (1974) *Child Welfare Services*, New York, Macmillan.

KAYANGO-MALE, D. and ONYANGO, P. (1986) *The Sociology of the African Family*, USA, Longman.

KEMPE, R.S. and KEMPE, H.C. (1983) *Child Abuse*, Oxford, Oxford University Press.

LEJEUNE, R. (1984) *Towards a European Convention on the Rights of the Child*, Vienna, Council of Europe Forum, I.

LIVINGSTONE, A.S. (1969) *Social Policy in Developing Countries*, London, Routledge and Kegan Paul.

LOBO, S. (1982) *A House of My Own: Social Organization in the Squatter Settlements of Lima, Peru*, Arizona, University of Arizona Press.

MACPHERSON, S. (1982) *Social Policy in the Third World*, Brighton, Wheatsheaf Books.

MACPHERSON, S. (1987) *Five Hundred Million Children, Poverty and Child Welfare in the Third World*, Brighton, Wheatsheaf Books.

MARTINEZ DE DURAN, S. (1983) 'A South American perspective on legislation affecting minors', in Covenant House/UPS Foundation *Shelter the Children '83–International Symposium on Street Youth* (proceedings), New York.

MEYER, P. (1983) *The Child and the State*, Cambridge, Cambridge University Press.

MICHEL ZINZOU, E. (1985) 'Pour une nouvelle famille africaine', in *International Child Welfare Review*, **64/65**, pp. 5–13.

MIDGLEY, J. (1986) 'Participation and social work services', in MIDGLEY, J. *et al.*, *Community Participation, Social Development and the State*, USA, Methuen. pp. 126–144.

MILLER, B. (1981) *The Endangered Sex*, Ithaca, Cornell University Press.

MINISTERIO DE JUSTICIA (1983) *Los Menores en las Comisarias de Lima*, Peru.

MINISTERIO DE JUSTICIA (1984a) *Menores de la Calle*, Peru.

MINISTERIO DE JUSTICIA (1984b) *Los Menores Maltratados: Un Estudio de los Menores Atendidoes en la Oficina Medico Legal de Lima*, Peru.

MINISTERIO DE JUSTICIA (1984c) *Los Menores de Edad que Consumeny/o Trafican Drogas a Nivel de los Juzgados de Menores de Lima y Callao*, Peru.

MINISTERIO DE JUSTICIA (1984d) *Menores Abandonados en Hospitales de Lima Metropolitana*, Peru.

MORGAN, P. (1987) *Delinquent Fantasies*, London, Temple Smith.

MUNCIE, J. (1984) *The Trouble with Kids Today*, London, Hutchinson.

MUNDAY, E. (1979) 'When is a child a child? Alternative Systems of Classification', *Journal of the Anthropological Society of Oxford*, **10**, 3, pp. 161–72.

NELSON, N. (1978/9) 'Female-centred families: Changing patterns of marriage and family among Buzaa brewers of Mathare Valley', in *African Urban Studies*, **3**, Michigan.

NEWMAN-BLACK, M. (1989) *How Can the Convention Be Implemented in Developing Countries*, in report from RADDA BARNEN, UNICEF Seminar on the UN Draft Convention on the Rights of the Child held in Stockholm October 1988, pp. 36–41.

OYEMADE, A. (1986) 'Child abuse and neglect — The Nigerian experience', in UNICEF *Child Labour in Africa* proceedings of workshop held at Enugu, Nigeria, 27 April– 2 May, pp. 193–8.

PALEN, J.J. (1981) *The Urban World*, New York, McGraw-Hill Book Co.

PATIL, B.R. (1986) *The Urban Industrial Working Child in India*, in Lawasia Conference on Child Labour and Child Prostitution, February, Kuala Lumpur, pp. 247–88.

PEARSON, G. (1985) *Hooligan: A History of Respectable Fears*, London, Macmillan.

PHILLIPS, M. (1912) 'The school as a means of social betterment', in WHITEGOUSE, J.H. (Ed) *The Problems of Boy Life*, London, King, pp. 206–27.

POFFENBERGER, T. (1983) 'Child rearing and social structure in rural India: Toward a cross-cultural definition of child abuse and neglect', in KORBIN, J. (Ed) *Child Abuse and Neglect: Cross Cultural Perspectives*, California, University of California Press.

PROUT, A. and JAMES, A. (1990) 'A new paradigm for the sociology of childhood?: Provenance, promise and problems', in JAMES, A. and PROUT, A. (Eds) *Constructing and Reconstructing Childhood: Contemporary Issues in the Sociological Study of Childhood*, Basingstoke, Falmer Press.

QVORTRUP, J. (1985) 'Placing children in the division of labour', in CLOSE, P. and COLLINS, R. (Eds) *Family and Economy in Modern Society*, London, Macmillan, pp. 129–45.

REPPOND, L. (1983) *An Overview of Street Youth in the Pacific North West*, New York, Convenant House/UPS Foundation.

RIALP, V. (1993) *Children and Hazardous Work in the Philippines*, Child Labour Collection, Geneva, ILO.

SANDA, A.O. (1987) 'Nigeria' in DIXON, J. (Ed) *Social Welfare in Africa*, New York, Croom Helm, pp. 164–83.

SCHEPER-HUGHES, N. (1989) *Child Survival: Anthropological Perspectives on the Treatment and Maltreament of Children*, Dor-drecht, Reidel.

SCHILDKROUT, E. (1981) 'The employment of children in Kano', in RODGERS, G. and STANDING, G. (Eds) *Child Work, Poverty and Development*, Geneva, International Labour Office.

SCOTT, A. (1987) 'Working class people, working class lives', Unpublished manuscript, Essex.

SEN, I. (1986) *How Threatened is the Female of the Species? — Time Trends in Indian Population*, Paper presented at World Conference of Sociology, New Delhi.

SINGH, M. and DE SOUZA, A. (1980) *The Urban Poor: Slum and Pavement Dwellers in the Major Cities of India*, India, Manohar.

SINGH, N. (1995) 'Promoting the Convention on the Rights of the Child; Thomas Hammarburg's visit to India and Pakistan', *South Asia's Children*, **6**, pp. 13–16.

SMYKE, P. (1979) 'The rights of the child in the international year of the child', Unpublished Manuscript.

SOMMERVILLE, J. (1982) *The Rise and Fall of Childhood*, New York, Sage publications.

STEIN, T.J. (1981) *Social Work Practice in Child Welfare*, New Jersey, Prentice Hall.

STEPHENS, M. (1996) 'Between the State and insurgents an exploration of reasons why children do not attend school in a rural Tamil village in the East of Sri Lanka', Colombo, Save the Children Fund (UK), Unpublished report.

STEPHENS, S. (1995) 'Children and the politics of culture in late Capitalism', Introduction to STEPHENS, S. (Ed) (1995) *Children and the Politics of Culture*, Princeton, NJ, Princeton University Press.

SUMNER, C. (1982) (Ed) *Crime, Justice and Underdevelopment*, London, Heinemann.

SWART, J. (1989) *Community and Self-perceptions of the Black South African Street Child*, in Symposium on Theory and Practice Street Children in the Third World, Amsterdam, 20–1 April, Caritas Neerlandica, Werkgroep Ontwikkelingsvraagstukken, Universiteit van Amsterdam, Holland pp. 49–56.

SZANTON BLANC, C. *et al.* (1994) *Urban Child in Distress: Global Predicaments and Innovative Strategies*, Florence, Gordon and Breach Scientific Publications, New York, in Association with UNICEF, International Child Development Centre.

TACON, P. (1981) 'My child minus two', Unpublished report for UNICEF.

THEIS, J. (1996) *Children and Participatory Appraisals: Experiences from Vietnam*, PLA Notes 25, London, IIED.

UNICEF (1985) 'Situation study of abandoned and street children in Olongapo City, Philippines', Unpublished report, Manila.

UNICEF (1987) *The State of the World's Children*, Oxford, Oxford University Press.

UNICEF (1994) *The Progress of Nations*, New York, UNICEF.

VEGA FUENTE, A. (1983) 'The maladjusted child is powerless in the face of drugs: A survey carried out in a juvenile remand centre and reformatory in Spain' in *International Child Labour Review*, **59**, pp. 23–34.

WARNOCK FERNEA, E. (Ed) (1982) *Women and the Family in the Middle East: New Voices of Change*, Austin, TX, University of Texas Press.

WHITE, B. and TJANDRANINGSIH, I. (1992) *Rural Children in the Industrialization Process: Child and Youth Labour in 'Traditional and Modern' Industries in West Java, Indonesia*, The Hague, Institute of Social Studies.

WHITEHOUSE, J.H. (1912) 'Street trading by children' in WHITEHOUSE, J.H. (Ed) *Problems of Boy Life*, London, King, pp. 163–9.

WINN, M. (1984) *Children without Childhood*, Harmondsworth, Penguin.

YOUNGHUSBAND, E. (1981) *The Newest Profession: A Short History of Social Work*, London, Community Care/IPC Business Press.

ZELIZER, V.A. (1985) *Pricing the Priceless Child: The Changing Social Value of Children*, New York, Basic Books Inc.

ZIETZ, D. (1969) *Child Welfare: Services and Perspective*, New York, John Wiley and Sons Inc.

Chapter 10

Re-presenting Childhood: Time and Transition in the Study of Childhood

Allison James and Alan Prout

Introduction

In this final chapter we focus on the issues of time and childhood touched upon briefly in the first chapter of this volume. The social construction of time in and through social relationships is a relatively neglected theoretical theme within contemporary sociology. In recent years, however, there has been a re-awakening of interest in the temporal dimension of social relationships (see, for example, Young and Schuller, 1988) and in this chapter we will take up the invitation implicit in such work to suggest that the social construction of time may be crucial to the study of childhood. Such a move is important, we suggest, in facilitating a wider and more critical thinking about childhood as a social institution and about the lives of children themselves.

We will approach this task from two directions. First, we will show how, in each of the separate contributions to this volume, 'time' has been implicitly, if not always explicitly, addressed. This underlines our suggestion of the centrality of time to concepts of childhood. In surveying the previous chapters it is possible, for example, to discern two main temporal themes. Sometimes both have been touched on and combined in a single paper for, as we shall to show, they are mutually dependent. The first theme involves consideration of the 'time *of* childhood': here the periodization of the life course is explored as the social construction of the ageing process. Time exerts sets of constraints upon our biological selves, which are interpreted in different cultures as different 'times' of life. Western societies, for example, might be thought of as being constructed around the following sequence: childhood follows infancy and is succeeded by adolescence, adulthood, middle age and old age. Each 'time of life' is understood to confer particular qualities and attributes upon its incumbents so that cultures can have their own periodizations and draw such boundaries differently. A second set of issues emerging through this volume revolves around the theme of 'time *in* childhood.' Here, consideration is given to the ways in which time is used effectively to produce, control and order the everyday lives of children. This is shown to be crucial to the very concept of childhood itself. To put it simply, what emerges from this set of papers is the suggestion that the 'time of childhood' both defines and is defined by 'time in childhood'. In this chapter we shall, then, trace both these threads as they emerge through the various contributions to this volume.

Our second task goes beyond this. Using a variety of illustrative sources, including our own ethnographic fieldwork material, we will explore in further depth the importance of time in the study of childhood and begin to tease out the temporal underpinnings of different representations of childhood. One useful starting point for accomplishing such an analysis is the currently fashionable social constructionist perspective within the social sciences. This approach, though not without its critics (for example, Bury, 1986), has contributed greatly to our understanding of the cultural relativity of social phenomena. Such 'natural' categories as 'women' and, more lately, 'children' and 'the elderly' have been effectively deconstructed by pointing out the social shaping of biology in a wide variety of ways. The temporality of these shaping processes, however, rarely features in such accounts. The timing of constructions — past and future — and their present tempo in the rhythms of everyday life, whilst imminent in such analyses, are not always directly addressed as *ongoing* historical processes. In the title of this volume with its emphasis on construct*ing* and reconstruct*ing* we have endeavoured to capture just such a processual spirit. The making and breaking of concepts of childhood is itself a continuing and changing social activity in which people themselves — men, women and children — are created, facilitated and constrained. By way of conclusion to this volume, then, we wish now to address the subject of time and childhood in a more direct way for, we would argue, it is during childhood (and incidentally its extreme opposite, old age) that time and perceptions of time have perhaps the greatest social significance.

Time and Childhood in This Volume

Hendrick, in his historical survey of changes in concepts of childhood from 1800 to the present day, deals the most explicitly with the impact of time on ideas of childhood. He shows the dialectical processes which have shaped and reshaped social thinking about children during this period, illustrating the effect which time has had on the life experiences of children at each historical moment. Mediated by class, and to some extent gender, each historical present created a novel version of 'the child': romantic, factory, delinquent, schooled, psychological and welfare children provided the images against whose form the lives of contemporary children were measured, interpreted and assessed. These images were not simply abandoned over time but as Hendrick shows remained as fragments which were incorporated in succeeding ideas of childhood. Concepts of childhood — and their attendant practices, beliefs and expectations about children — are shown to be neither timeless nor universal but, instead, rooted in the past and reshaped in the present. They may also prefigure the future in a number of profound ways, as is illustrated in the later discussion by Hunt and Frankenberg. Concepts of childhood and of children must take account therefore of the temporal and cultural specificity of ideas and social constructions.

This latter point is brought home most dramatically in Boyden's paper. Her identification of the impact of the historical legacy of western ideas of childhood on the life experiences of Third World children through the operations of international welfare agencies challenges our thinking about children. She shows how the globalization of ideas of childhood promoted from the west — as a culture free and timeless concept — takes no account of the conditions of existence of children in poor communities where such concepts may be totally inappropriate. The wholesale exportation of sets of ideas about children, out of time and space, into other contexts and times can have, as she shows, severe social consequences. This point is given concrete illustration in Glauser's ethnographic account of street children in Paraguay. He shows through detailed examples that these children's lives are largely shaped — in terms of the help or assistance they receive — by definitional criteria developed at other times and in other cultures.

This dialectical relationship between ideas and social action is discussed in greater detail by Woodhead in his critique of the concepts of children's needs. Rather than postulating children's needs as a universal, psychological necessity, Woodhead shows these to be social constructions reflecting different views of what a child, an adult and their relationship ought to be. He demonstrates that the concept 'children's needs' is the result of a particular patterning of adult responses to children which can be temporally and culturally located in twentieth century western cultures. The underlying normative character of 'needs' is disguised by ideas of age (calculated as years of time passing) in relation to childhood. It is here that the study of time in and of childhood is perhaps most important. Age fixes the limits and boundaries to western conceptions of childhood and, although these limits are largely context specific and may vary, 'age' nevertheless exerts a powerful and constraining force on the daily activities of children. Solberg's paper is most interesting in this respect. She shows in her ethnographic account how age (time passed), despite its apparent fixity, can be conceptually expanded and contracted through negotiations between parents and their children. This negotiation alters time present, for concepts of age and its associated concept of 'maturity' affect what parents allow their children to do. For some Norwegian school children negotiating an older conceptual age gives them time during the day which is under their own control.

The importance of age in childhood study is further underlined by Qvortrup who shows in his analysis of statistical data how children are continually omitted from such accounts. This lack of information available from statistical sources about the lives of children — for example, their levels of poverty, their social and material experience of the consequences of unemployment — suggests, he argues, a particular conception of children as always represented by another agency — the family, the welfare system or the educational system. They are not present in their own right, reflecting the practice and ideology of lived experience if not the rhetoric of contemporary western constructions of children as being marginal to the social order. That statistical data about children's lives is not available suggests that it has little conceptual value. Time in childhood — children's daily life experiences — is in effect made secondary to the time of childhood, when children are seen as dependent upon and protected by the adult world. Issues of dependency and protection, then, are linked to ideas of age and predominate as themes of the time of childhood. In Kitzinger's paper they are of central concern. Her analysis of child sexual abuse explores the ways in which constructions of childhood innocence and dependency are entwined and submerged within ideas of the family. Revelations of child sexual abuse rupture these associations leading to reconstructions of the time of childhood itself. Finally, then we are returned to the 'time of childhood', as a socially constructed time in an individual's early life, a construction which is the culminated product of past, present and future understandings of what children have been, are or should be. This mythology and mythologizing is addressed by Hunt and Frankenberg in their account of Disneyland, which in all its symbolic splendour constructs and reconstructs childhood in an endless series of images in which time future, present and past is a central theme.

Time and the Re-presentation of Childhood

Whilst the breadth of the issues drawn out above *illustrates* the ways in which concepts of time play a key role in shaping and contextualizing the lives and activities of children, close attention to the temporal problems of other accounts of childhood provoke further areas of enquiry. In particular, we shall argue that in much sociological analysis, children are not 'present' in their own right and that as a corollary, the 'present' of childhood is systematically down-played in favour of theoretical frames of reference which place the importance of childhood in either the past or the future. Alternatively, sociological accounts locate childhood in some timeless zone standing as it were to the side of mainstream (that is adult) history and culture. Childhood appears to be, so to speak, lost in time: its present is continuously banished to the past, the future or out of time altogether.

This is not to argue that temporal reference points in the past, future or out of time are of no theoretical or empirical utility. On the contrary, they illuminate aspects of childhood which otherwise might remain hidden; in the next section we shall assess their contribution to the study of childhood. Nevertheless, the sociology of childhood will remain incomplete, we suggest, whilst the 'present' of childhood (and therefore often the presence) of children remains a suppressed component. Indeed we would argue that the promise and potential of what in the Introduction we refered to as the emergent paradigm for the sociology of childhood will remain unfulfilled until this temporal dimension is theoretically and empirically integrated into it. We suggest, in particular, that the frequent transitions of childhood provide strategic points of analysis since during them past, present and future are symbolically represented. In the next sections, we shall illustrate these reflections by reference to time and childhood in contemporary western cultures, primarily that of England. Although this limits the scope of our analysis we hope that it will stimulate discussion elsewhere, for to reiterate the main theme of this volume, other times and other places structure other childhoods.

Time Passed: Concepts of Age and Maturity

A first common representation of childhood in contemporary English society is, we suggest, located in time passing, that is in the past. It is however an image of childhood which is closely tied into the other locations — time future and timeless time — for it is through the passage of time itself that their meanings reverberate. 'Time passed by' — the past — is marked out in an individual's life through the concept of age, but it is during childhood that 'age' has a particular significance. For example, adults on first getting to know children frequently ask their age; parents are asked how old their children are and children themselves often state their ages with formidable accuracy: six and a half, ten and three-quarters. Such an expressed interest in a person's 'age' during adulthood would be considered at best rude and at worst intrusive. The insistent demand of children that their age be made public rests, we suggest, on a set of implicit constructions of the position of children in the life course. Contained in questions about age are others: how many years have passed since you were born, are you growing up, will you soon be grown up? Indeed, the other standard question which adults ask of children is: what to do you want to be when you are grown up? This questioning thus denies time present in the life of the child, focusing as it does on the interrelationship between time past and time future. Indeed, as each year passes by, its passage is ritually noted in the birthday celebrations performed by adults for children[1]. Each year lived through is recorded by the number of candles on the birthday cake, for it is this past upon which the child's future is deemed to rest. It is therefore to an examination of the significance and structuring of ideas of age, maturity and social status that we first turn our attention.

It is anthropology which has probably made the greatest contribution to the analysis of age as a structuring principle in society through demonstrating that conceptions of age and maturity vary in their significance and meaning both through time itself and cross-culturally (see, for example, Bernardi, 1985; La Fontaine, 1979). We give particular predominance to this issue here not only because we consider ideas of age to be a central feature in the social construction of childhood but also because it is assumed by many commentators that, in comparison to class or ethnicity, age plays but a minimal role in the social stratification of western industrialized societies. Bernardi in his cross-cultural survey of age systems states, for example, that in western societies 'age is conceptually employed to define certain categories of person but is not used as a basis for constructing social structure' (1985: 1). This is, we suggest, misleading with respect to childhood, a point which once again bears witness to the muted role which the study of children has long played in the social sciences. Far from being absent from social structure concepts of age are the main scaffolding around which western conceptions of childhood are built and it is through reference to concepts of age that the daily life experiences of children are produced and controlled.

However, as Janet Finch (1986) has recently reminded us, age is one of the most elusive social variables of sociological analysis; the most collected but the least used. As she notes, '... moving beyond

Allison James and Alan Prout

simple correlations to the use of age in ways which are theoretically
informed as well as empirically rigorous is relatively uncharted territory'
(Finch 1986: 14).

Age is most commonly dealt with through the idea of age groups.
These sometimes form the basis for conceptual categories such as 'childhood' or 'adolescent' and, at other times, are used as more or less
arbitrary configurations which group together chronological ages (e.g.,
1–4, 5–14, 15–44, 45–64, 65–74, 75–84, 85 +). Both methods are, however, problematic as sociological devices: the latter groupings, usually the
basis of statistical analyses, may reflect particular biases in relation to the
data being collected. For example, age groupings which are used for
analysis of employment data may not be sufficiently stratified for information about health care and extra or different significant groupings
may have to be used (see Qvortrup, this volume). On the other hand,
the vague and uncertain boundaries between the former groupings
make them problematic for sociological analysis precisely because they
are used as a powerful and changeable means of inclusion and exclusion. The uncertain position of teenagers in western, industrialized societies, neither children nor adults, with a multiplicity of different cut off
points in different social contexts is a case in point. As Finch concludes,
although age, like gender, is based on biology, this tells us little about
the social meaning and significance that is constructed around it and to
use age as a unidimensional category can be extremely misleading. Age
groups as social categories need to be seen in relation to their intersec-
tions with other important variables such as class, gender, and ethnicity.

Within anthropology, where most of the sociological interest in
age has occurred, two main analytical concepts have been developed
for distinguishing between societies which use age as a structuring principle. These classifications — age grades and age classes — although
developed primarily in relation to non-western cultures are nevertheless useful, we suggest, in gaining some purchase on the ways in which
age operates as a constitutive element of childhood itself. The former
concept — age grade — refers to a formal or informal grouping which
has associated with it particular rights and duties which define the relationship of an age grade member to the social structure and polity. In
England, although this system is informal and relatively imprecise in its
application, with the boundaries between childhood, adolescence and
adulthood being unclear and fragmented, the concept of age-grades
has some use for examining the symbolic import of these social classifications. For example, the anomaly which teenage pregnancy creates
indicates that an age-grade type of system does indeed operate at the
level of social relationships if not social structure (Murcott, 1980). The

236

teenage mother is construed as a social problem, as an individual who is literally out of time with the expectations of her age grade.

Age classes, on the other hand, are very apparent in the construction of childhood in English society (and other western) cultures. Used to refer to a group of coevals who progress through the age structure together, an age class structure finds embodiment in the school system. In many instances it continues beyond it, with coevals continuing their loyalty to one another in adult life, exemplified best in the yearly ritual reunions and old boy network to be found in the English public school system (see Gaythorne-Hardy, 1977). Promotion through the school age class system takes place at regular scheduled intervals and is involuntary; that is, individuals are promoted through the system irrespective of their individual characteristics. In any particular school, the different age positions carry with them differential status and responsibilities; their school work is different and they carry with them different rights, duties and privileges. In this respect the National Curriculum, being implemented in English schools, represents further consolidation of the age class system as a structuring principle of English society. Educational attainment targets for each aspect of the curriculum are being linked to particular biological ages which are, nationwide, to be represented by particular year groupings in the schools:

> According to Department of Education and Science guidance notes, the average child will reach about level 2 by the age of seven, level 4 by 11, level 5 or 6 by 14 and level 6 or 7 by 16. The higher levels from 8 to 10 will be reached only by the brighter pupils (*The Independent*, 7.11.89).

This emphasis on an age class system, however, creates problems, particularly in relation to ideas of social and educational maturity. For an individual child, the relationship is potentially stigmatizing: it risks being interpreted in terms of immaturity or precocity, backwardness or giftedness. 'Holding down a year' in school, for example, when a child fails to keep up the same academic progress as his/her peers has, in the past, occurred only rarely in England and after much negotiation between teachers, parents and education officials. Similarly the premature advancement of a pupil to a higher than normal class is also extremely unusual, as is shown by the debate which took place in the media in 1981 when a 10-year-old girl achieved a Maths 'A' level, normally achieved at the age of 17 or 18. Significantly, she had been taught by her father at home, not in school, and opinions were voiced about the extent to which both her education and her achievement could be construed as 'normal'. Demotion *and* advancement are therefore both tinged with social stigma — despite the normally positive value placed on academic success — for such children are treated as anomalous for their 'age'. They are out of time with their contemporaries.

There is then a temporal duality structuring childhood in England. First the system of informal age grades structures the movement over time of children from infancy through childhood into adolescence and the second, more formal system organized around schooling, groups children into age classes within which they move sequentially as year succeeds year. The discussion which took place about 'gifted' children that is referred to above illustrates well their intersection. Journalists and letters from the public, located the debate firmly in the arena of the social construction of childhood. The 'normality' or otherwise of such success was largely interpreted in terms of the implications which it had for other aspects of childhood. This conception of childhood is neatly summarized by Ennew (1986: 18):

> The modern form of childhood has two major aspects. The first is a rigid age hierarchy which permeates the whole of society and creates a distance between adults and children. The status difference is enhanced by special dress, special games, special artefacts (toys), special language and stories, which are all considered appropriate to what Aries calls the 'quarantine' period of childhood. The distance is further enhanced by the second aspect which is the myth of childhood as a 'golden age'. Happiness is now the key term associated with innocence — childhood must be a happy time as well as a time of separation from corrupt adult society.

Through educational precocity had such childhood happiness been forsaken? The relationship between the two structuring processes of age classes and age grades is, as such examples reveal, both ill defined and tense, for the two systems are not directly related to each other in contemporary English culture. Rather, links are forged in subtle and ambiguous ways which only become apparent through their breach.

Time passing and time past, thus, gains a particular potency during childhood. Through the explicit structure of the school system, age classes operate to regulate the times for and of infancy, childhood and adolescence through setting the ages of entry into and exit from different parts of the school system: nursery, primary and secondary schools. The somewhat ambiguous and blurred boundaries to these periods of time in an individual's life thus become more distinct and acquire meaning through the interlocking of biological age with social status, a mechanism provided primarily through the institution of schooling. The 'time of childhood' therefore structures and is structured by 'time in childhood'.

Time Future: The Moonshot Model

The location of childhood in time passing is inextricably linked to time future for, as suggested above, the importance of age during childhood is that it indicates movement towards adulthood, the child's future. In this other sense, then, childhood is frequently represented in the 'past' as something to be remembered, as a time to look back upon during later life. It is the older people who remark to the younger that 'school days are the best days of your life'. This constitution of childhood as memorabilia is, however, double-edged; there is a darker side. Childhood, in contemporary western societies, is also popularly regarded as the potential antecedent for adult neurosis (see Hendrick; Woodhead, this volume). This means, therefore, that in such representations childhood becomes most important with respect to the *future*. This is, of course, where until the late 1970s most academic study of childhood was situated: child development and socialization theories concentrated predominantly on childhood as a sort of 'moonshot', a highly complex and engineered trajectory towards adulthood (Holt, 1975). Only in terms of this future period of life was childhood of importance, (see Prout and James, this volume).

But the inevitability of physical ageing, combined with the conceptions of mortality of what now are largely secular western cultures, does in fact place upon children a particular responsibility for the future. It is children rather than 'fate', 'gods' or 'demons' who will most likely endure to shape and participate in any future social world: they are the 'next generation,' 'the guardians of the future' on whose shoulders time itself sits. It is a rhetoric which crops up in a wide diversity of social contexts, from politics to commerce. For example, in 1936, Sir Percy Alden remarked that the child is 'the foundation of the State and the first line of defence. We cannot lay too much stress upon the importance of the child if the state is to endure' (Pinchbeck and Hewitt, 1973: 347–8). And, in 1990 it is still the child who provides the visual mnemonic for the future, in advertisements and other cultural representations. In such constructions childhood does not have a 'present' although children themselves have an undeniably potent and powerful presence: in an advertisement for financial investment for example, a mother, clutching her naked child to her breast, looks dreamily away from the camera into the future; in another advertisement for coal, we observe a mother and daughter walking hand in hand towards a group of trees in the far distance. In both cases it is children, depicted as providing the continuity between generations, who are used to underline the prospects for the future, suggesting that it is there, more than now, that their importance will lie. To protect the future (the child's adulthood) means however, as the small print suggests to their parents, investing now during the child's childhood.

The denial or underplaying of the present of childhood through focusing on its importance for the future is not restricted to the schemes of politicians or ad-men, for a comparable case can be made in relation to more recent sociological representations of childhood. It is pertinent, for example, to discussions of the relationship between schooling and the reproduction of capitalism in western societies: here again the 'present' is only discussed as it relates to the future rather than as being of interest in itself. This is done through the conventional counterposing of concepts of work and school which in historical, sociological and (especially) social policy discourses are often implicitly mapped onto the categories of adult and child. 'Work' (usually used in a sense which restricts the term to paid employment) in regarded as the province of adults and 'school' as the arena for children. Seeing children's schoolwork and the social relations within which it takes place as a form of work therefore becomes problematic. This dichotomous mode of thought means that characteristically, but often unselfconsciously, analysts are forced to draw a distinction between 'work' and work, between the activities of children and those of adults. There is then an unstated temporal relationship between the present and future of children's lives, between children's present school 'work' and their work as adults.

An example is found in Sharp (1980: 124), who in a discussion of the ideological consequences of pupil-teacher relationships, comments that: 'Pupils carry out their "work" individually rather than collectively and are encouraged for their diligence, social conformity and deference to the teachers' authority.'

The distinction that is being signified here by the quotation marks around 'work' has two aspects. First is the implication that work can be identified with waged or salaried employment and that 'work' (at school) is in many ways *like* work (in factories and offices). It has some of the same characteristics; for example, in the way pupils are placed in a subordinate position, under the authority of the teacher. This, and other features such as the externally imposed nature of the tasks, their regulation and monitoring, and the evaluation of performance, are seen as preparing pupils for a position in (usually capitalist) relations of production. Second, and as a consequence of this definition of work being employed, the social reproduction framework entails a particular ordering of time in the interpretation of the relationship between schoolchildren and work. It could be summed up as follows: 'work'/work: present/future. Work, in such analyses, exists therefore only in the future of children's lives; their present is constituted through 'work', a sort of virtual image of the 'real' thing, a preparation only[2].

Clearly, the social reproduction framework of education outlined above is based however upon a particularly narrow view of work. It is one which has been criticized by feminists and others who have shown the need for the inclusion of all types of work — for example, housework, unpaid work — in the definition. To this list we should also like to add schoolwork, for this too can usefully be seen as a form of work and not only as 'work'. Wadel's (1979) and Wallman's (1979) expansion of the definition of work to include all activities which involve the production, management and conversion of resources — whether these be materials, ideas or people — is one way in which the significance of children's activities at school could be assessed for their present rather than just their future lives. For example, schoolwork involves taking raw materials (the things, ideas and people available in the classroom) and applying physical and mental skills in a process which is characteristically defined, imposed and regulated externally[3]. Such a redefinition of work means that the meaning of children's schoolwork can be located in *both* their present and future lives. It has a part to play in the kinds of adults they are to become but at the same time their work also has meaning, relationship and consequence for the present. Whilst therefore not questioning the importance that schooling plays in the processes of social reproduction, we suggest that the sociological analysis of childhood also requires that the 'present time-frame' be recognized. Just as we suggested in our earlier critique of socialization approaches, social reproduction analyses also tend to neglect children's present lives and children's active role in them.

The Timeless Culture of Childhood

Our discussion of this illustrative material, shows that it is sometimes hard to separate the location of childhood in time past from its referential position in time future for, in one sense, they define each other. It is possible, however, that the reason for this conceptual interdependence is the existence of yet a third dimension in which childhood is represented as outside time. In such representations childhood is both enduring and universal (see Boyden; Hunt and Frankenberg, this volume). This characteristic — timelessness — contextualizes the themes of innocence and purity as being the essence of childhood. For example, it is precisely their freedom from the relentless passage of time that characterizes the adult world that guarantees children their sanctity in childhood. As Holt observes, people who believe in the institution of childhood . . . see it as a kind of walled garden in which children, being small and weak, are protected from the harshness of the world outside until they become strong and clever enough to cope with it' (1975: 22). However, as he goes on to show, for many children, childhood 'as in Happy, Safe, Protected, Innocent Childhood, does not exist' (see Kitzinger, this volume) despite the rhetoric which, in effect, silences their protests. For other children, childhood plainly just goes on too long (see Solberg this volume).

Despite the critiques of childhood which have been variously offered since the 1970s the 'separate haven of childhood' remains a predominant representation and children are often stranded in a kind of time warp. It is a function of what Boas (1966) has, in his depiction of the cult of childhood, termed a form of cultural primitivism: a nostalgia for time passed which sees 'the child' (a resonant symbol for children which children themselves have to negotiate in their everyday lives) as inhabiting a timeless cultural space. Like primitive man, the child as primitive adult is in harmony with nature, set free from the ravages of the time driven modern world. It is an attractive ideology which casts children into a mythical past or a magical present and has been, until fairly recently, a favourite literary theme, for both adults and children alike. As Ennew notes, in England it is A.A. Milne's Christopher Robin who represents 'the archetypical innocent childhood whiled away in complete isolation in the Hundred Acre Wood, accompanied by sexless woolly animals' (1986: 11).

As an ideological representation this model of childhood appears to find support in the Opies' (1977, 1984) magnificent work on children's games, lore and language. In their terms the culture of childhood is a storehouse or repository of things past, a treasury to be explored: a playground rhyme 'has passed along a chain of two or three hundred young hearers and tellers, and the wonder is that it remains alive after so much handling' (1977: 28). In this sense the culture of childhood is timeless. It is 'primitive' if not 'primaeval' in form:

> The folklorist and anthropologist can, without travelling a mile from his door, examine a thriving unselfconscious culture (the word culture is used here deliberately) which is as unnoticed by the sophisticated world and quite as little affected by it, as is the

culture of some dwindling aboriginal tribe living out its helpless existence in the hinterland of a native reserve (*ibid*: 22).

Children, they say, are 'tradition's warmest friend':

> Like the savage they are respecters, even venerators, of custom; and in their self-contained community the basic lore and language seems scarcely to alter from generation to generation (*ibid*: 22).

And yet as the Opies readily acknowledge elsewhere, children, at the same time, also eagerly and enthusiastically comment upon the contemporary world around them, quickly incorporating new material into the old forms of their lore and language. It is a vibrant, adaptable culture responsive to the nuances of the adult world. There appears, then, to be a tension here between a mythical past and a modern present.

A similar and comparable tension is apparent in the early work on the culture of childhood from within the social sciences. In the preface to the social psychological series on the Social Worlds of Childhood, Harre's description of the aim of the series recalls the Opies' words:

> The frame of mind cultivated by the authors as investigators is that of anthropologists who glimpse a strange tribe across a space of forest and millennia of time. The huddled group on the other side of the playground and the thumping of feet in the upstairs room mark the presence of a strange tribe (1979).

In both extracts childhood is constructed as separate (conceptually and physically) from the adult world. It is as if individual children pass into and out of the time machine we call 'childhood' with no contact between that and the adult world.

This strict separation of the world of children from the world of adults was understandable given the context of the late 1970s, the time when the study of childhood was beginning to emerge. In attempting to give children a voice authors (including ourselves) were battling against a longstanding tradition in which, as suggested in the introduction to this volume, children were passive bystanders in discussions about socialization processes. As Harre continues:

> This frame of mind is deliberately different from that of the classical investigators of child psychology who have brought adult concepts to bear upon the understanding of children's thoughts and actions and have looked at childhood primarily as a passage towards the skills and accomplishments and distortions

of adults. In these studies the authors try to look upon the activities of children as autonomous and complete in themselves (*ibid*).

The casting of children into a timeless culture of childhood was a crucial step towards incorporating children within the discourses of social scientists — and indeed an understandable reaction to the past obscurity of children — but claims to authenticity were, like those to noble savagery, misplaced. This 'time capsule' model of childhood ironically reflects and contributes to the very universalization of childhood which it is attempting to deconstruct. Potentially it feeds the globalization of childhood, which on the surface it seems to contradict, by its very effort to demonstrate the supposed cultural autonomy of childhood from adult society. For this reason, then, it is crucial to consider how temporality can be reintroduced into the social construction of childhood and the culture of childhood situated within, rather than outside, the world of adults. The 'world we have lost', 'the lost world of childhood' can be reclaimed not by archaeology but by ethnography and it is through recognition of the temporarility of social phenomena that this can be achieved.

Re-presenting Childhood

We suggest, then, that the empirical study of childhood and its more effective theorization (tasks which we see as linked) will be aided by a careful consideration of the temporal dimension. In particular we wish at this point to emphasize the need to 're-present' childhood. The elision of time and signification here is, of course, deliberate; we wish to suggest that by focusing on the present of childhood, by grasping it as a continuously worked upon interactional and cultural construction, sociology may find new ways of representing childhood. We advocate this despite the recent (1983) strictures of Johannes Fabian against the, ethnographic present, a mode of discourse which he identifies with the 'othering' of ethnographic subjects/objects. The use of the present tense in ethnographic accounts, he argues, allochronically fixes them; it takes them out of the flow of time into a limbo, such that (as Frankenberg points out) as a teacher of anthropology he tells his students that 'the Dinka *are* raided by the Nuer and absorbed into their lineages', despite this statement actually being based on what Evans-Pritchard deduced from his observations between 1930 and 1936 (1988: 138). Such reifications are similar to those in the Opies' work which we have criticized above and clearly we do not advocate such a practice. On the contrary, one of the main thrusts of this book is to argue that childhood is a shifting social and historical construction and the corollary of this position is that *all* accounts of childhood must be carefully placed in their proper temporal and spatial context. As such what we do advocate is a *theoretical* perspective which can grasp childhood as a continually experienced and created social phenomenon which has significance for its present, as well as the past and future.

Such sociological work is being and has been done, much of it reviewed in the Introduction to this volume. As an exemplary instance we would cite the work of Myra Bluebond-Langner (1978). It is her relocation of children into the present through an examination of their daily life as patients on a children's cancer ward which gives such power to her account of dying children. As she shows, the contemporary ideology of childhood which locates its importance firmly in the future is violently disrupted by the development of terminal illness during childhood. The conception of the 'untimeliness' of death during childhood has been encouraged by a corresponding decline in child mortality and, as she shows, it is adults who fail to deal conceptually very effectively with the situation. Her ethnography demonstrates that the children are well aware that they are dying, that they have no future, despite adult ploys to hide their mortality from them. In acknowledging their own untimely deaths these children explode the concepts of childhood which nurses, doctors and parents try to place upon them.

It should be clear from this example that re-presenting childhood does not mean the complete rejection of socialization and social reproduction theories. On the contrary they both remain important areas. But what is vital is to focus on children not only as protoadults, future-beings, but also on children as beings-in-the-present. The importance of some contemporary accounts of socialization lies therefore in the way they see the future shaping of a child's adult life in and through present adult constructions of childhood. For example, exploring the critical meshing between age and social status is a key area in which the emergent paradigm for childhood could be moving these debates forward. In everyday life age is used as a dividing line to legally exclude children from all kinds of 'adult' spaces. Inconsistent though these lines of demarcation are in English culture, age sets boundaries and limits to children's activities. It prohibits 14-year-olds from marrying, 15-year-olds from betting, 7-year-olds from being prosecuted, and 3-year-olds from going to school. A fruitful avenue for exploration could be to examine how this structures childhood and constitutes children, including their own view of themselves as well as the strategies of resistance.

Such an approach might, for example, explore the 'age-prohibited' activities of children, such as smoking, drinking alcohol and gambling. Another avenue could involve looking at the ways in which time during childhood is passed by children and, as Solberg has shown, to consider the power relationships, say of the family or the school, which delineate who has control over time itself.

Two examples taken from educational research on gender development further demonstrate the value of such approaches. They point to the existence of the 'hidden curriculum' of school life whereby the 'ideal type' of girl is described as nice, kind and helpful in contrast to 'active' boys (see Walkerdine, 1984). Elsewhere Steedman (1982) shows how much and in what ways little girls prefigure their own future as wives and mothers in their play. It is a future which is factual, an explicit and detailed working knowledge of the adult world. Such accounts of the relationship between present childhood and future adulthood provide meaningful insights into the process and not just the product of socialization. Children can thus be thought through as active beings in a social world at all points in their growth and development.

Transition Time

The transition from childhood to adulthood in contemporary English (and most western) society is characterized by a series of small transition points rather than a single initiation into adulthood. Nevertheless, for children themselves these points of partial transition, such as their moves through the schooling system which we discussed above, can take on quite intense meaning. Within the school system the movement from nursery school to primary school, for example, implicitly recognizes and reflects the movement out of infancy into childhood, from the domestic world of the family to the culture of children. A study of friendship groups amongst primary school children carried out by James (1993) reveals that 4-year-old children themselves are aware of this implicit patterning of their lives. In the last few weeks at nursery school children talked of their move to 'big school' when they would themselves become 'big': a 'big boy' or a 'big girl'. Later, during their first few weeks at primary school, they looked back on the time they had passed in the nursery as the time when they were at the 'little school' for little children. This was safe in the knowledge that this time had passed. As one boy put it: 'I'm big now aren't I'. Becoming 'big', over time, is linked to movement into the world of school children, away from the home and the nursery.

The forging of links between two structuring systems — age classes and age grades — in this example is an ongoing, complex and messy process, involving a struggle to make the two systems of meaning mesh together and make sense. Thus, the nursery children were given glimpses of their move into childhood by the staff through the adoption in the last few weeks of procedures with which they would have to become familiar in the reception class in 'big school'. They were instructed, for example, in how to answer at registration and taught the words of the Birthday Song which is sung during Birthday Assembly in the big school. The phrase 'when you are in big school' was also used to curb undesirable behaviour through stressing its inappropriateness in that future context.

If James's study suggests that transitions into and during childhood are key points at which rich ethnographic data can be collected, then the classic framework for understanding social transitions, developed by Van Gennep (1960) and later elaborated by Victor Turner (1968), suggests some ways in which theoretical advances in the understanding of childhood might also be made. In this last section we shall discuss Turner's concept of liminality during transition processes and demonstrate its theoretical utility for the study of time in childhood.

In his well-known work on the rites of passage Van Gennep pointed to their three-fold structure: rites of separation during which passagees are stripped of their previous social roles; rites of liminality during which they occupy an ambiguous zone out of social time and space; and rites of re-aggregation during which they are conferred with new identities and roles. Turner elaborated this schema by paying special attention to the liminal zone, pointing to its complex combination of, on the one hand, condensation of dominant ideologies (often expressed by demanding feats of endurance from those being initiated), and on the other, permissions to treat the dominant culture and social relationships ludically, literally allowing them to be 'played around with' and re-ordered in novel but temporary ways. In Turner's view dominant symbols play a central and complex role during the liminal phase. As symbols they act as condensers of ideology, concentrated representations of dominant but contradictory social practices; but they are also polysemic, having a wide range of referents, shifting over time from dominant to subordinate aspects of ideology and practice.

Such a framework is highly suggestive in relation to contemporary British childhood and its transition points, even though these are scattered, gradual and not even usually performed at specific moments of ritual drama. Therefore, to be useful as a theoretical framework, Turner's concepts need considerable adaption. Most important here is the recognition that many of the most important transitions which children make are, like those of the children in James's nursery school, extended over considerable periods of time rather than being concentrated into ritual moments. What appears, therefore, are not usually rites of liminality but a more prolonged period or process of transition during which the features of ritual liminality are, so to speak, stretched out.

Prout (1987a, 1989) has shown this in his study of the sickness absence among children undergoing the transition from primary to secondary schools in England, a move which loosely reflects the shift out of childhood and into adolescence. He argues that movement through the school system involves a complex series of changes in both pedagogy and expectations of social maturity which are enmeshed with and inextricable from the move out of childhood. The very inexactness of this relationship means that the transition to secondary school is loaded with a symbolic meaning that goes far beyond those concerned with the institution of schooling in a narrow sense. The transition is lived through by children, parents and teachers both as an important social process in itself and as expressive of future transitions which the children will make during their life course, especially the transition from school and onto the labour market. Tensions, conflicts and contradictions about each of these present and future transitions are shown to symbolize gender divisions in school and work discipline, paid employment, domestic work and emotional labour in personal relationships.

Although Prout's ethnography takes in the general features of the transition process it focuses on how the children (and their parents and teachers) performed sickness absence from school. Sickness, seen as a form of culture performance, is analyzed as a dominant symbol in the transition process. For one period in the school year sickness absence from school was restricted and controlled by teachers and parents, inducting children into ideas about the intensified work disciplines of the 'big school' and echoing the instrumental demands of the labour market and domestic responsibilities later in their lives. For a shorter period, later in the school year, after the children had completed a series of examinations which decided their academic ability range at the secondary school, controls on sickness were relaxed and rates of sickness absence increased markedly. At this stage sickness symbolized ideological themes opposite to those earlier in the year. They resembled more the ludic aspect of liminal processes, as children were allowed to explore some of the undercurrents in the ideology of work discipline: that there is more to life than work and that leisure and recreation are necessary. Sickness as a dominant symbol was therefore polysemic: referring forwards in time to the children's future as participants in the labour market, whilst at the same time recalling their past life in primary school.

If such is the case then the study of transition points into and out of, as well as during childhood, must form a fertile point of growth for the emergent paradigm for the sociology of childhood. They are strategic points for analysis, allowing the focus on the present of childhood, which we have argued for in this chapter, whilst at the same time maintaining firm links with the past and future of the life courses on which children are embarked.

Notes

1   Hockey and James (1993), in their discussion of ageing and the life course show how during extreme old age, birthdays are also significant.
2   This section summarizes an argument made in Prout (1987b).
3   The work of children in school can perhaps be best placed in the same category as that sometimes referred to as 'people work' (Stacey, 1984). In all such settings there are 'clients' who are both objects to be worked on and active working subjects themselves.

References

BERNARDI, B. (1985) *Age Class System: Social Institutions and Polities Based on Age*, Cambridge, Cambridge University Press.

BLUEBOND-LANGNER, M. (1978) *The Private Worlds of Dying Children*, Princeton, Princeton University Press.

BOAS, G. (1966) *The Cult of Childhood*, London, Warburg Institute.

BURY, M. (1986) 'Social constructionism and medical sociology', *Sociology of Health and Illness*, **8**, 2, pp. 137–69.

ENNEW, J. (1986) *The Sexual Exploitation of Children*, Cambridge, Polity Press.

FABIAN, J. (1983) *Time and the Other*, New York, Columbia University Press.

FINCH, J. (1986) 'Age', in BURGESS, R.G. (Ed) (1986) *Key Variables in Social Investigation*, London, Routledge and Kegan Paul, pp. 13–30.

FRANKENBERG, R. (1988) ' "Your time or mine?": An anthropological view of the tragic temporal contradictions of biomedical practice', in YOUNG, M. and SCHULLER, T. (Eds) (1988) *The Rhythms of Society*, London, Routledge, pp. 118–53.

GAYTHORNE-HARDY, J. (1977) *The Public School Phenomenon*, London, Hodder and Stoughton.

GIDDENS, A. (1979) *The Central Problems of Social Theory*, London, Macmillan.

HARRE, R. (1979) 'General editor's preface', in MORGAN, J. *et al.* (1979) *Nicknames: Their Origin and Social Consequences*, London, Routledge and Kegan Paul.

HENRIQUES, J. *et al.* (Eds) (1984) *Changing the Subject: Psychology, Social Regulation and Subjectivity*, London, Methuen.

HOCKEY, J. and JAMES, A. (1993) *Growing Up and Growing Old*, London, Sage.

HOLT, J.C. (1975) *Escape from Childhood: The Needs and Rights of Children*, Harmondsworth, Penguin.

JAMES, A. (1993) *Childhood Identities*, Edinburgh, Edinburgh University Press.

LA FONTAINE, J.S. (1979) *Sex and Age as Principles of Social Differentiation*, London, Academic Press.

MURCOTT, A. (1980) 'The social construction of teenage pregnancy', *Sociology of Health and Illness*, **2**, 1, pp. 1–23.

OPIE, I. and OPIE, P. (1977) *The Lore and Language of Schoolchildren*, London, Paladin.

OPIE, I. and OPIE, P. (1984) *Children's Games in Street and Playground*, Oxford, Oxford University Press.

PINCHBECK, I. and HEWITT, M. (1973) *Children in English Society, Vols 1 and 2*, London, Routledge and Kegan Paul.

PROUT, A. (1987a) 'An analytical ethnography of sickness absence in an English primary school', Unpublished Ph.D thesis, Centre for Medical Social Anthropology, University of Keele, Staffordshire, England.

PROUT, A. (1987b) 'Work, time and sickness in the lives of some English schoolchildren', Unpublished-paper presented at the Conference of the Association for the Social Study of Time, Dartington Hall.

PROUT, A. (1989) 'Sickness as a dominant symbol in life course transitions: An illustrated theoretical framework', *Sociology of Health and Illness*, **11**, 4, pp. 336–59.

SHARP, R. (1980) *Knowledge, Ideology and the Politics of Schooling: Towards a Marxist Analysis of Schooling*, London Routledge and Kegan Paul.

SHILDKROUT, E. (1978) 'Roles of children in urban Kano', in LA FONTAINE, J.S. (Ed) *Sex and Age as Principles of Social Differentiation*, London, Academic Press.

STACEY, M. (1984) 'Who are the health workers?: Patients and other unpaid workers in health care', *Economic and Industrial Democracy*, **5**, London, Sage, pp. 157–84.

STEEDMAN, C. (1982) *The Tidy House: Little Girls Writing*, London, Virago.

TURNER, V.W. (1968) 'Variations on a theme of liminality', in MOORE, S.F. and MYERHOFF, B.G. (Eds) (1968) *Secular Ritual*, Assen van Gorcum.

VAN GENNEP, A. (1960) *The Rites of Passage*, London, Routledge and Kegan Paul.

WADEL, C. (1979) 'The hidden work of everyday life', in WALLMAN , S. (Ed) (1979) *The Social Anthropology of work*, London, Academic Press.

WALKERDINE, V. (1984) 'Developmental psychology and the child-centred pedagogy: The insertion of Piaget into early education', in HENRIQUES, J. *et al.* (1984) *Changing the Subject: Psychology, Social Regulation and Subjectivity*, London, Methuen, pp. 153–202.

WALLMAN, S. (Ed) (1979) *The Social Anthropology of Work*, London, Academic Press.

YOUNG, M. and SCHULLER, T. (Eds) (1988) *The Rhythms of Society*, London, Routledge.

Notes on Contributors

Jo Boyden works internationally as a social development consultant focusing on policies and programmes for especially disadvantaged children and youth. She has recently been involved in training practitioners in the methodologies and methods of participatory research with children and in preparing background reports on education and psychosocial issues for the UN study on the Impact of Armed Conflict on Children. She is now participating in a cross-cultural project analyzing perceptions of and responses to children's work among welfare practitioners, policy makers, parents and working children. Recent publications include 'Children's experience of conflict related emergencies: Some implications for relief policy and practice', in *Disasters* (1994); *Exploring Alternative Approaches to Combating Child Labour* (UNICEF, 1994); *The Relationship Between Education and Child Work* (UNICEF, 1994).

Ronald Frankenberg is notionally retired but teaches Medical Anthropology part-time at Brunel, Keele and occasionally elsewhere. He is currently involved in research projects related to children's vulnerability in sickness and health and to general practice and in writing about children in film, AIDS literature and about representations of death in the twentieth century. At home he shares a lived reflexive praxis and ongoing seminar with, amongst others, Pauline Hunt and Adam and Rebecca Frankenberg.

Benno Glauser has been active in grass-roots social work with different underprivileged groups in Latin America and particularly in Paraguay, where he has lived since 1977. In the 1980s, his work was dedicated for several years to street children, as an independent social researcher, a street educator and also a co-founder of a Paraguayan institution working with street children. Presently, he is working freelance as a social analyst and counsellor, writer, teacher and consultant. He is the author of several publications on street children: 'Proyecto de la Convencion de las Naciones Unidas relativa a los Derechos del Nino/ Evaluacion Critica' ('Critical Evaluation of the UN Convention Project on Children's Rights') (CDE, Asuncion, 1989); 'Ninos y Jovenes de la Calle: Sentidos desde la Sociedad' ('Street Children and Street Youth: Significance for Society') (NATS, Verona, April 1996).

Harry Hendrick is a freelance lecturer in British Social History, specializing in social policy, childhood and youth. He is author of *Images of Youth, Age, Class and the Male Youth Problem, 1880–1920* (Clarendon Press, 1990); *Child Welfare, England 1872–1989* (Routledge, 1994); and *Children, Childhood and English Society, 1880–1990* (CUP, 1997). At present he is working on a comprehensive history of young people from the eighteenth century to the present.

Pauline Hunt studied sociology at Sussex, Edinburgh and Keele. She was a tutor–organiser for the WEA and published articles and a book in gender studies in domestic and industrial relations. Her current project concerns the making visible of ancient stories through text and painting and the recreation of rituals in daily practice. Like Ronald Frankenberg, she shares a house with their now teenage children, Adam and Rebbeca.

Allison James is Senior Lecturer in Applied Anthropology at the University of Hull and has worked in the sociology/anthropology of childhood since the late 1970s. Her interests include work on children's language and culture in relation to theories of socialization and more recently has explored children's attitudes towards sickness and bodily difference. Her current work, together with Pia Christensen and Jenny Hockey, is a generational study of relations of dependency within farming families. She is author of numerous articles and books on childhood, including *Growing Up and Growing Old* (with J. Hockey, Sage, 1993); *Childhood Identities* (EUP, 1993) and *Theorising Childhood* (with C. Jenks and A. Prout, Polity Press, 1997).

Jenny Kitzinger graduated in social anthropology from Cambridge University in 1984 and subsequently worked as a researcher there looking at NHS staffing structures and obstetric services. She is now Senior Research Fellow with the Glasgow Media Group, based in the Sociology Department at Glasgow University. Her research includes work on media representations on AIDS, the Zero Tolerance campaign against male violence and public understandings of child sexual abuse. She is just completing a study of media/policy reactions to 'false memory syndrome' and currently starting a project examining how research findings about breast cancer are processed into public and professional consciousness.

Alan Prout is Senior Lecturer in the Department of Sociology and Social Anthropology at Keele University and currently Director of the ESRC Children 5–16 Research Programme which is a major initiative aimed at developing the theoretical, empirical and methodological understanding of contemporary childhood. He has long-standing interests in the social study of childhood. He has written extensively on childhood and forthcoming publications include *Theorising Childhood* (with C. Jenks and A. James, Polity Press, 1997) and *Childhood Bodies* (MacMillan, 1997). He has also worked in medical anthropology and sociology, including research on the cultural performance of childhood sickness, cross-cultural studies of childhood medicine use, family health practices and childhood asthma, see for example *Children Medicine and Culture* (Haworth, 1996).

Jens Qvortrup is Research Director for the Department of Social and Health Studies, South Jutland University Centre, Denmark, and Co-director of the European Centre's Childhood Programme, Vienna. He is president of International Sociological Association's Working Group on Sociology of Childhood and directed the large international project 'Childhood as a Social Phenomenon (1987–1992)'. He is Editor of a special issue of *International Journal of Sociology* on the sociology of childhood (1987) and co-editor of *Childhood Matters* (Avebury, 1994). He has written numerous articles in journals and books and his latest book in Danish is about childhood in the Nordic countries, *Children Half Price.*

Anne Solberg is currently a Research Manager at the Norwegian Institute for Urban and Regional Research in Oslo. Her main research interest is in the sociology of childhood — particularly children's work and everyday life — and in qualitative methods. Author of numerous articles on childhood, her most recent publication is 'The challenge in child research from "being" to "doing"' in J. Brannen and M. O'Brien (Eds) *Children in Families* (Falmer Press, 1996).

Martin Woodhead took degrees in psychology and sociology, and carried out research into early child development and education, before joining The Open University in 1977. He is now Senior Lecturer in the Centre for Human Development and Learning and Chair of the MA course 'Child Development in Social Context'. Major publications relate to early childhood, especially the way theory and research relates to social and educational policy and practice. He has been a Fulbright Fellow in the USA and a Series Adviser to the BBC series 'All Our

Children'. Martin has also worked in residential special education, as a houseparent caring for children with emotional and behavioural difficulties. Most recently he has been exploring the role of theory and research in global child development issues, and prepared a report for for the Bernard van Leer Foundation on 'quality issues' in large-scale childcare programmes. He is currently coordinating an international project for Radda Barnen (Swedish Save the Children), exploring children's perceptions of their working lives.

Index

Lightning Source UK Ltd.
Milton Keynes UK
UKOW032205240912

199565UK00003B/77/P